MALAIKA AND THE SEVEN HEAVENS

Malaika AND THE Seven Heavens

A MEMOIR OF MY ENCOUNTERS WITH ISLAM

Toyin Falola

UNIVERSITY OF MICHIGAN PRESS

ANN ARBOR

Published in the United States of America by the
University of Michigan Press
First published October 2025

A CIP catalog record for this book is available from the British Library.

Library of Congress Cataloging-in-Publication Data

Names: Falola, Toyin, author
Title: Malaika and the seven heavens : a memoir of my encounters with Islam / Toyin Falola.
Description: Ann Arbor : University of Michigan Press, 2025.
Identifiers: LCCN 2025011614 (print) | LCCN 2025011615 (ebook) | ISBN 9780472077670 (hardcover) | ISBN 9780472057672 (paperback) | ISBN 9780472905270 (ebook other)
Subjects: LCSH: Falola, Toyin. | Muslims—Nigeria—Biography. | Islam—Nigeria. | Christianity and other religions—Islam. | LCGFT: Autobiographies.
Classification: LCC BP80.F26345 A3 2025 (print) | LCC BP80.F26345 (ebook) | DDC 297.09669—dc23/eng/20250521
LC record available at https://lccn.loc.gov/2025011614
LC ebook record available at https://lccn.loc.gov/2025011615

DOI: https://doi.org/10.3998/mpub.14469709

The University of Michigan Press's open access publishing program is made possible thanks to additional funding from the University of Michigan Office of the Provost and the generous support of contributing libraries.

Cover Image: Portrait of Ibrahim, Baba Ajara, in front of Ojaba mosque, Ibadan, Nigeria by Ekeolu Oyetunde Kazeem. Toyin Falola Private Art Collections.

Authorized Representative: Easy Access System Europe, Mustamäe tee 50, 10621 Tallinn, Estonia, gpsr.requests@easproject.com

In memoriam
Mama Ida Gaye of The Gambia
Who gave me a name: Ebrahima, the son of the womb,
"father of multitudes, father of a nation."

O God, forgive her and have mercy on her, keep her safe and sound and forgive her, honor her rest and ease her entrance; wash her with water and snow and hail, and cleanse her of sin as a white garment is cleansed of dirt. O God, give her a home better than her home and a family better than her family.

If a person were given the entire world and everything in it and then said, الحمد لله (*Alhamdulillah*, All praise belongs to Allah), the blessing of being inspired to say الحمد لله (*Alhamdulillah*) would be greater than receiving the entire world itself.

This is because all worldly pleasures fade, but the reward of الحمد لله (*Alhamdulillah*) lasts forever.

—Ibn al-Qayyim رحمه الله

Contents

Digital materials related to this title can be found on the Fulcrum platform via the following citable URL: https://doi.org/10.3998/mpub.14469709

Figures

Preface

IBADAN

Listen, hear a stirring tale!
A tale to be declaimed
In many mouths of Africa
Listen!

To Ibadan, my Ibadan
Berth and cradle of rich culture
Home of heroes and heritage
Exploits of courage and honor.

Listen and hear Ibadan!
Stories of mettle and pride
Familiar yet exceptional tales
Of hustling, bravura, and bravery!

Day and night against
Hunger and starvation
Ibadan hustle and bustle
Oluyole of conquerors!

Sweetly, Ibadan thrives
City of eternal optimists
Strivers making a living
Indomitable, hopeful, surviving.

Ibadan, thrilling tale of the best edibles
Where hot *amala* and *ewedu* dance down the throat
With juicy goat meat that embraces the palate
Longing for a frothy keg of *oguro*.
Take me to Ibadan!

The city of worldwide civilization
Take me to the house of Oluyole
The home of many *firsts* and *bests*.

Ibadan!
Take me to Ogunmola's town
The abode of happiness and joy
Radiant with beautiful scenery.

I've been to the East and West of the world
From the North tower to the southern coast
But there is none like the tapestry
Of russet and ochre rooftops.

Ibadan, my heart, my home!
Though our stories have been molded
This is where my heart knows
It's here my soul finds contentment.

This memoir chronicles my journey with Islam, from childhood to the present, framed in a historical/comparative context. It begins with my childhood encounters in the city of Ibadan and extends through my later years as a teacher, researcher, and resident in the predominantly Christian United States. Sometimes, our environment can fundamentally shape our perceptions, challenge our presumptions, and open our hearts to new possibilities in a world marked by religious diversity and cultural complexity. My lifelong encounter with Islam is a testament to this empirical experience.

Come with me on a personal journey as I share the events, engagements, and conversations that have shaped my understanding of Islam, with both Muslims and non-Muslims. This memoir is not an academic exercise or an attempt to fully explain Islam's complexity. Rather, it is a personal narrative, influenced by my upbringing, environment, and values, that reflects how these elements have molded my perspective on Islam.

I have been enthralled by the beauty and profundity of this faith as I explored its complex beliefs. Through interpersonal relationships, dialogues, and moments of humanity, I discovered a richness that transcends language, ethnicity, and nationality. I found a religion that values kindness, fairness, and the tremendous interconnectedness of all creation. Yet there were times when these values seemed to falter.

In this memoir, I recount the stories of the extraordinary people I met along the way—men and women who lived their faith with steadfast dedication,

FIG. 1. *On the Streets of Ibadan* by Dr. Kazeem Ekeolu. Growing up in Ibadan, the marketplace, occasions, and streets were never short of the Yoruba Muslims, whose mode of dressing and communication portrayed many aspects of their identity.

opened their hearts to others, and demonstrated the values of Islam through their actions. Their experiences serve as a powerful reminder of the power of empathy, the force of unity, and the potential for change that each of us holds.

My interactions with Islam were not without difficulties, internal disputes, and uncomfortable moments. This narrative aims to capture the complexity and subtleties of these encounters—highlighting the moments of uncertainty and insight that shaped my evolving understanding of Islam and other religions.

The opening chapter, "The Masquerade, the Imam, and the Pastor," begins with me witnessing a masquerade festival. This event serves as a backdrop to explore how Islam came into Ibadan and how it intertwined with the indigenous practices, including the use of charms rooted in the African Òrìṣà religion. My encounter also reveals the complex interactions between the three prominent religions in the community—Islam, Christianity, and the African Òrìṣà religion—highlighting the relationships between the pastor, the imam, and the *babalawo*.

Chapter 2, "One Wudu and Ninety-Nine Tasbih," delves into my observations of the Muslim mode of prayer and the various interpretations others hold of these practices. In this chapter, I relate how the Òrìṣà religion became intertwined with Islam, reflecting the blending of cultural and religious traditions. I also discuss the formation of different Islamic sects and Islamic associations, each with a distinct worldview, particularly within the Yoruba contexts.

Additionally, I narrate how Muslims in my immediate community held a deep reverence for the pilgrimage to Makkah and Madinah, fantasizing about the journey and the honor and respect bestowed upon those who completed it. The chapter also covers the origin of the titles Alhaji and Alhaja, the significance of pilgrimage in Islamic injunctions, and the activities that take place in the holy cities of Makkah and Madinah during this sacred journey.

In chapter 3, "A Cane of Memory and the Joy of Pain," I recount my experiences at the madrassas I attended, using these memories to narrate how the learning system of Islam and Western education relate. This chapter is set in an Islamic learning center, a Western school, and a fusion of both.

In chapter 4, "Lips of Angels," I delve into the power of music and recitation in Islam, using sing-along Islamic songs in Yoruba and Arabic to illustrate their influence.

My journey will not be complete if I do not talk about Oja Oba in "Our Mecca and Medina," chapter 5. Here I explore the symbolic significance of religious conquest, detailing the coming of Islam and its dominance in that part of the city. I describe the existence of Muslim communities in Ibadan and how Oja Oba—a place I regularly visited as a teenager—was regarded as the Makkah and Madinah of the city.

As part of my itinerary, in chapter 6, "Sir Sabo and *Conc Juju*," I narrate the story of the sheikh and his amulets. This chapter delves into the figure of the medicine man at Sabo, known as *oni juju*, and recounts my observations of spiritual leaders who used and believed in "voodoo" for healing and other spiritual problems, using Islam as a vehicle. Here I draw a comparison between Sufism in Islam, Yoruba traditions, and Western medicine.

In chapter 7, "Alhaji Many, Alhaja Money," I narrate my encounters with Islam, focusing on women, polygamy, domestic matters, and conflicts. These experiences are well detailed, covering my visits and journey to Ilorin, which inspired this chapter.

In chapter 8, "In the City of Double Conscience," I take a closer look at the story of Usman Dan Fodio in Ilorin, as well as the Yoruba-Fulani clashes. While some Yoruba will argue that Ilorin is a city that betrayed the Yoruba, or perhaps the Yoruba betrayed the city, my focus is on the unique Islamic practices in the city of Ilorin as I observed them.

Centered on the mosque and madrassa, chapter 9, "Baba Agege Is Dead!," is written to extol the ulama—Islamic scholars and spiritual leaders. This chapter focuses on the responsibilities of imams and alfas, tracing how Islam arrived in Lagos and the significant roles these leaders have played over time in shaping the religious landscape of the city.

Chapter 10, "Slaughtering the Living Elephant," addresses religious crises and contemporary conflicts facing Islam today, including anti-Islamic sentiments such as controversies over the hijab and declining ecumenism.

The final chapter, titled "The Last Sermon," centers on my experiences, lectures, and frequent visits to Islamic universities in Nigeria. Drawing inspiration from the last sermon of Prophet Muhammad (PBUH), this chapter showcases the essence of inner vision, the realm of dreams, and the pursuit of set goals. It also explores how advancements in technology and the internet age have influenced the spiritual realm, highlighting the intersection of traditional beliefs and modernity in today's society.

This memoir explores the integration of Islam with Yoruba cultural elements, as well as the success of Islam's establishment despite occasional tensions over what is deemed acceptable for worship. The poems at the start of each chapter convey the depth of my personal connection to the themes and my respect for how the religion is organized, as well as the behaviors and values it promotes.

I write from a dual perspective, both as an insider and an outsider, sometimes adopting an anthropological voice and gaze. While some Nigerian Muslims might perceive some of my judgments/assessments of behavior as coming from an "outsider" and a voice of difference, I believe the overall intent of my work remains intact: to promote unity and acceptance of Islam as a faith that has been Yorubanized or indigenized.

I am aware that my experience is only one thread in the great tapestry of encounters that people have had with Islam. This memoir does not claim to reflect all experiences or viewpoints, nor does it seek to compel the reader to agree with my views. Instead, it offers an opportunity for personal exploration, challenges preconceptions, and promotes an atmosphere of communication and understanding.

It is my earnest hope that this memoir serves as a catalyst for conversations that bridge the gaps that separate us, enhancing our collective understanding of diverse human experiences. I pray that it inspires us to seek common ground, recognize our shared humanity, and set out on our quests for self-discovery. This is my hope, my aspiration, and my heartfelt prayer.

Inshallah!

Acknowledgments

I am humbled and grateful for this opportunity to write my third memoir, *Malaika and the Seven Heavens: A Memoir of My Encounters with Islam*. This work would not have been possible without the help, inspiration, and guidance of many individuals who have made a significant impact on my life.

I owe a debt of gratitude to my family and friends for their encouragement and support. Your unwavering confidence in me and your steadfast support have continued to encourage and inspire me. Thank you to everyone who supported this project and offered insightful criticisms and contributions, which shaped the final presentation of this memoir. Completing this memoir has been made possible by your wisdom and commitment to excellence.

I must also express my heartfelt appreciation to my Muslim and Christian friends with whom I had the privilege of sharing my childhood and teenage years. The adventurous and blissful memories we created together provided the foundation and insights to write this memoir. I will always cherish these friends and neighbors, some of whom I have known for over fifty years.

This book is not just a reflection of my experiences and encounters but also a recounting of the profound impact of my maternal Muslim background. As a teenager, I made various oaths, which I have continued to respect. Through this memoir, I aim to acknowledge and appreciate the huge impact that Islam, as well as Christianity and Yoruba religion, have had on me from childhood to date.

Several dedicated "researchers" worked with me on this project, some of whom I entrusted with the task of exploring contemporary situations in various locations. Kaosarat Aina was in Sabo and Ojaba; Wale Ghazal went to Agege; Yemisi Obaleke was in Ilorin; Habeeb Adisa covered Abeokuta; Bello Muhammad did the Kaduna research; while Yusuf Wahab oversaw Kano and various neighborhoods in the city. While the data they gathered were revealing, they primarily served to jolt my memory rather than being directly used for this memoir.

The draft of the memoir benefited immensely from the keen eyes of notable individuals, including Bola Dauda, Michael Afolayan, Vik Bahl, Cassamance Boy, and Habeeb Adisa, among others. Special thanks to 'Tayo Keyede and Adebukola Bassey, my editorial consultants, who meticulously checked for possible errors in the manuscript.

As I rewalked the paths of my life across decades, through cities and villages that have shaped my journey, I enjoyed the invaluable contributions of many people, too numerous to mention here. To each of these individuals, I owe a debt of gratitude. Their efforts remain vivid in my memory, and their support has left an indelible mark on this memoir. For that, I am eternally grateful. I still have many voyages to report but . . . I am not a Muslim!

SHOULD THIS BE OUR LAST RAMADAN

Ya Allah
We know YOU own the heart of kings and chiefs
And as we propose, YOU sometimes dispose
But should this be the last holy month YOU will grant us
Please, count us worthy before YOU.

Ya Rabb
Should this be our last night for *Tahajjud*
Purify our souls, cleanse our hearts, and purge our minds
Let our breath be more pleasant before YOU
That we may hear YOU when YOU call.

Oh Allah
Should this be our last *Dua* at this early hour
Cause us to remember to say *Astaghfirullah* again
We know our ways are not pure before YOU
And our hearts are stronger than stones
But please forgive a slave like us.

Ya Rabb
Should this be our last delicious *Sehri* and *Iftar* food
May we remember to thank and praise YOU
And if our days go without food, may we be filled with YOUR power
And should our days go without water, may we be quenched
with our *Nafl prayer*
But above all, that YOU remember us in YOUR mercy.

Oh Allah
Should this be our last Ramadan
Let our good deeds be multiplied in manifolds
Let YOUR crescent from above descend on us
That we may find favor in YOUR sight
And lead us to YOUR *Aljannah*.

CHAPTER ONE

The Masquerade, the Imam, and the Pastor

The Beginning
In the ancient realm of sacred tales,
Where diverse voices find their trails,
In my dream, I wandered upon a path unknown,
With an eager heart, I sought to be shown.

Through whispering winds, I heard a call,
A melody echoed through the empty hall,
It beckoned me toward a sacred land,
Where Islam's light would gently expand.

I met the faith that breathed in the sand,
Carried by the footsteps of the ground,
I walked through the verses of the Quran's page,
Where I discovered wisdom's eternal sage.

I discovered Christianity before Islam. By the time I knew what Islam was, I had become an admirer of the masquerade cult and its elegant annual festivals and carnivals. I attended a madrassa before I joined the Anglican choir. I heard the stories of the spread of religion before I read about them. My practices preceded my knowledge derived from Western education. Let me thrash what I learned in school and tell you what my eyes saw and what my ears heard. I am a storyteller, doing it for free. I am no longer a scholar writing to get my income once in thirty days. If I lie to you, may my two eyes shift to the back of my head to see the past and forget about the present and future. If I alter falsehood, may my tongue disappear, and the teeth follow to make the mouth hollow!

Originally, before Islam came into Yorubaland, the indigenous Òrìṣà religion was the order of the day. Hence, the saying: *Aye la ba 'fa; Aye la ba 'male;*

osan gangan n'igbagbo wole (there was Ifa before we were born; there was Islam before we were born; it was only much later that Christianity came). This was common knowledge until modern-day religious fundamentalists revised the story to say that Jesus had always been here, only that you and I rejected him. It was in anger that he left Africa to relocate to the Middle East. The miracles that we didn't allow him to perform in Africa for thirty years, he did them within three years in the Middle East. As a consequence, Jesus and Muhammad, who came after him, went elsewhere, developed new practices, forgave us, and returned to us, no longer in person but by sending their Assistants.

All Yoruba older religions, like Ogun, Omi, Osun, and Egun worship, had their styles of worship and *aajo*: the sacrifices. Ibadan, being a Yoruba city, was predominantly inhabited by the Yoruba ethnic group. However, similar to other major cities in Nigeria, different ethnic groups have settled in Ibadan in considerably large numbers over time. The spread of Islam and Christianity came through interactions and the migrations of people far and wide into Yoruba territories, now known as southwestern Nigeria.

I wasn't born when those people began to arrive, yet the migration continued even long after I was born. Today, they keep coming from far-flung countries such as Niger and Chad, and you better believe that a human being can walk over a thousand miles. If you are not chasing something, but something is chasing you, you can keep walking and running for the rest of your life!

For people more interested in my stable growth, approbation, and maybe a few lashes of the cane, might have followed my "bold" rejection of adult wisdom. At the very least, it became a command when someone said, "Toyin, go and pack your things and relocate to the house of your late father's cousin." This was to follow the principle that *aburo baba eni, baba eni ni nse*—your father's brother is your father—and that would have been the end of the matter as far as they were concerned. After all, Baba Olopa, my late father's cousin, could hardly refuse to foster me, especially since I had my inheritance—a quarter of my father's property in Agbokojo—held in trust until I could manage it myself.

That was how I left Agbokojo, dominated by Christians, to Ode Aje, a zone of greater plurality and ecumenism. I left the Christian world and St. James Cathedral to land in the world of masquerades and mullahs. My body could now be sliced into three: one part Christian, one part Muslim, and one part Sango, the god of thunder. I could pray with the Quran, curse with the Bible, and repent with Ogun, the god of iron. I didn't know whether I had three gods or one God in three forms. And it might even be more appropriate to say or think that it seemed that three gods had me!

Ode Aje became my home in 1963. With a tiny bag filled with a few pieces of worn and dirty clothes, I left for my new home, located east of Africa's big city,

Ibadan. It was unannounced, and I lost the friends I had made in the previous ten years of life. No regrets, as I can accumulate friends and lose them. Due to my loose and detached relationships, a friend described me as *Eni o ri, ba lo!* (Go with whomever you find). I didn't cry, as my children were later to do when we moved from one house to another in the 1980s.

Settling in at Ode Aje wasn't difficult despite my fears about living with new people and making new friends. Baba Olopa's no-nonsense attitude kept drama at bay to some extent, and I quickly adjusted to the rhythms of life in this place, which my old friends had assured me was less than Agbokojo. The Ode Aje that I knew while growing up can best be described as the countryside. To those in the city, it was considered a village. The new public school had children of people experiencing poverty and parents who struggled to buy school supplies. Today, this part of the city has become so densely populated that even the government has no record of the number of people living there. You can easily disappear into one of the houses and never be seen again.

The Ode Aje of my youth was going through an uncomfortable morphing process required of most colonized places to achieve the status of "civilized," for which all populated areas aimed. Individuals, especially younger people, were lured by the siren call of the shiny solutions (something of amusement) that Europeans brought with them as they traversed the world in search of valuables to improve their situation and, by extension, their countries. My friends were sure that anyone moving from Agbokojo to a place like Ode Aje was being downgraded from civilization to the jungle. Of course, they were right if they measured civilization by the number of drinking places, prostitutes, and modern houses!

In my youth, Ode Aje wasn't "cool." I do not think cool would be the apt word to use for it even now, compared to other parts of Ibadan, but it has certainly acquired more of the trappings of modern Nigerian society—multistoried homes, some tarred roads, small stores offering different wares or services, the now ubiquitous commercial motorcycles called *okada*, and lots of other religious houses where adherents pray to the deities of their choice.

Religion has always been a prominent feature in the area, and it is probably the only thing that has not changed in Ode Aje. There are still genuine and fake pastors and alfas—if your head guides you to know the difference—and all of them would collect your money. If Nigeria is the poster child for poly-religiosity, Ode Aje is its small-scale version. Muslims, Christians, and Òrìṣà worshippers all inhabit this crowded area. It has always had that religious-pluralistic setting that gave us many festivals to look forward to as children, teenagers, and adults.

The Ode Aje Christian saw nothing bad in joining the masquerades in

FIG. 2. *The Babalawo, the Imam, and the Pastor* by Dr. Kazeem Ekeolu. A portrait featuring the heads of an imam, a pastor, and a *babalawo*, each with his respective emblem.

dancing during the annual festival. If one were to evaluate the followership of the masquerades, I believe that more than half of them belonged to the Abrahamic religions. The masquerade festival was one of the highest points of the year at Ode Aje, and not taking part meant denying oneself the great pleasures that one had grown quite fond of over the years. One way or the other, every Christian or Muslim in Ode Aje belonged to an extended family whose ancestors were represented by the masquerade. In the same manner, Christians would participate in Islamic festivals, joining the Islamic faithful in the annual ram fight competitions and other events that accompanied the occasions. Unbothered with any thought of difference, we feistily partook of processions, dressed up, and feasted as appropriate. I now describe those communal events as vacations.

In today's Nigeria, it often seems like people have daily vacations, not by leaving the country but simply by waking up to unpredictable events. A witch can suddenly appear on a Monday, and you become alarmed and gather on the streets to witness the spectacle. On Tuesday, as the story spreads that a former governor in the country has allegedly spent over one billion nairas to pay for his children's school fees five years in advance, you run to social media to read people's comments on the issue while silently praying for the door of *japa* (immigration) to open to you.

On Wednesday, stories circulate that a popular young artist has committed suicide, prompting emotional responses from Nigerians. The streets and social media are filled with people trying to analyze his life and claiming they knew the exact period in his life when he fell into depression and became suicidal. A few hours later, the "dead artist" releases a new song, and then you hear again that the suicide was a hoax. It turns out that he orchestrated the fake story and made his family and friends spread it in order to promote his new song.

Thursday is even more fun as the politician seeking reelection distributes rice and sardines to would-be voters. The next day, the thugs of two *agberos* (bus conductors) competing to take over a local taxi park would slug it out, breaking beer bottles to stab one another until they bleed to death. Saturday is too holy to give up the fun: The coffin carrying a corpse falls from the truck, and instead of the dead, a "ghost" comes out. And on Sunday, as you are watching soccer and shouting Liverpool and Chelsea, a lorry load of "scorpions" can descend on you, and what you remember is that you fled and some three young boys wearing dreadlocks were taken away, probably the last you'd hear of them.

I lived in a community of wonders. A mosque wasn't far away from a church, and an Ifa priest lived behind both. Daily, the call for prayer wouldn't allow you to sleep past 5:00 a.m., and the campaign for the redemption of your soul by the itinerant Christian preacher would not give you peace at night. If you complain, the devil has possessed you. Yes, you may even be the devil, and you need the evil spirit to be cast away by the Pentecostal pastor with his hut-like church within walking distance. Everybody is holy except for the other person, who is a sinner. Only one person is righteous: Me! Like most Yoruba communities and towns, Ode Aje accepted everyone and anyone with their religion. Stories were told so that we could understand the significance of various aspects of Ode Aje's socioreligious system.

Ode Aje was the abode of hunters and farmers, so I was told while growing up there. I saw the hunters in the town and at Elepo, a village I visited many times. It became a residential abode for the first set of original settlers and, by default, home to various indigenous religions. These hunters, as expected of them, worshipped various deities and gods. It would be irrational to go into deep forests without paying homage and offering propitiations to the entities that governed these spaces.

The obstacles encountered by the hunters in the jungle were not only physical, as they confronted more than wild animals in the forest. Our forest wasn't a place for the lily-livered, and our hunters were quick to embrace better and faster weapons that got the job done. With most of the animals now in extinction because they have been killed, consumed, and digested, the forest has gone too, pushed far away as the hideout for the new occupation of kidnapping, far more lucrative than chasing snakes and rats.

Back in the 1960s, hunter groups going into the dense forests engaged in prayers and propitiations, sometimes for days at a stretch, with the belief that some animals can transform into humans. Passing by a man who was an animal wasn't a risk for people who had spiritual protection or magical powers. If the antelope could turn into a man, so could the hunter turn into a lion. However, you would be killed and swallowed if you didn't change fast enough. And if you boasted too much about your prowess, the powerful one with the most potent magic may turn you into an *ado*, a small gourd, and swallow you.

I have heard stories of men being swallowed by another man, but not about how they eventually escaped, whether through the anus or mouth, to regain their manhood. I knew the most potent juju man who collected his power from the spirits of the forest. He must never cross a river, or he would lose his power. Encounters with mysterious creatures made it imperative for hunters to arm themselves with charms and other spiritually potent materials in their search for wild animals as food and hide. This became part of the reality of living.

The hunters in Ode Aje often doubled as herbalists and operated within the confines of religions, including deity worship. The gods and goddesses at Ode Aje were celebrated at intervals, some weekly, some annually. Invariably, cults were formed, increasing the secrecy surrounding religious practices. The various *agbole*, the family compounds in Ode Aje, worshipped the deities that their ancestors worshipped before them, sometimes even after they had converted to other religions. Their mindset was adequately expressed in the common song during processions for their deities, warning that a new faith, whether Christianity or Islam, could not stop them from their inherited practices:

Awa o s'oro ile wa o
Awa ó s'oro ile wa o
Igbagbo o pe k'awa ma s'oro
Awa o s'oro ile wa o

We will hand in our tradition to our child
We will teach him our tradition
Being converts to the new religions does not stop us from that
We will hand in our tradition to our child.

With this song, those who had temporarily exchanged the Bible for the god of thunder effectively announced that their newfound faith didn't obstruct them from participating in their clan's traditional rites.

From its inception, Ode Aje was home to witchcraft, magic, and masquerades. I knew some sorcerers and heard about some, like the case of a woman who allegedly killed her children and those of her co-wife because her husband took a second wife without her permission. She was stoned to death on the street, and the silly husband died in loneliness.

Egungun festivals were a time of high excitement in any town, and Ode Aje was no exception. I used to wish the festivals were a daily affair so I wouldn't have to go to school. These festivals dented my original commitment to Christianity because of their singing, dancing, and processions, which were far more entertaining than the Christian Sunday worship. The processions were solemn and prayerful and could be used to show off participation skills.

I would wonder which of the dead we were watching and which particular ancestors were visiting. I knew many people who had passed to the great beyond; any of them could choose to visit us during these festivals. But it was impossible to tell if the *ará ọ̀run* was who they said he was while such festivals were going on. In the church, we received no visitors from heaven, and our piano music could not compete with the energetic drumming at the festivals.

In preparation for one such festival, Ojelabi, who lived a few houses away from mine, bent over to come out of the *igbale*, a sacred room where women and *ogberi* (non-initiates) should not enter for any reason lest they face dire consequences. Our classmate was there, and he spent weeks telling us the incredible story. Ojelabi had just finished consulting with his forefathers, represented by the magical masks.

As the *Alagbaa* of his clan, Ojelabi was the custodian of all the masks and the regalia, just like his father and forebears before him. This time, he came out with a calabash half-filled with well-ground darkish powder. It was time for him to bring his son into the fold and teach him the ways of their father. Masquerading was their way of life, a tradition passed from generation to generation. His name, Ojelabi, translates to "We have birthed a masquerade."

Ojewale, the son, sat on the floor in front of his father, who was seated on a slightly elevated stump of wood. Ojewale's back was turned to his father, who brought his thumbs together to part the boy's hair from the forehead to the back of his neck. As the skin of Ojewale's head came into view, Ojelabi let out a satisfactory sigh before picking up his *abe* (a small knife with a small wooden handle). He started making incisions on the parted path of his son's head while singing an occultic song followed by a series of incantations, not minding the wincing and the fuss from Ojewale:

O wa la be aso, ogberi o mo o o
O wa labe aso, ogberi o mo o o
Omo kekere ti a bi si oje oo
O wa la be aso, ogberi o mo o o
Omo kekere ti a bi si oje o o

He is under the garb; a novice doesn't know about it
He is under the garb; a novice doesn't know about it
A small child born to the home of masqueraders
He is under the garb; a novice doesn't know about it
A small child born in the home of masqueraders.

It became a school song to play with.

After Ojelabi checked every place he marked with his knife and ensured they were bleeding, he carried his calabash in one hand and pinched the black powder with his index finger and thumb. He rubbed the powder into the bleeding spots on Ojewale's head. The boy winced more now, and Ojelabi empathized with him as a father, but this was compulsory if his son would ever grow up to wear the masquerade garb of his forefathers. Satisfied with his work, Ojelabi asked his son how he felt. Ojewale said his head felt heavier than usual and ached. With a dry laugh, his father said, "Well done," and implored him to lie down and rest before they continued the rest of the ritual.

That headache was the last Ojewale would ever experience for the rest of his life. We all heard the story. It was their tradition in their clan. After taking the incisions on the head, they were rid of all headaches stemming from spiritual attacks or medical issues. They were also eligible to wear the *tika-tore* (evil and good) mask and its regalia. Anybody from Ojelabi's bloodline who wore the mask without head incisions would suffer severe headaches and might die if they were not quickly taken care of.

Fifty years earlier, the family story kept repeating: they had lost four men to this error. A steeper consequence awaited a stranger who was bold enough to don the mask, as such a person would drop dead immediately after the mask touched the center of the head. While I didn't see anyone drop dead myself, one must be careful because if the ritual didn't work, a club could do the same job. A sane person does not challenge the wish of a mad person threatening him with a machete.

When Ojewale finally woke up, his father welcomed him back to the land of the living. That short sleep was said to be Ojewale's visit to heaven. Now that he was back, he was no longer an ordinary man; he was an *ara orun* (heavenly person) like his fathers. And when he wore the masks, he could proudly answer the name of *ara orun*. The *eku*, the masquerade's garb, came in assorted colors of rich texture, which was the hallmark of Yoruba fashion.

I often wondered why there was a need for complicated attire for someone believed to be one of my ancestors residing in heaven. Why not appear as an angel in white, which the church later told me was their dress? Only Blacks, we were told, wore black, as they were satanic. The exclusivity of those who acted as guardians of the symbol or custodians of the clan's occult activities was preserved in costumes and rituals. In other words, the guardian of the *eku* represented the de facto custodian of the specific divinity, whose annual return from the world beyond was kicked off through panegyrics and rituals, followed by a carnival-like movement around the town. Our schoolbooks could be more expensive than the *eku*, but they contained knowledge, not magical power. I wanted an *eku* for myself.

The visiting ancestor under the *eku* was expected to offer prayers and curses as deemed appropriate. This was one of the important renditions done by the visiting spirit. Knowing where to offer prayers or otherwise was a function reserved for the followers or initiates of the Egungun. The uninitiated were usually warned against coming too close or touching them lest unfavorable incidents happen to such violators. The *eku* was a living garb and often displayed the attributes of living things, such as breathing or making sounds.

Invariably, an uninitiated who found himself within the location that housed the *eku* might experience its ethereal sounds and movements. In essence, the power of an Egungun was embedded in its *eku* or costume. I wanted to wear one, but I was just too small to carry the heavy load. The *eku* created an occult aura, one that ensured that the spiritual essence of the visiting ancestor remained a mystery. This knowledge was different from what the schoolteacher taught us. The *eku* formed an elaborate part of the Egungun's essence, indicating social power and prestige. The multilayered piece, expensive lappets made of luxurious textiles, expressed the status and wealth of the particular ancestors from the Egungun clan.

Also, the *eku* offered unique protections for its wearer. As spirits, the ancestors under the garb needed as much protection as possible to prevent the people from doing something irrational that might impede the visiting ancestor from returning to wherever it came from. Although not visible, the *eku* is lined with amulets that have performative powers, providing protection against unfriendly and negative influences.

With the costume, it was difficult to analyze the *ara orun*'s specific parameters like body mass, height, and looks. I realized the more I tried, the more it seemed like I was chasing the wind. The ancestors and those charged with ushering them from the spirit realm back to earth appeared to have blocked all avenues for deciphering these details. How best to hide the face of the visiting ancestors other than to cloak them in garbs of varying patterns and styles, sometimes to elicit fear and other times to signify their opulence.

The garbs were often kept in a secluded portion of the clan's shrine or with carefully selected town members who dedicated their time and effort to ensure that the visiting spirits wore outfits that were not spiritually stained or rendered impotent by the touch of the uninitiated. Interestingly, the flowing gowns of the imam and the reverend father didn't have such power; they even put plates of rice on them while eating.

Ode Aje was the home of the Oloolu, the preeminent masquerade in the city that no one must compete with and that women must never see, making the place the unofficial capital of the Egungun clans in Ibadan. For those in the city who had no compunction to visit Ode Aje, the stories they heard were often fearful or bizarre. Among the most popular stories was that of the most famous masquerade, Oloolu, from another clan. Ile Oloolu housed this masquerade belonging to the most powerful cult in Ode Aje, even up to the four corners of this huge city.

During a visit to the clan, I was told the story of how a warrior named Ayorinde Aje defeated the first Oloolu in the masquerade community. This particular masquerade was encountered at Ogbagi, Ondo State, during the civil wars that ravaged the Yoruba kingdoms in the nineteenth century. With nobody powerful enough to defeat the Oloolu, Ayorinde Aje stepped forward and emerged a winner, which led to Oloolu's enslavement and his subsequent relocation to Ode Aje, the abode of his conqueror.

Back to the initiation story. Ojelabi picked up his *abe* again and started another set of incisions. Three under each eye, three under each ear, six on each shoulder blade, six on each chest, three on his knees, and one on each foot. I know these were difficult to endure as my mother had once taken me to an herbalist who made many incisions on my head and told me not to bathe or shower for three days for the medicine to penetrate my body. These incisions were covered with different black powders and concentrated *agbara*, both seen and unseen magical powers to produce physical prowess and things I didn't know then and still don't know. *Ajesara* (fortification) was what Ojelabi called them. They would protect Ojewale from the evils plotted against him by his enemies and rival Oje/Egungun clans. The ones on his chest, knees, and shoulder blades were for protection from beatings that took place during Egungun festivals.

Some rivals, seeking mischief, would spike their canes with evil charms or whip their rivals with juju to test the potency of their magic or their rival's strength, or simply to cause harm. As a result of the incisions his father gave him, Ojewale would have protection from all of these, including hacks from cutlasses, stabs and cuts from knives, and other sharp objects. The incisions below his eyes and ears would help him see and communicate with spiritual beings, witches, wizards, ghosts, or jinns. Small cuts made on the body with a small knife and rubbed with some kind of powder could produce the effects of turning night into day.

After his father finished the second round of the incision ritual, Ojewale made another journey to heaven. The word spread that he was in a trance, undertaking a journey. When he returned, small clay pots filled with a mixture of things he could not relate to were waiting for him. This was called *aseje* (a meal for spiritual fortification). Ojewale was required to eat everything in the pots, followed by shots of dry gin. Once he finished this, there was celebration and fanfare in their household. Ojewale had come of age and became an initiate, and his father was eager to show him off at the coming Egungun festival. He was confident that his son would make him proud as he showcased everything he had been taught since he was a toddler.

The time for the annual Egungun festival was quickly approaching. Ojelabi's household buzzed with preparations. There was a lot to buy, cook, set up, and a lot of fortifications to do. But they had to visit the ritual room first to appease the Egungun and seek help and advice for the coming festival. This would be taken care of by Ojelabi and his heir, Ojewale. They took *akara* (fried bean cakes), *ekuuru* (steamed bean cakes), gin, and palm oil to the sacred room. One after the other, they saluted and worshipped each Egungun and gave them propitiations to guarantee the success of the festival. I could only see them from a distance, but the rituals inside the room were well known to our schoolmates.

Ojelabi's clan housed five masquerades. Two were for magic and fanfare, two were for fear and horror, and the fifth embodied both good and bad. Eegun Onidan (the magician masquerade) had a nice regalia of bright colors and gold, his mask was colorful and not scary, and he could perform many breathtaking and unbelievable stunts. Eegun Okiki (the popular masquerade) was well known for his magic, and he could transform into anyone and anything to entertain people. Eegun Elegba or Olumoyan (the cane-wielding masquerade) was one to fear. With a scary mask and regalia mostly made from raffia, it was popular for the long canes it carried to whip people.

It was the norm for Egungun clans to meet during festivals and whip one another. Whenever Eegun Elegba was out to perform, only those from his bloodline could come closer and dance with him, holding canes to flog the crowd. Spectators not from the masquerade's bloodline could only watch from afar. Eegun Madurodee (the masquerade you should not behold) was the scariest of all the masquerades. Aside from the masquerade's families, no one knew what he looked like; others were not allowed to see him for their own good. Those who proved recalcitrant and tried to see the masquerade either didn't survive to recount the experience or lived to tell a sad tale.

"This person died three years ago, and that person died seven years ago," I heard.

Tika-Toore was the most special of these masquerades for varied reasons. He was the most powerful of all the masquerades, yet his regalia made him look like an ordinary covered man, much like the superhero Spiderman. He would go around town praying for the community and healing the sick, then retired to Ojelabi's family house, where those who were sure of their own goodness would gather to receive prayers and prophecies. This gathering was exclusive to good people only because Tika-Toore could peer into the hearts of individuals, and if they were bad, he would curse them. Also, while strangers could be initiated into masquerading and become eligible to wear the masks of other masquerades, only people from Ojelabi's bloodline could wear the mask of Tika-Toore.

After the meeting with the gods in the gorge, Ojelabi and his son prepared to start the Egungun festival. A messenger would be sent out to notify the community of the date the festival would begin. This period would last for days so that the message circulated throughout the community. Simultaneously, preparations were made to provide food and drinks for families and loved ones who would join in the celebrations. It was always a time of abundance for the Ojelabi family, as those who came to felicitate with them never arrived empty-handed.

On the sixth day, as dusk settled, messengers from Ojelabi's house would disperse into the community with gongs in their hands, beating them loudly to signal that it was time. Those outside would scamper home, and those at home would quickly bolt their windows and doors from behind. Children sought protection in the bosom of their parents, and silence would fall upon the community.

Once it got darker, Eegun Madurodee would be brought out amid incantations from several initiates. His legs were chained to each other, and so were his wrists. I didn't understand why a visitor from heaven would be treated like a prisoner, but he probably brought so many blessings that he must not be allowed to escape. He was surrounded by initiates who kept their distance from him as they patrolled the length and breadth of the community. If Eegun Madurodee stopped moving, it meant a non-initiate was looking; the belief was that such a person could get leprosy, lose sight in both eyes, or become insane. The nightly walk was for the masquerade to cleanse the community of afflictions; only those he had cursed didn't receive his favor.

Early the next day, cooking would start at Ojelabi's place as soon as Eegun Madurodee returned to the gorge. Before noon, people would begin to make merry while expecting Eegun Onidan to make an appearance. He always made explosive entrances with somersaults and flips like a gymnast. Everyone watched in awe as he did his stunts, and when it looked like the people were getting bored, he would transform the color of his regalia. One wondered how many materials were used to make the regalia when he switched from one color to another. It was an incredible sight to behold, especially when he started a stunt in one color and ended with another. People were always happy to gather around and watch this.

The day after, Eegun Elegba would take to the streets with long whips and an entourage of males unclothed from neck to waist. They would carry long canes, too, and dance around the community. So long as you were not in their path, you were saved. Anyone who got too close or stood in their path would get flogged as a way of blessing them. The act of flogging was more intriguing when two different cane-wielding masquerade groups encountered each other. The masquerades competed among themselves over the path, and their followers would whip one another till one party conceded to the other. Some of the followers would have laced their canes with evil charms and would harm anyone who wasn't fortified enough; hence, non-initiates were less likely to not engage.

The appearance of Eegun Okiki on the day after was always anticipated. Nobody knew how, where, or when he would appear. He could also come in any form. Sometimes, as a maiden, as a snake, a sheep, or even as something as small as a locust. He thrilled people with his dance moves, then disappeared into thin air only to appear where people were not looking. While doing that, he could also transform into anything that caught his fancy. This act was one of the propagators of his popularity because, with Eegun Okiki, you never knew what to expect next. After his show, everybody retired, and people rested the next day. I never missed the chance to watch our magician of the year perform.

Eegun Tika-Toore would come out at night with initiates and pray around the community. People could watch from their windows or doors, and those who were not scared of the dark would sit in front of their houses and receive blessings from Tika-Toore's prayers. By dawn, he would be seated in front of Ojelabi's family house, praying for good people and prophesying to them. Once Tika-Toore peered into your heart and saw evil within, he whispered a curse in the individual's ear and they became doomed for the rest of their life. There were always wild jubilations when someone met Tika-Toore and he prayed for them. I knew a long time ago that I wasn't evil, as Tika-Toore would have killed me!

Hunters and farmers might have founded Ode Aje, but how some of these hunters chose to jump ship by abandoning their Òrìṣà faith for other religions was beyond my understanding in those early years of life. Perhaps the hunters and farmers were forced to abandon their indigenous faith when it could not protect them against the superior might of Usman dan Fodio's religious descendants, who aimed to overrun many communities and towns south of Ilorin.

Children born to African parents automatically adopt the religion of the household. For me and a whole lot of children growing up at Ode Aje, one way to kill boredom was to embrace all religions, whether our parents agreed. Well, they wouldn't disagree since most of them also practiced varying degrees of religious syncretism. For some new converts, their names before embracing Islam were not befitting of their new status, so they adopted Arabic names like Abdul Jalil, meaning "Servant of the Majestic God." Some had to change their faith when they encountered Sufi Islam. The Sufi Muslims came into their society and started to preach Islam to anyone who cared to listen.

Initially, some people paid no attention to the Sufi preachers and focused on the religion they were born into, but they could not ignore that the Muslims were powerful, and people started to patronize their enclaves, reducing the influence of the local religion. In some encounters with Isab Sufi Muslims, they realized that the differences between them were not that much.

The clerics did their best to convert a lot of them to Islam, even though they were always reluctant. Nevertheless, they became friends and started to share ideas. Little by little, the bond between them became so strong that it began to blur the religious lines. During the next masquerade festival, some Islamic preachers tried to watch the activities of the masquerades and their worshippers. The dances, chants, and incantations were surprising to them, as their mode of worship was different from what they saw from the Òrìṣà people.

I remember an occasion when I witnessed an encounter between an imam and one of the senior masquerades. The imam regarded these worshippers as pagans and gave stern warnings to new Muslim converts at the festival about *shirk*, pointing to the fact that they could not worship any other god except Allah.

Can these intervals go?
Five calls, numerous Makkah
Rosaries of worship, cast away evil
Oh, you servants of Allah,
What will shirk bring forth? Doom!
Want to create a rival for the Almighty? Laaa!
He is Ahad! Allahu Samad, lam yalid wa lam yulad
He begets not, nor was he begotten.

After becoming consistent in using Solat as a means of connecting with Allah, some realized that the Islamic religion didn't allow for them to bow to any god except Allah, and if they continued, they would be committing *shirk*, and their prayers wouldn't be answered. Many of these Òrìṣà worshippers abandoned their father's gorge, and the family masquerades to become Muslims. Following the Sufi way of Islam, balancing their traditional religion with the new faith was relatively easy. They could consult the jinns for answers to help people who came for a solution to a problem, and he could prepare charms for them, too.

Ode Aje never relinquished its tie to the religions of its ancestors. Those regarded as pagans in Ode Aje let others practice their beliefs. It would be difficult to point to a particular Muslim household without one or two elders who still upheld the religion of their ancestors. This allowed Muslims in Ode Aje to share their hearts with more than one religion.

As a child, I was oblivious to the dissimilarities between these religions; the uniformity and unity of the adherents made me believe they were all one. For people like me, I saw nothing wrong in participating in as many religious festivals as possible, even though I could only claim one religion at any given time. For the fun of it, I became a Christian during the Easter and Christmas seasons and a Muslim during the small Eid and big Eid.

Being a devout Muslim in society was related to the capacity to embark on pilgrimages to Mecca, which conferred on the sojourner the famed title of Alhaji, meaning a traveler, a title Alhaji Onigolu wore with pride on his sleeves. Muslims like Alhaji were in abundance in the city. Armed with amulets and juju, they never needed to make use of the mosque to fight spiritual battles. The five obligatory daily prayers were only an avenue to fulfill all righteousness; to truly be protected, amulets, charms, and *igbadi* seemed more potent.

Alhaji Onigolu was tough, and this often elicited fear from his children. Any of his children who weren't afraid of him was regarded as a bad child. The principle of respect for the elderly became a sin when not done to the letter. This meant Alhaji's children adhered to every word he spoke like it was the law.

Despite fathering plenty of children, Alhaji Onigolu acted like he owed none of them anything. Nothing was guaranteed except food. He married four wives, as he believed that was the ideal number permitted by the Prophet. Even though his fourth wife tried to persuade him to marry one more, Alhaji had reached his maximum. For him to marry another wife, he must either lose one of them to death or a divorce. He cannot marry more than four wives at a time; this is what the sharia teaches.

I recall the time when Alhaji Onigolu battled a prolonged illness and was dying. The previous year, he had lost one of his four wives to what was believed to have been a spiritual attack. Eleha, Alhaji's wife, was said to be the family's most devout Muslim because she completely covered her body in the niqab. Eleha had chosen to wear the niqab, as Alhaji never made it mandatory for his wives. Except for her husband and close family members, no one could brag about having seen Eleha's face after she began wearing the niqab.

Eleha's tragic experience with a masquerade resulted in her death. Her garment had always interested the followers of Egungun, and they believed that by dressing like them (masquerade), she was making fun of their gods and ancestors. Although the *eku* and the veil of Eleha are both used to cover the entire body, they are not the same and do not serve the same function. The only thing that makes them similar is the fact that they both have religious significance. Moreover, if you've never seen the face of the person wearing the niqab, you can't identify the person, just like the *eku*.

On this fateful day, the masquerade got confrontational with Eleha, asking her questions that infuriated her as she replied angrily.

In his thick, deep voice, as always, the Egungun asked, "Why are you dressed like us? Where are the other layers? Which heaven are you from? Is this a mockery of my fathers? Who are you?"

Before Eleha responded, she murmured some words that the masquerade assumed were incantations:

بِسْمِ اللَّهِ الرَّحْمَنِ الرَّحِيمِ
الْحَمْدُ لِلَّهِ رَبِّ الْعَالَمِينَ
الرَّحْمَنِ الرَّحِيمِ

Bismillaahi ar-Rahman a-Raheem (In the name of God)
Al hamdu lillaahi rabbil 'alameen (All praise belongs to Allah, Lord of all the worlds)
Ar-Rahmani ar-Raheem (The All-compassionate, the All-merciful)

She replied with a brave voice, not discouraged by the sticks and reactions from the masquerade's followers who were harassing her, knowing fully that the masquerade would be more confused. This raised their anger toward her as they thought she was still mocking them and trying to use charms on them, too.

"I am a servant of Allah, a member of this world. May Allah not send me to death."

She was holding her tasbih, the Muslim rosary, as she uttered those replies. The masquerade responded by laughing uncontrollably and expressing his amazement at her gender as well as his admiration for her daring and bravery.

"Oniyeye! Better undress and let me impregnate you. I have a well of sperm in my scrotum," the masquerade replied.

A few days later, Eleha fell ill and eventually passed away. It was believed that the masquerade or one of his minions had put a charm on her during their confrontation. Alhaji had pleaded with her to see the traditional healers for treatment, but she refused, turning down all local medicine till she died.

Eleha's sudden death taught Alhaji Onigolu a valuable lesson. When it looked like he wasn't getting better from his sickness, he contacted the traditional healers and diviners for treatment. While he continued Islamic prayers for healing, the diviners prepared various offerings, including *gbeere* and *aseje*. Alhaji maintained his adherence to the old faith to be healed, all the while having faith in his new belief. When he was healed, he would decide to whom he owed gratitude.

The Muslims at Ode Aje had some level of dependence on people they considered to be pagans. Traditional worshippers or "pagans" seldom visited the mosque to strengthen their spiritual lives. However, the Muslims visited the people who sell *ewe ati egbo*, herbs and various materials needed to prepare propitiations that were not intended for Allah.

Iya Lekuleja's store didn't discriminate against those who believed their religion forbade them from holding what they considered fetish materials. These people often sneaked down to the prominent herbal store, aware of the perceptions others might have if they were seen. However, the Òrìṣà people didn't need much from the imams and Islamic teachers. While the former had materials to perform various healing acts, the latter could only offer prayers and hope the prayers were accepted.

One thing that Islam brought to the Yoruba was the delineation of various times of the day. Since the obligatory five daily prayers were to be undertaken at specific times of the day, it was easier to schedule an appointment without worrying if the other party understood the timing.

The Muslims congregated five times daily to offer prayers in unity. And the timekeeper, who offered the call to prayer, possessed deep insight about using the location of the sun as well as its glare to affirm which time of the day it was. The call to prayer could be heard multiple times a day in a voice so sweet and melodious:

Allahu Akbar Allahu Akbar
Ashadu an Laa Ilaaha Ilal Laah
Ashadu anna Muhammadan Rasullullahi
Hayya alas-salah . . .

Hence, time wasn't measured by the hunters' three periods of the day but by a different five-period day. This was one positive aspect that no one dared to fault. It was beneficial to adopt certain elements of borrowed culture to reinvent social existence.

The hunters and farmers didn't need time since their engagements didn't fall within the auspices of social association. They only required abstract conceptualism of the periods of the day: morning, afternoon, evening, or night.

Conversely, the Christian missionaries brought with them timing machines, often ringing their bells in the evenings.

From the outset, the Abrahamic religions shared a peaceful coexistence with the "pagans," as they chose to call the Òrìṣà worshippers. Much like the earliest years of Nigeria's marriage, the three religions in Ode Aje didn't have any form of animosity against each other. For instance, even though their religious teachings were not on par, all three religions celebrated their dead. During Easter, Jesus would rise, and the Muslims would share in the joyous event. Although the other Abrahamic religions didn't set aside any date for the revisit of their famed progenitors, ancestors of several Ode Aje clans would come annually to offer prayers to everyone, regardless of their religious background.

However, one does not need a soothsayer to know that this won't last forever. The contrast in dogmas and ideologies, irrespective of how subtle, was a recipe to break the fragile peace existing among these distinct religions in Ibadan. Moreover, there was a fervent zeal in the hearts of the respective proponents to convert as many people as possible to the Abrahamic religions. In truth, those wrongly labeled as pagans had little recourse for advertising their religions or seeking converts like their imported counterparts. While they spread the gospel messages, albeit from two divergent perspectives, the Abrahamic religions focused on those we now call traditionalists, whose ways and activities they saw as contradictory to their monotheistic views of divinity.

In no time, Ode Aje began to witness powerful messages aimed at denigrating what the people upheld as their religious beliefs. Gospel songs sounded great, much the same way Islamic lore was accepted without scrutiny from opposing forces. A common one, which you could expect in many services, was the idea to drop the family ancestor as a savior to be replaced by another ancestor presented as the Prophet or one with a Yorubanized name of "Jesu" for Jesus:

Jesu ni Olugbala!
Igbagbo ninu Jesu ni iyee
O ku fun ese emi ati ire
(and they ring the bell continuously)

The bell must ring, especially when the wandering church workers walked the streets in search of converts. If the Muslims used the holy wars to make converts, the preachers used threatening language of death and hellfire. One killed with the sword, the other with words. When the second line was sung, it demoted the concept of ancestorhood in Yoruba to a mere mortal since Jesu was declared the ultimate salvation, the *iyee*, who, as proclaimed in the last line, died because of you and me.

Our ancestors didn't die because of us but were killed by Iku, a translation of death (*iku*) but with a different meaning. Iku was a being, a roving spirit, a living entity who traversed heaven and earth. Iku lived among us, carrying a club. When a sick man cries in pain, it is often not for the reasons you may think, but because Iku is hitting him with a club.

Pasito, my grandfather and one of the early Christian converts in the city, made me realize at a young age that Christianity, as brought by the missionaries to Ode Aje, would inevitably be diluted with African concepts. For example, my understanding of judgment according to the Bible was that the day set aside for it will not come until one is dead. This was in sharp contrast to the Yoruba belief that the wicked will surely be punished on earth for their deeds.

Even after rising through the ranks from a floor member to a clergyman, Pasito never relinquished this fundamental law of karma. He would tell his congregation that the wicked would face judgment and punishment on earth. Some of his alleged punishments were so bizarre that one began to evaluate if he was following the teachings of the Bible. Sometimes, the congregation would laugh at Pasito's messages, abruptly interrupted by his demeanor that didn't reflect that of a jester or clown.

Pasito's messages often ignited the congregation to curse and insult those whose actions seemed discordant with the progress of the church, contradicting the biblical injunction for Christians to pray for their enemies. The imam and the priest did want their so-called pagan neighbors to die!

Just as it was applicable in other Yoruba communities, those who brought Christianity to Ibadan were cunning. They arrived armed with Western education and a new religion, far different from what the people were familiar with. Any beneficiary would have to accept the "two gifts" simultaneously. Many parents in Ode Aje, eager for their children to learn the white man's ways through formal education, were not conscious of the fact that the Christian schools would eventually expose the children to a new religious culture, one that relegated the Òrìṣà religion.

Ironically, Christianity was unable to stop its converts from practicing polygamy. That aspect of culture was strongly adhered to since none of the Ten Commandments explicitly frowned on it. As I would later become aware, marrying a second, third, or fourth wife needed little or no ceremony; the man would simply bring a new woman home and proudly announce the latest addition to his wife or wives. The elders of the church could not persuade the converts in Ode Aje to shun a practice regarded as a macho ideal. Often, I wonder how the converts would have responded if both Abrahamic religions frowned on polygamy.

Baba Olopa and Alhaji were two strong converts who refused to part with the polygamist concept. Fortunately, one religion upheld it, while the other didn't—unlike the concept of Esu that the Abrahamic religions successfully equated to Satan, the evildoer. The Ode Aje Christians would wear their best clothes on Sunday, a practice that is still common among churchgoers in Nigeria today. While growing up in Ode Aje, it was normal to see a Christian wear the same clean clothes to church every Sunday, especially if such clothes seemed to be the newest. Since new clothes were bought either during Christmas or Easter, the repetition of perceived new clothes continued until the wearer outgrew them or they became worn or torn.

For the less privileged like me, owning one pair of shoes meant walking barefoot on school days and reserving the shoes for church on Sundays. The missionaries had taught the converts to see the Sabbath as not only a holy day but also a day to wear one's best attire. I attended church regularly, and nothing captivated me more than the songs and hymns. This led to my joining the choir, although I eventually lost interest and opted out.

One other thing that many Christians in Ode Aje never felt reluctant to do was to visit charm makers and diviners to seek insights into their future. The desperation to know the future or guide against impending failures wasn't something the Christians considered sacrilege. Despite the Ten Commandments explicitly warning against the worship or subjection to any other god, Christians trooped down to herbal stores to get various materials to produce charms and sacrifices, definitely not for the Christian God, who, as the Bible made clear, required none of these.

The Christians who visited Iya Lekuleja, the preeminent herbalist, needed protection from evil forces, failures, and unforeseeable events. Their Christian teachers and missionaries didn't have any amulet to protect them; instead, they told them to believe in the mere words written in the Bible. However, this wasn't enough for these new converts, as they required more than words to protect themselves against bad dreams, witches, illnesses, and other afflictions.

Just as the *ijala* constantly chanted by the hunters' guilds, charms, and other physical materials bolstered their courage, the missioners were expected to give the new Ode Aje converts materials for protection. While hymnals and worship songs may substitute for the *ijala*, and prayers substitute for incantations, Christians believe in bearing one's cross as a form of forbearance rather than a preventative measure against misfortunes. But the cross is nothing to substitute for the mystical powers of amulets and charms. Jesus is powerful, but his territory is extraterrestrial. Amulets are powerful, and their effects are observable in the real world.

For the newly converted Muslims, the recitation of the Kalima Shahada (profession of faith) was an affirmation that there was no other deity worthy of worship than Allah. In Islam, women are regarded as sacred, and it is forbidden for them to expose sensitive parts of their bodies. Islam condemns fornication and adultery and considers showing one's nudity to be a serious offense. Muslim women are encouraged to cover their hands and face with clothing and wear a long veil (niqab). These women are called *Eleha*, and I heard many Islamic preachers base the Eleha practice and belief on the *ayah* (a verse of the Quran) cited below that corroborates that women in Islam are seen as sacred and should dress modestly.

O Prophet! Tell thy wives and daughters,
and the believing women,

that they should cast their outer garments
over their persons (when abroad):
that is most convenient,
that they should be known (as such) and not molested.
And Allah is Oft-Forgiving, Most Merciful. (Quran 33:59)

There are several tales and stories about the adherents of the Abrahamic religion at Ibadan, and one of them is the account of some church officials who were alarmed by how quickly the Muslim faithful were able to convert followers of the Òrìṣà to Islam. To win souls for Jesus, they needed to find a means to also win over many people to their own religion.

Go ye therefore, and teach all nations,
baptizing them in the name of the Father,
and of the Son, and of the Holy Ghost. (Matthew 28:19)

Surprisingly, these church leaders consulted local diviners for assistance instead of stepping up their spiritual efforts to gain new souls. Everyone in the community was aware of Ojelabi's ability to use charms for a variety of purposes, both good and bad, and these church leaders rushed to him for charms to help them convert more people to their religion. Prior to this, the story of a merchant who sought Ojelabi's charm for commercial prosperity had gained notoriety after his exiled wife revealed the secret of his success.

It might even be worse at Iya Lekuleja's store because customers from all three religions came to buy various items to use as charms or as medicines. Most recent converts to the two Abrahamic religions held that their new faith didn't prevent them from seeking *aajo* from diviners during tough times or from inquiring about the future.

One Sunday, a devout follower of Egungun and a close friend of Baba Olopa visited him. During their conversation, Baba Olopa's friend asked him a few questions about his religion. He had heard that some Christians, particularly recent converts in Ode Aje, referred to Jesus as their savior and that he currently resided in heaven before he would return to earth, although they were unsure of the exact date.

"Your ancestors live in the same place (heaven), so you also worship *ará ọ̀run*." Since Jesus also resides in heaven, he is also *ará ọ̀run*, like our own gods. But why does your father hate you so much and doesn't bother to visit you? Our father visits us from heaven every year, but your father doesn't," the man noted.

Baba Olopa's reply left his friend more confused and even in greater doubt. "He will come on the resurrection day, a day in which all the dead will rise.

Many will go to hellfire, and a few will follow Jesus to glory to be with him on the right hand of God."

Now even more confused, Baba Olopa's friend smiled. "Please give me some palm wine, let me enjoy myself before your Jesus arrives and takes my life. Why wait to wake up already dead people for judgment when they could have been punished for their sin on earth before they died?"

That conversation stayed with me ever since.

In another tale that was very prominent in Ode Aje, it wasn't strange to see Muslim migrants coming to seek settlements in Yoruba territories in the nineteenth century. At first, they were met with stiff resistance as they were suspected to be spies for the jihadists to launch another attack. On their part, the migrants comported themselves and left without making a fuss in places they were rejected.

Eventually, a chief gave them the benefit of the doubt and gave them a parcel of land to settle on. Grateful for the opportunity, they remained peaceful and didn't trespass or break the rules of the land. They simply practiced their religion and subsisted. This opened the ever-accommodating Yoruba people to welcoming the Muslim migrants who, in turn, projected themselves as good neighbors.

One of the fascinating attributes of these people was how they worshipped. Beginning with a small bath, someone would then step up to rally others to the prayer location, speaking a language the Yoruba didn't understand. While these were all amusing, the prayer itself was intriguing.

A man would stand in front, and the others would maintain a straight line about two feet behind him. A separate row accommodated the women who were always covered. The man in front, acting as the leader, called out in a low tone and changed posture, and the others replicated his move after his assistant repeated the leader's words, albeit louder. Fascinated by the uniformity, coordination, and focus they put into their prayer, some adherents of the Yoruba traditional religion started to join the Islamic religion.

The early spread of Islam that I witnessed was hard, and I believe it must have been even more complicated before I was born. It wasn't an easy task to preach a new religion to your landlords, who were already suspicious of you, without causing further suspicion. This was one of the issues faced by the Muslims who settled in the area where Ojelabi resided. The area was dominated by Egungun clans, who were devout adherents to their religion. They also were amused by the Islamic way of life, but rather than do away with them, they learned how to use the timing for Muslim prayers to their advantage, transforming it into a clock they used to make appointments.

Frustration set in for the new Muslim migrants, but they persisted, using prayers and actions to gain converts, although not as much as they desired. Launching a jihad in Ode Aje wasn't possible, as it would mean one family member killing another.

At some point, I heard that someone insinuated that the *olorìṣàs* were spiritually fortified, which was why it had been difficult to convert them to Islam. He then proposed that the best way to get them would probably be to use the people's voodoo against them. To buttress his point, he explained that he had witnessed the *olorìṣàs* during their Egungun festivals and saw how they harmed themselves with voodoo despite being fortified against it.

While they saw sense in his reasoning, the challenge lay in how the Muslims could approach the Egungun worshippers to ask for the charm that would make them leave their traditional religion to follow Islam. Many Muslims eventually gave up, and we later discovered that Bello or Ibrahim was also the one inside the *eku*.

Then, one day, Ojelabi was approached by a self-proclaimed merchant from a neighboring town, who sought help to attract more customers to his trade. After deliberations between the two, they settled on making *aworo* (crowd puller), a charm that would pull people to where it is invoked and would be made from an unusual ingredient—*igbe eegun* (masquerade feces).

To get this, they needed a masquerade to come out and perform. Once the regalia and mask had been returned to the gorge, the first solid waste of the individual who donned the mask and regalia would be collected and burned with some selected leaves to make the *aworo*, which would now be taken to the place it was needed and then buried.

After getting the charm, the merchant left. However, instead of leaving town, he headed for the Muslim settlement under the cover of night. There he presented what he had gotten to the others. As instructed, the powder was buried at the back of their yard, and everyone retired for the night.

As if by magic, the following day brought an astonishing transformation. Immediately the early dawn calls for prayer began, people started trickling into the mosque one after the other. It was unprecedented to have that many "pagans" at once for prayer, and they had to teach them to take the ritual bath (*ghusl*) before they could pray. They were received with warmth and urged to say the *Kalimatu Shahadah* as an attestation to Islam as their new religion.

Ojewale was one of those new converts.

By 1967, four years after I arrived at Ode Aje, my world had undergone a profound transformation. I had now become fully Yoruba, able to tell the differences between the stings and poisons of the bee and the wasp, running from the one bite to escape the multiple bites of the other. I knew that a house wasn't about the bricks and the roof but was intricately woven with culture.

I recognized that my earthly fathers could provide for me, but they were less powerful than the witches and sorcerers. I knew that my mother in heaven was more important than my mother on earth. I had a father who was both a wizard and a witch whom I must appeal to, as his pouches were full of charms and magic.

When confronted with troubles brought by the wizards at home, I learned how to make invocations to the wizards in the outer world. I knew that imams and pastors could be traducers that I must appease. I knew that the Bible and the Quran could serve the same purposes as charms, that the lines in them were no different from incantations, and that they could all be used for invocation.

I learned that the diviner, pastor, and imam could share the same space in an esoteric cult, translating the words of God in ways that transcended human understanding. Jesus Christ shed blood, the Prophet of Islam shed blood, and Ogun, the god of iron, also shed blood. That blood had to be placated. Everyone must invite the cosmic to agree on peace and to prepare for battles.

As the 1970s unfolded, my experience with Islam taught me that you have not succeeded in killing the cobra until you have cut off its head; that you cannot kill the elephant with a small sword, that you cannot kill the buffalo with a kitchen knife; and that you must slit the bowel of a python to see its end.

I am not reciting a surah here, but the incantations from the Òrìṣà emphasize that, in later years, Islam became so big that all the Egungun combined could no longer overpower it.

FIG. 3. *Al-Wudu* (ablution) by Dr. Kazeem Ekeolu. Muslims perform ablution before prayer at the mosque.

CHAPTER TWO

One Wudu and Ninety-Nine Tasbih

In the bustling streets of Bodija's charm,
I met the faithful, their spirits warm,
From Oja Oba to Mapo Hall's might,
Ibadan's heartbeat pulsed with Islam's light.

In the bustling markets of Oja Oba,
Where cultures melded, without a flaw,
I heard the call to prayer, sweet and clear,
An invitation to Allah, drawing near.

In the songs of praise that filled the air,
I heard the echoes of Allah's care,
From the lips of worshippers devout,
A symphony of faith, there was no doubt.

Through the tales of Balogun's past,
I witnessed resilience that would forever last,
Yoruba heritage intertwined with Islam's grace,
Weaving a rich embroidery in a sacred place.

In the sanctity of the ancient Oke-Are,
I found solace; my heart laid bare,
From the towering Olubadan's throne,
To the streets where faith had grown.

Ibadan, a city that stands so tall,
Where Islam's spirit would never fall,
A beacon of unity, a home for all,
In the heart of Yorubaland, clear writings on the wall.

During the early years of my stay in Ode Aje in the 1960s, there was no disruption of worship or even an outright forceful prohibition of practicing a particular religion by another religion. Instead, it was common to see churches and mosques in Ibadan situated not far from each other. Naturally, the churches were bigger since they preferred to cluster all their members in one spot as if to show the advantage of size.

In contrast, the Muslims built many mosques, strategically placing them to encourage worshippers to quickly leave their homes, worship, and promptly go back to their businesses. You cannot ask people to pray five times a day and then locate the abode of Allah far away! However, determining the dominant religion between the two was a challenge. If you base your data on the number of mosques, there were more Muslims. The Christians were more if you took your census on a Sunday at the entrance of a church as they trooped out at the same time.

For a more precise figure, you could approach government officials at the secretariat, and a Muslim official would tell you they were more, while a Christian one would claim the Christians had the greater number. The government itself wasn't a mediator since everyone involved was interested in exaggerating the numbers. Official censuses in Nigeria counted people and goats together to swell up regional and ethnic figures.

Both Christians and Muslims looked alike, except for one or two ladies who had bleached their skin, which made them look like apparitions from strange lands, and who were tactlessly mocked as prostitutes. Those with the longer beards were Muslims, as Christians tended to prefer shorter beards, with the exception of the socialists among them who needed to make a point by pulling at their unkempt beards during conversations. There was a relatively balanced relationship and existence.

We had the Anglican church to the West and the Catholic to the East. The Baptists were located a few miles away, with the Aladura church only a few steps away. Given the way their pastors talked poorly about one another, it seemed that salvation couldn't be in all three churches.

To the people in my Anglican church, Catholics were pagans worshipping the photograph of Mary and the effigy of Jesus. To the Aladura, the prayer warriors, the cornerstone in the corner of a church couldn't have been Peter but Jesus. To the Baptists, the Anglicans had too many members in the Ogboni fraternity, alleged to use human skulls to drink human blood in order to seal deadly oaths.

I didn't fully understand why the hymns of all the dueling churches were the same, and their "Holy Communion" used the same cup to take less than a teaspoon of red wine, with a minuscule bread that disappeared on the tongue, leaving nothing to be swallowed.

Muslims in those days saw one another as members of a single religion, which meant total submission to the will of Almighty Allah. Islam does not have different forms of worship; its goal is worshipping Allah and accepting Prophet Muhammad (Peace Be unto Him) by adhering strictly to his commandments.

While the Christians urged us to keep to the Ten Commandments, we were never sanctioned for breaking them. For the Muslims, defying their laws was equivalent to the loss of faith, the end of life. And they insisted on not breaking the core instructions. Various organizations and movements arose because of individual differences, giving rise to varying views, perceptions, interpretations, and understandings.

Despite these differences, however, Muslims have always been united in the mode of worship. For instance, regardless of the sect, salat (prayer) must be observed the same way across all societies and races. Likewise, it is compulsory to recite Suratul Fatiha before any other surah while praying. There is no Islamic society whatsoever that can decide to modify this or even choose to increase or decrease the number of *rakah* (supplications and body movements) already stipulated for every prayer.

In Ode Aje, preaching and theology were available on the streets, and recorded sermons were everywhere, played at such volume that even if you tried to block your ears, a sentence or two would find their way through. You would encounter preachers who would force themselves on you.

We had our preeminent educator, tutor, and librarian, known as Baba Ula. He was among the ulama, which they shortened to Ula. His real name, no one knew. A devout Muslim, Baba Ula was well versed in history and the Quran, which was why he was said to be among the ulama. I don't know how he was appointed to that position because there was a clause that required any member of the ulama to be a historian, the transmitter of knowledge, and the guardian of facts.

Not everyone regarded Baba Ula as a real member of the ulama, and many Muslims doubted he had the requisite training. I trusted him, though, together with my classmates and schoolteachers, perhaps because he had a library with many books written in Arabic and Ajami—the use of Arabic scripts to write in the Yoruba language. The public and high school teachers consulted him, and this was an open secret.

As I grew up in Ode Aje, I developed an awareness that everything had a genesis, a backstory. I was intrigued by the Islamic religion, so I tried to find its backstory. I had always understood that Islam spread to the southwestern part of Nigeria (Yorubaland) from the north through the Fulani during the Sokoto jihad. Wanting to get a broader scope of knowledge, I inquired around and was directed to Baba Ula, the oldest member of the ulama in the area. An *alim* (a young member of the ulama) told me that Baba Ula was a human library and had knowledge that dated back centuries. Some of this knowledge was based on what he witnessed, while others came from stories told to him by his forebears.

My eagerness to meet Baba Ula was unmatched, but my repeated attempts were thwarted as his family consistently denied me access to him, giving various excuses like, "Baba Ula is sleeping," or "Baba Ula is an old man; he should not be disturbed."

I was relentless, and they realized my determination. Eventually, the matriarch of the family took pity on me and scheduled a meeting with me. I was so happy. What would we do without mothers? Nothing!

On the appointed day, I arrived as responsibly as I could, bearing gifts of a few oranges for Baba Ula and the matriarch and some groundnuts for the children—a token of appreciation for the wisdom I hoped to acquire.

When Baba Ula began sharing his insights, I knew immediately that the wait and persistence were worth it. He said my knowledge about Islam wasn't entirely incorrect but wasn't totally right either, as Islam had gotten to Yorubaland before the Fulani arrived. I was persuaded and listened more attentively. According to him, Islam had penetrated Hausaland through trade with the Arabs who settled in East, West, and North Africa, actively participating in the trade across the desert. Few of these Arabs were explorers, and they eventually reached the southwest from the north, preaching Islam.

As explained by Baba Ula, the Yoruba name for Islam, *imole*, was derived from one or two sources. The first source attributed the name to the preachers who came to Yorubaland from the ancient Mali empire, leading to the religion being dubbed "the knowledge from Mali" (*imole*). The second possible source was that when Islam was preached, it had many guidelines that were quite strict and life-changing, so the Yoruba called it "strict knowledge" (*imole*). My head shook softly in response as I absorbed the information.

Islam was mixed with the Hausa indigenous religion. Africans, proud of their culture, were unwilling to forsake it to pick up a foreign one; instead, they married Islam with their traditional religion. That was what the Fulani jihadists, who were more into Islam than their roots, tried to change in the north while also trying to spread it southward. They were unsuccessful in the southeast, but Islam was able to gain more ground in Yorubaland, with followers continuing to mix it with their traditional religion.

The jihad created a divide. On one side were those advocating for the pure practice of Islam, and on the other side were those who believed there was nothing wrong in mixing it with their local religion. "It incurred profit for some people and a great loss for others," Baba Ula concluded with a momentary pause as if waiting for me to take in all he had said.

At that point, I remembered the story of one of Baba Ula's colleagues, Alfa Abdulkareem, from whom I had first learned about Islam. When the man wanted to get married, the lady he loved was from a family who practiced the Òrìṣà religion. Defying the wishes of their imams, Baba Ula's friend married this lady, and his friends predicted that the union would not end well.

But they were wrong. Alfa Abdulkareem's in-laws proved to be good and accommodating. Over time, he embraced some of their practices and became successful. Unlike his friends, who often suggested prayers as the only solution to every problem, Alfa Abdulkareem went the extra mile. He would check first by divination to seek a suitable solution that often had nothing to do with prayers. Most times, he just needed to burn or cook herbs and prescribe their usage for his customers. His practice looked more realistic, and more people patronized him, establishing him as a force to reckon with among his fellow Muslims.

As a bonus, his wife had a big stall in the market where the roots, leaves, dried animals, and other ingredients needed for his potions were sold, which he directed his customers to. The more customers for the husband, the more customers for the wife, allowing them to quickly build their fortune.

There were also great losses caused predominantly by those who took an overdose of Islam. Some individuals were adamant about practicing Islam in its purest form and didn't want to mix it with the indigenous religion. But some took it a notch higher by refusing to take simple traditional medicines like herbs, citing Islam as their excuse.

But Baba Ula, remembered that Alfa Abdulkareem's family refused to have anything to do with him due to his involvement in divination and selling herbs. "Were the Muslims not justified to disassociate with him?" I wanted to hear the older man's thoughts about the juxtaposition of prayers with herbal remedies.

With pain in his eyes, Baba Ula replied, "Not all herbs are driven by spiritual motives. Some are just leaves boiled in water to treat 'stubborn' ailments and have been used long before the arrival of Islam, but people chose to discard them for something new."

Baba Ula continued with the tragic story of a woman who suffered from recurring fever during pregnancy. She would be bedridden yet refused medicinal herbs prepared for her, saying it was against her belief and that Allah would cure her. According to Baba Ula, the herb was potent, made from mango leaves boiled in water and nothing more. She kept turning it down, asking for Islamic prayers to be done for her instead. Her mother worried to no end; she couldn't persuade her daughter to reconsider her decision.

Despite the woman's persistent rejection of the herbal remedy, her alfas didn't reprimand her and continued to pray in a cup of water for her to drink. When the sickness continued to get worse, she finally listened to her mother's pleas to take the herbal remedy. Regrettably, she died with her unborn child before the first batch of concoctions was ready for her to use.

Baba Ula shared additional insights about Islam with me. He explained that during the lifetime of Prophet Muhammad (PBUH), Allah revealed a chapter of the Quran to him when idolaters who were ready to convert to Islam came to him, but on the condition that he had to accept some of their practices. In response to the idolaters' proposal, Allah instructed the Prophet (PBUH) to reject their offer and to tell them to practice what they believed in while he did the same because he served a God different from theirs. The final verse of the chapter reads thus:

لَكُمْ دِيْنُكُمْ وَلِى دِي

You shall have your religion and I shall have my religion. (Quran 109:6)

Baba Ula continued, "Don't meddle in the affairs of others. Don't impose your ideals on them, the same way they should not force theirs on you. If you are a Muslim, believe in Allah alone. Follow his instructions, believe in the last day, and do good deeds for everyone. During the time of the Prophet, Muslims and non-Muslims lived together peacefully, and the Muslims protected everybody like they were the soldiers of the territory.

"As Muslims, we are not to disrespect, argue, quarrel, or raise our voices at Christians without cause. Unless they behave unjustly or try to claim what does not belong to them, Islam encourages peaceful coexistence. In fact, it is possible to live with them for years without any issues because we are to coexist peacefully and respectfully. Anybody who goes around killing, slaughtering, and disturbing innocent people on the basis of religion is not a Muslim and shall be among the losers on the Day of Judgment. The best way to avoid religious intolerance is to follow Allah's injunction that we should let them be while we uphold our practices. We have to stop here now. We will revisit the lifetime of the Prophet another time."

From my interaction with Baba Ula, I deduced that Allah wants nothing but peace; after all, the very essence of Islam is peace. Allah could have ordered the Prophet to reject the offers of the *mushriks* (idolaters) and *Kafirs* (unbelievers) and forced them to accept Islam. However, he told the Prophet to tell them to maintain their lane while Muslims maintained theirs as well. Muslims are not permitted to condemn or disrespect non-Muslims at any point, except in extreme cases, as explained in the Quranic verse below:

وَلَا تُجَادِلُوٓا اَهۡلَ الۡكِتٰبِ اِلَّا بِالَّتِىۡ هِىَ اَحۡسَنُ
اِلَّا الَّذِيۡنَ ظَلَمُوۡا مِنۡهُمۡ وَقُوۡلُوۡۤا اٰمَنَّا بِالَّذِىۡۤ
اُنۡزِلَ اِلَيۡنَا وَاُنۡزِلَ اِلَيۡكُمۡ وَاِلٰهُـنَا وَاِلٰهُكُمۡ
وَاحِدٌ وَّنَحۡنُ لَهٗ مُسۡلِمُوۡنَ

And do not dispute with the followers of the Book except by what is best, except those of them who act unjustly, and say: We believe in that which has been revealed to us and revealed to you, and our Allah and your Allah is one, and to Him do we submit. (Quran 29:46)

Baba Ula quoted another verse of the Quran that commands Muslims to be just and relate fairly with non-Muslims:

لَا يَنۡهٰٮكُمُ اللّٰهُ عَنِ الَّذِيۡنَ لَمۡ يُقَاتِلُوۡكُمۡ فِى
الدِّيۡنِ وَلَمۡ يُخۡرِجُوۡكُمۡ مِّنۡ دِيَارِكُمۡ اَنۡ
تَبَرُّوۡهُمۡ وَ تُقۡسِطُوۡۤا اِلَيۡهِمۡ‌ؕ اِنَّ اللّٰهَ يُحِبُّ
الۡمُقۡسِطِيۡنَ

Allah does not forbid you respecting those who have not made war against you on account of (your) religion, and have not driven you forth from your homes, that you show them kindness and deal with them justly; surely Allah loves the doers of Justice. (Quran 60:8)

At that time, my goal wasn't to verify the accuracy of Baba Ula's stories and ideas. Given his quiet and easygoing nature, the Christians had no problems with him, and even the masquerades visited him each year, and he gave them money. Fellow Muslims made cynical remarks about him: how could someone who had not performed the hajj claim so much knowledge? Nevertheless, I stood firm in my admiration of Baba Ula and my acknowledgment of him as my imam!

After spending a holiday at my grandmother's place, my journey back to Ode Aje was relatively short, albeit boring, on that particular hot and humid day.

Upon my arrival, I started cleaning and dusting. Then my schoolmate, Wasiu, knocked on my door.

Wasiu was the mischievous son of an Islamic leader and the grandson of the late imam of the biggest mosque located in Ode Aje. The mosque stood at the intersection of three roads leading to three neighborhoods. It was a junction famous for the placement of *ebo* (ritual sacrifices), such as food, sugarcane, and coins for ritual sacrifices. People earnestly prayed never to be the first to stumble upon an *ebo*, as one would inadvertently absorb all the afflictions and curses battling the person who left it there. Essentially, seeing an *ebo* was believed to be a potential transfer of misfortune, allowing the shifting of one's bad luck to another person.

Wasiu was popular at school as he often shared money he claimed was given to him by worshippers. However, the truth was revealed the day he was caught stealing from the mosque's offering box and was beaten to a pulp. The children of some great prophets in the Bible were also thieves and miscreants, as I read in many biblical passages. Eli's children are good examples, and even the children of Samuel, the prophet whom God used to warn Eli, didn't fare any better.

Wasiu and I exchanged numerous visits. I taught him arithmetic, a subject he was struggling with. For Wasiu, four plus four could be six today and thirteen tomorrow. Once we got tired of studying, we would switch to the fun part: telling stories about the adults in our lives. If adults spanked us with a cane, we took our revenge by spanking them with our tongues. Sometimes, we searched for the dregs in the palm wine bottles the adults had consumed the previous day. Although the Quran asked Muslims not to drink, this didn't apply to palm wine for some of them. Guinness wasn't beer, and the alcoholic fermented palm wine was fruit juice.

I knew all of Wasiu's large family members, including his mother and her co-wives, his half brothers, half sisters, and even those he didn't know how they were connected to him. I knew his grandfather, Alhaji Agba, father of the Khalifa, Wasiu's father.

Alhaji Agba's first name, Alhaji, was the title given to someone who had undertaken the pilgrimage to Mecca—and his last name was his age, since *agba* meant the senior or elderly. His real name was unknown, as he needed no credentials to be self-employed. Before he died, he rarely came out. Rumors had it that he had paralysis of the legs, but I had seen him standing while praying. Some said he had testicles the size of his head. The Yoruba call this *ipa*, which is considered a social stigma. Some also said he was blind and only pretended to see. People saw him as a man of mystery, but I thought he lived in misery.

Alhaji Agba was an intelligent man from a long line of Òrìṣà worshippers.

He was expected to take over the worship of the gods that his father had worshipped before his birth. Just as Christians transferred Christianity to their children, the Òrìṣà people did the same. But when Islam began to penetrate the land, Alhaji Agba bolted. As a teenager, he interacted with the ulamas and alfas, who taught him that he was practicing the wrong religion and would go to hellfire unless he became a Muslim. Becoming a Muslim was pretty tough, and Alhaji Agba must have endured a lot. They told him about the prophets in the Quran and how they had come to rescue several generations from the torment of hellfire in the afterlife.

I sat in total silence, listening as Wasiu carefully narrated his grandfather's genesis.

Alhaji Agba lectured on the five arch-prophets of Islam and the four holy books. The process involved nine levels, nine lessons, and nine things to memorize all at once. If you stayed in Ibadan long enough, you would know all the *malaika*—the angels who guided heaven and earth. Your hope in life, your salvation in heaven, and the avoidance of hellfire required you to pray, the *wudu* of life (cleanse), and you must ensure enough credentials to overcome the seven heavens before you could eventually get to Allah. We saw them perform ablution every day, just as we heard that the *malaika* did. We needed the *malaika* as we needed our parents. We were cursed by the *malaika*. We prayed by the *malaika* and aspired to become like them.

As I learned from Wasiu and the street preachers, the first of the arch-prophets was Nuh (Noah for the Christians), whom Allah sent to warn his people of impending wrath if they didn't turn away from their sinful ways. I heard a similar story in church. The people, however, didn't listen to Nuh, who looked different from them, wearing white and covering his head and body. Allah then gave Nuh instructions to build an ark that would save the people from a massive flood.

The people regarded the arch-prophet with suspicion, labeled him a fake prophet, and questioned the authenticity of his message. Consequently, they refused to board the ark. Undeterred, Nuh filled his ark with male and female animals of each species. The deluge came and washed all the people away, sparing the animals and those who had heeded Nuh's warning. In literature, this would have been called a tragedy.

There is also the story of Ibrahim, another arch-prophet who was from an idol-worshipping clan like Alhaji Agba. Ibrahim went against his idol-worshipping family and almost sacrificed his son in obedience to Allah. This narrative marked the beginning of Eid, a festival of rams when two innocent animals are made to fight with their horns until one of them is tired. Eid, which is called *Ileya* in Yoruba, is one of the most anticipated festivals of the year. Back in Ode Aje, the rams' fights provided so much excitement, and on the day they were slaughtered, our favorite portion was fat.

The long stories also included that of Musa, whose mission was to deliver the Israelites from the tyranny of the pharaohs in Egypt and the Egyptians. A particular pharaoh proved stubborn, and he faced the wrath of God on more than one occasion. One of the peaks of Musa's story was when he split the Red Sea into two so he could escape with the Israelites. I once thought that Musa was one of the most powerful magicians in the world. We hoped to recover that rod and harness its conjuring powers.

Another significant moment in Musa's story was when Allah gave him a tablet inscribed with commandments for the guidance of the people's affairs. That tablet, known as the Decalogue, had the Ten Commandments written on it. Isa, known as Jesus to those of the Christian faith, had the *Injil* (Gospel) book or the New Testament written about him, although he was reading the Torah, the collective term for the first books of the Bible. Isa's birth was a miracle as his mother was a virgin when he was conceived, and he continued the miraculous works when he was born.

Then came the greatest of them all, the most revered prophet to the Muslims—Prophet Muhammad (PBUH), presented to us in Islam as the seal of the prophets as there would be no other prophet after him. I thought that prophets come and go, as the Bible lessons in Sunday school presented the story to us: Moses came, followed by John the Baptist, then Jesus Christ, and others mentioned in the gospels excluded from the Bible.

When we call the name of Jesus Christ, it is followed by a period. However, for Muslims, every mention of Prophet Muhammad, Allah's messenger, must be followed by the phrase "May the peace of Allah be upon him," shortened to "PBUH." A similar phrase, *Alayhi salam*, is uttered for other prophets before Muhammad. It took me many years to understand why.

I remember how the madrassa teacher at Adeoyo, a lean and stern-looking man, narrated the story in a way that any preteen could understand. According to him, the Prophet preached using the Quran, which was revealed to him by Allah through Angel Jibril (Gabriel for Christians). But it was in later years that I learned that the Prophet didn't preach the Quran during his lifetime, as it was yet to be compiled by the caliphs.

Another prophet who had a book from Allah, albeit not one of the archprophets, was Dawud (David), who received the Sabur (Psalms). It was the same David in the Bible, the father of Solomon, who composed some of the Psalms. We used some of the Psalms for magic and read some others as the diviners recanted incantations. The Sabur held significant power, was regarded as holy, and contained grail messages.

All of these prophets' stories were narrated to a younger Alhaji Agba before he was lectured on the angels, pillars of Islam, and how to perform *wudu* (ablution), which is the cleansing of the body before prayer using clean and odorless water. Wasiu was also learning some of these while attending a formal Western school. Some days, the poor boy was tired and confused.

Growing up in Ibadan, you couldn't escape the presence of several Islamic societies. Some were missionaries doing good work, while others provided free meals to the community. In the Aladura church, the precursors of the Pentecostals criticized the Anglicans as being too religiously soft to enter into the kingdom of heaven. In contrast, members of the Islamic associations coexisted in peace and harmony and didn't abuse one another. They all deferred to the chief imam of the city as the leader, based at the Central Mosque at Ojaba. In later years, the title was expanded in scope to become the chief imam of Ibadanland, making him a sort of the emperor of a kingdom.

Everyone saw what the Muslims did and how they carried out their activities. For instance, they must all fast during Ramadan and break the fast in the open, with many of them sitting in front of their houses to devour large meals. I remember some of our schoolmates who would cheat during Ramadan, stealing from our lunch, drinking water, and eating outside the permitted times set by Allah and his Prophet. But they would return home to join the *iftar*, the breaking of the fast, pretending as if they had almost died from fasting during the day.

Whether you liked it or not, the Muslims would wake you up every day during the fasting period with the early morning prayer and the preparation of the *suhoor* (the meal taken in the early morning), which the Yoruba call *saari*. Regardless of your inclination, you would witness the *iftar* and all the quick and busy work in the kitchen.

There were several local leaders, each heading different organizations—one as the secretary and another as the president. They talked about Allah but did other things, mainly social. The differences among these organizations were peripheral; the fundamentals for worshipping were nonnegotiable because Almighty Allah and his Prophet explicitly laid them down. As we all know, you can't be a Muslim if you don't submit absolutely to the will of Allah.

Some of these societies started as groups of friends praying together in their different homes, gradually evolving into larger associations that accommodated more people; for example, the Istijabah prayer group of Nigeria. I had a friend whose family were pioneer members. Other societies came later, including the Ansar-ud-Deen, Nasirullah Fatihi Society of Nigeria (NASFAT), Tijjaniyah, Qadiriyyah, Tableeq, Ahlu Sunna, and Ahmadiyya, among others.

It's noteworthy that these societies are not restricted to Ibadan alone but exist in various parts of the country, particularly across different states in the southwest. A man could belong to more than one of them, and you would see his joy as he proudly adorned his new attire to commemorate the annual anniversary of any of the societies.

The associations were often unstable, as politicians sought their support. Some members borrowed money from their treasurers and refused to repay the loans. Of course, minor internal conflicts, which are an indisputable feature of any human grouping, could arise due to individual differences in temperaments and personalities.

Friendship at Ibadan wasn't necessarily long-lasting, as little things created crises. If you had money and you didn't give, you were seen as miserly; if you lent money and weren't repaid, forget about the loan. If you built a big house, the one who had yet to buy a plot of land would resent you. If your wife was beautiful, you were in trouble, and if your wife was unattractive, you were scorned. Whether heads or tails, you made a friend or you lost a friend.

Islam united people as one, while human behavior divided them into particles. Once they all became particles, the association would collapse, leading to the formation of new ones. The bitterness lingered for years, sometimes forever.

During fights, Muslims would cast aside their Quran and turn to the Yoruba god Esu. Interestingly, rather than blame Shaytan (Satan), they stigmatize our one and only Yoruba god, Esu. Then and now, I still don't get why Esu has to be empowered. Islam has its devil, Iblis (Shaytan), who defied the Creator and was thrown out of heaven. Iblis established an alternative kingdom with his servants, engaging in fights with the angels. It was the clash between evil and good, with Iblis so powerful that he could lead men and women into temptation. Iblis was even the one who ruptured the biblical Garden of Eden, leading Adam and Eve into sinning.

Since Iblis left heaven to live among us, he became our enemy. But the Muslims in Ibadan never blamed Iblis, but our Esu, who was never thrown out of paradise, never fought with Olodumare our God, didn't bear false witness and didn't deliver errands of evil. For the Christians in my church, Esu was the Satan. I thought then that Iblis was more powerful than Esu, and they dare not mention his name as the instigator of crises and downfall.

I recall one time Iblis misled Saliu, our neighbor, on the worst day of his life. Saliu was caught having sex with his friend's wife. He received the beating of his life, was expelled from the house naked, and thrown onto the street. As he tried to run away, neighbors didn't see him as a thief but as a *werè* (a lunatic).

"Weré! Weré! Weré!" everyone shouted until Saliu found a small bush where he took cover to escape the humiliation. He vanished from sight and was never seen again. His disappearance left us with many questions: Was he bitten by a snake and died? Did he take his own life? Or did someone give him clothes, enabling him to get to the motor park to catch a lorry to Lagos? The mystery of his disappearance remained unanswered.

All the stories Wasiu told me he heard from his father were also stories I had heard multiple times. Alhaji Agba also taught him about the existence of angels as servants of Allah who are not human and were created from light for the sole purpose of serving and worshipping Allah. Ordinary human eyes cannot see them unless Allah has anointed you as a prophet or a wali (a friend of God). In my attempt to understand, I compared them to gnomes (*iwin*), the spirits believed to live in the forest around us and visit us regularly even though we can't see them.

However, I was told I must not call *iwin* an angel. Fearful of being whipped, I only referred to angels as *iwin* among my classmates. Angels were clean, and *iwin* were not, although they had the same attributes. *Iwin* were numerous, countless, just as there were millions of angels in Islam. Among the angels, the most prominent ones, as I memorized the list, included Jibril, Mikail, Israfil, Azrail, Munkar, Nakir, Raqeeb, and Atid.

Angels were heads of departments with allotted responsibilities. Jibril (Gabriel) is the leader of all angels, and he is the link between the angels and Allah, carrying messages back and forth. In my understanding, Jibril convened and presided over all the meetings of the angels. I didn't know their agenda and wasn't privy to their meetings. But I imagined they were spying on us who live on planet Earth. Another angel, Mikail (Michael), is in charge of rain, and we must remember to pray to him as we do to Osun and Yemoja, the goddess of fertility.

The other angels really scared me and made me sleepless, like Israfil, who would blow the trumpet to signify "the end of time." Wasiu and I decided we were going to close our ears when he blew the trumpet, assuming that if we didn't hear the sound, we would not die. Those who heard the tune and sound would die a minute later. They would be transferred and collected by Azrail, the angel of death, who is more powerful than Israfil because he carries a club. It is believed that every time a human dies, Azrail is at work. He hits you so powerfully on the head that you will bleed to death, but no one will see your blood.

As if Allah does not trust us, we are daily policed by Raqeeb on our right side and by Atid on the left. Raqeeb is in charge of documenting people's good deeds, and Atid documents the evil deeds. Both of them deliver their reports to two no-nonsense and unforgiving angels, Munkar and Nakir, who will visit the dead in the grave and brave his body rotting while families and friends are still eating and drinking to commemorate his passing.

Munkar and Nakir followed up with questions, interrogating the deceased about how they spent their life and posing difficult questions.

"General Abacha, is it true that you stole all of Nigeria's money when you were president of Nigeria?"

"No," Abacha replied. "I stole only a third."

I still don't know the questions the terrifying angels would ask me.

After hearing all of the ulama's lectures, the younger version of Alhaji Agba started to slowly deviate from the traditional faith of his forefathers to the Muslim faith. He was leaving behind Ogun and Sango and moving more toward Prophet Muhammad. They taught him many ritual baths, with *wudu* being the most prominent. *Wudu* could be done several times every day, but it was required five times a day before every salat (prayer). His best friend must be water. For the *wudu*, he needed sparkling, crystal-clear water that was odorless, colorless, and tasteless. This would not be a problem if you could fetch it from the river or collect rainwater. Some had pipe-borne water, but it was unreliable. We were not that blessed as our Ogunpa River was so dirty that even the fish were unsafe to eat.

I must confess my sin, though Allah may never forgive me. I once started the rumor that I smelled alcohol in the kettle that our Muslim neighbor was using for ablution. We were playing soccer, and our ball fell into his backyard. He refused to return it. In anger, I went about telling everyone that he used beer for ablution, which was why he was always smelling. This is the work of Shaytan, not of Esu. Angel Atid has already recorded this sin against me, and there is no opportunity for forgiveness except on one condition: if it was true that there was beer in the prayer kettle!

A Muslim signals his readiness for the *wudu* ritual bath by saying *Bismillah* (in the name of Allah). Before his saliva dries up, he must thoroughly rinse his palms three times, as if removing bacteria, then also rinse his mouth three times to clean it of all smell and dirt. Prayers cannot reach Allah with a dirty mouth. Next, he briefly sniffs water into his nostrils and rinses his nose three times, after which he rinses his face three times, too. The next step is for him to rinse his forearms (right arm first) from wrist to elbow, three times each, and then he will wipe his head from his forehead to the nape of his neck just once. Following this, he cleans his ears using his thumbs to reach the back of his ear and his index fingers to clean his earlobes once. Lastly, he would wash his feet (right foot first) to the ankle thrice each.

Before I forget, there should be no urine or ammonia smell in any part of the body, and they must not fart during this process because that would mean redoing the entire ablution! Cleanliness is next to godliness.

We didn't do ablution in Christianity. In our church, we just didn't pay attention to this.

Wasiu boasted about the religious piety of his family. According to him, since Alhaji Agba was an intelligent man, he quickly got the hang of the numerous sacred rites of the Muslims. To show their support and encouragement, Muslims in the community collectively decided to sponsor him for the hajj pilgrimage to the house of Allah, the Kaaba in Mecca.

Hajj, the last of the pillars of Islam, is compulsory for Muslims who can afford the journey. Everyone, even our masquerades, knew this injunction.

وَأَذِّن فِى ٱلنَّاسِ بِٱلْحَجِّ يَأْتُوكَ رِجَالًا وَعَلَىٰ
كُلِّ ضَامِرٍ يَأْتِينَ مِن كُلِّ فَجٍّ عَمِيقٍ

> *Call all people to the pilgrimage. They will come to you on foot and on every lean camel from every distant path.* (Suratul Hajj verse 27)

The hajj pilgrimage is a one-time obligation, but individuals can choose to perform it as many times as they can afford or send those who don't have the financial means. Hajj is performed on the first ten days of the twelfth month on the Muslim calendar, Dhul-Hijjah. As an adult, I sent relatives from my mother's family to hajj.

The prestige that comes with being an alhaji or alhaja (the title received upon return from Saudi Arabia) among the Muslims in Yoruba communities will make even non-Muslims want to perform the pilgrimage for the associated respect and honor. Upon returning from hajj, an alhaja would often have a gold tooth and adorn herself with beautiful gold necklaces, while an alhaji would be well dressed. The respect is enormous.

I once asked a Muslim friend why he wasn't wearing a gold tooth after he returned from the hajj, and he replied, "Toyin, it is not compulsory to do that; it is your *niyah* (intent) and *ibadah* that matter."

"If I ever go on hajj, I will fix up two golden teeth, labeled *eyin Meccah* (Mecca's tooth), and smile at all times to show them off," I told him, and I meant it.

Some of those who returned from hajj shared stories of the miracles they experienced there. One alhaji described to us how he was catching live birds during the flight. They told us about the power of an elevator that took people to the sixth floor while they remained in one spot. One even claimed a washing machine was "so polite" that it washed all his clothes for him. Some of them even claimed that Allah had forgiven their sins just by going on the pilgrimage. These stories were embellished to such an extent that we became inferior to the Middle East, and we revised many of our origin stories to claim ancestral origins from there.

For those who traveled by airplane, it was usually their first and last experience. For all those who successfully returned, a grand celebration ensued, with food, beverages, rejoicing, dancing, sermons, and music. Returning as an alhaji or alhaja signified success among my people.

The party wasn't without expenses and troubles, which we call *wahala*. Guests expected gifts brought from Mecca. These gifts were mostly the rosaries, tasbih, niqab, hijab, *jalamia* (a long robe outfit) adorned by both men and women primarily for prayers, and *zam-zam* (water attributed to Hajar, the second wife of Ibrahim (Abraham) and the mother of Ismail). It all started when Prophet Ibrahim (Abraham) left Hajar and the infant Ismail in the desert between the peaks of Safa and Marwah.

To put Abraham's faith in him to the test, Allah ordered him to abandon his wife and son in the desert. Ismail started to cry as the day grew hotter, and he became increasingly thirsty. Hajar feared because she had brought nothing with her. Seven times, she circled back and forth between the hills of Safa and Marwah in search of water. Suddenly, water sprouted from the earth on the seventh circle.

Hajar mouthed, "Zam-zam" as the water continued to flow.

The history of *zam-zam* is well known in the Yoruba communities through teachings and narration. The water is regarded as spiritual due to its curative, healing, and health benefits.

No one could live among the Muslims in Ibadan and not recognize the significance of going to Mecca and Medina. While the people in French Dakar say, "See Paris and die," our highest aim in Ibadan was to see the tomb of the Prophet in Medina and be cleansed of our sins. Paris didn't come with any spiritual blessing. No one prayed for me when I went to London or upon arrival. For years, Muslims have nurtured the desire and plan toward pilgrimage. They pray about it; they beg Allah for it. They work for it and even slave for it.

Without having stepped out of Nigeria or reading any book about it, I knew about the procedure to become an alhaji or alhaja. I think everyone knew, and we even tested ourselves on all the steps. Questions like "Which one came first?" could be answered by anyone; even the less brilliant boy would answer.

The stories about Mecca and Medina were more common at Ode Aje than those of London, where their king was a queen! How can a king be a queen? Our queen was the wife of a king.

I don't know the steps and procedure for the hajj today, but I remember those that were told and retold in the 1960s. Mecca must receive you as a new person, a requirement not imposed by London and Paris. In Mecca, you must stop at the Miqaat and change your clothes to the ihram, a pure white garment for men in two pieces, one to be used for the loins and the other for their upper body, with no underwear. For women, the ihram is neither color-bound nor piece-bound, and they are allowed to use their underwear.

A ritual bath must precede putting on the ihram. Wearing the ihram is a value changer: once worn, all evil thoughts must be banished, and all acts of indecency must be eliminated. The punishment for violation is draconian: the hajj becomes invalidated, and the violator is demoted from a pilgrim to a tourist.

Proudly adorned in your ihram, you walk with others to enter the house of Allah (the Kaaba) through "the door of peace." Your lips must keep proclaiming the Talbiyah, chanting till you enter the Kaaba. Make a right turn toward the right pole, Ruknu Yamani, the point of departure for *Tawaf*, kiss the black stone, and say, "Bismillah Allahu Akbar." You are making progress.

Next is to do the *Tawaf*, circumambulating the Kaaba seven times counterclockwise. Be careful not to fall, as someone can climb onto you! Once this is completed, you must now ask for all the blessings by performing voluntary units of prayer behind the place where Prophet Ibrahim's footprint can be found. You have to be physically fit as you are expected to run between the valleys of Safar and Marwa seven times!

You have to cut your hair, then proceed to Munah to spend the night in your ihram. Talbiyah will be completed after the stop at Arafat (the mountain upon which Prophet Muhammad [PBUH] delivered his farewell sermon). The Muslims not in Mecca are required to fast on that day. Missing the Arafat ritual makes the hajj invalid. Arafat is so important to the Muslim Yoruba that climbing the mountain is one of the crucial symbols of the pilgrimage.

From Arafat, you go to the open space, "Musdalifah," to rest and pray. It is also where you pick forty-eight pebbles to throw at Jamarat for the next three to four days. Chant "Bismillah Allahu Akbar," throw seven pebbles at the symbol of Shaytan, and then face the Qiblah and pray. After praying, you'll start chanting the Talbiyah on your way to Muna, where you will remove the ihram, take your bath, and slaughter a ram for Eid before returning to Jamarat. Did you carry a ram with you? No! Someone in faraway Abeokuta or Kano could slaughter it on your behalf. Over the years, professional agents in Saudi Arabia have commercialized this aspect by collecting cash to handle the ram for you.

Afterward, you return to Muna the following day to continue throwing stones at Shaytan for about three days. The shaving of hair and removal of ihram is the final step for the pilgrims, and this is done in their different hotels or destinations. Women don't need to shave their hair, but they do a symbolic cutting of some strands. As new hair grows, it is believed that good luck and abundance will follow.

The month of Ramadan is usually an eventful period for the Muslims. To me, it was my month of enjoyment, singing in the middle of the night, collecting coins and free food. Today, it is common to see different societies holding several programs like Ramadan lectures, iftar sessions, and so on. Muslims move from one lecture to the other, from one *tafsir* (Quranic exegesis) to another, to maximize the purpose of the holy month.

I attended some of these programs, joining the band of Muslims who sing melodious songs around the neighborhood to wake people for *suhoor*. We sang and mentioned the names of Muslims around the neighborhood to wake them up to pray, prepare *suhoor*, and eat before Fajr. Singing wasn't only an interesting exercise that showed the unity among people of different religions in the community but also the enthusiasm that came with the period. The songs, called *were*, became a precursor to the rise of fuji superstars, notably Alhaji Ayinde Sikiru Barrister, who started his music career in this small way. Barrister and I coincidentally ran into each other in the 1960s on the streets singing.

I joined them for the last ten days of Ramadan vigil prayers, particularly the Laylatul Quadri (Night of Majesty), even though I wasn't fasting. I was told that during those ten days, angels come closer to humans to take their prayers and requests straight to Allah and that they will be granted. This is attributed to the fact that it was during this period that the first verses and chapters of the Quran were revealed to the Prophet by Angel Jibril. Some boys even claimed that they saw angels!

We enjoyed the tempo during the prayers. After the salat, other recitations done in Arabic sounded like incantations to those of us who were not well versed in Arabic or didn't know the meaning of those words. We saw them as akin to the incantations heard during the Egungun festivals in Ode Aje.

Adults engaged in discussions and debates about the strange Quranic verses for long hours. Some of us, including myself, began to imitate the imams, reciting fake passages, pretending to be speaking in Arabic, just as we pretended, as Christians, to pray, receive the Holy Ghost, and speak in tongues. It dawned on me that these religions all have their style of chants or incantations, be it the Yoruba herbalist, the Aladura, the pastor, or the imam. They all use languages and words that people don't understand, and they will attach importance to whatever you say, even going as far as paying for the translation of their messages.

As Christian churches improve their organizational capacity to engage the youth, Muslims across the country have adopted similar strategies. I have observed the Jalsa, an annual end-of-the-year program organized by the Ahmadiyya Society in Ibadan. This program is held on a campground for three days. Muslims, young and old, male and female, come together from various regions for this spiritual gathering, fostering relationships and creating avenues for different people to meet and establish connections. The Jalsa not only serves as a platform for spiritual upliftment, but it also acts as a catalyst for individuals to come together. There are countless testimonials from couples who met at this program.

These societies also organize programs such as youth conferences and sisters' circles for females, among other programs, even going as far as organizing marriage counseling for intending couples. Some of these organizations have taken it a step further by establishing schools and businesses. Each society is under a spiritual leader who provides leadership and guidance, contributing to the overall growth and impact of the society on communities.

Christian Pentecostals do the same thing in their engagement with witchcraft—there can be no Sunday service without a prayer directed at a witch. Witches and idols are scattered all over the country, depicted in Nollywood films and tabloids. Even television programs dedicate segments to exposing witches and evil herbalists and feature testimonies of how they were conquered. Despite efforts to suppress African traditions and history, both Christianity and Islam haven't been able to entirely disentangle themselves from the rich tapestry of African culture.

Wasiu, for instance, told me that when his grandfather returned from Mecca, he was a new man and no longer tolerated his father's "idols," constantly pressuring the old man to abandon his traditional practices. Alhaji Agba did all he could to show his father that the idols were powerless and ineffective, but the older man staunchly defended his gods.

Frustrated and determined, Alhaji Agba set out to burn the wooden idols, but he was stopped midway by his father. He knew he couldn't carry out the act in the presence of his father, but he still needed to do something to demonstrate how ineffective the idols were. He grabbed one of the idols and smashed it on the hard floor, and it split into two. Before Alhaji Agba could turn around to ask his father why the idol didn't defend itself against the assault, the older man had dropped to the floor. Reacting swiftly, Alhaji Agba rushed at his father, who was gasping for air. Despite attempts to resuscitate him, the die was cast, and the older man was already on his journey to the afterlife.

In his final moments, as the older man was surrendering to the inevitable, he urged Alhaji Agba to find a way to be at peace with the gods of his forefathers while he continued with his new religion. Alhaji Agba regretted the role he played in the death of his father, and because of this, he never forced Islam on his children. He left his distant cousins, who were still Orìṣà worshippers, in charge of the house so they could take care of the needs of the gods, and then he moved to another place where he could peacefully practice his newfound faith. He respected the first rule that should guide a Muslim in the pursuit of peaceful coexistence: There is no compulsion in religion.

لَآ إِكْرَاهَ فِى ٱلدِّينِ ۖ قَد تَّبَيَّنَ ٱلرُّشْدُ مِنَ
ٱلْغَىِّ فَمَن يَكْفُرْ بِٱلطَّٰغُوتِ وَيُؤْمِنۢ بِٱللَّهِ
فَقَدِ ٱسْتَمْسَكَ بِٱلْعُرْوَةِ ٱلْوُثْقَىٰ لَا ٱنفِصَامَ لَهَا ۗ وَٱللَّهُ سَمِيعٌ عَلِيمٌ

> *There is no compulsion in religion; truly the right way has become clearly distinct from error; therefore, whoever disbelieves in the Shaytan and believes in Allah he indeed has laid hold on the firmest handle, which shall not break, and Allah is all-Hearing, all-Knowing.* (Quran 2:256)

From that time, Alhaji Agba responded to those who tried to enforce Islam on others by quoting the verse above and emphasizing that Islam forbids intervening in other people's business. Ibadan Muslims were probably unaware of the jihads when they publicly said that Islam forbids forcible conversion. At madrassa, the tutor always warned the students to shun forced conversion, as Allah himself had said that there is no compulsion in religion.

Perhaps this message is for the Yoruba that Allah has sent apostles and books to clearly communicate his words and that whosoever wishes to follow should do so, and anyone who disbelieves is free to do so too, as Allah will judge everyone equally on the last day. So, the preachers in Ibadan would say it is not the place of a Muslim to forcefully impose Islam on others but to embody it as a good example and inspire people through it.

While being virtuous may attract people to a religion, in some other places, souls had been won through the use of the sword. It was the practical mode of conversion in Yoruba towns. During the jihads, the wars were so serious that the Yoruba couldn't fight with ordinary power and needed spiritual fortifications to combat the jihadists. Of course, they had brave warriors who could use swords to slay their enemies, but even the sword could do more with the help of charms.

In Ilorin, an Islamic city, I learned that Yoruba charms became part of Islam as Muslims realized their effectiveness, as well as the war between Afonja and Alimi during the conquest of Ilorin. According to my source, Afonja, an Ogbomoso man, was well fortified with charms, while Alimi, his Fulani counterpart, had a sword engraved with the name of Allah. Afonja could perform magic and kill people easily, and Alimi had to step back and collaborate with him to conquer Ilorin. They formed alliances, and when Ilorin was conquered and Islam spread, the people believed that religion couldn't be practiced without traditional magic fortifications. They believed tradition and religion were inextricably linked, which is why charms entered Islam.

The Muslims who came with Alimi believed that though they could have eventually won the war, it was easier for them because Afonja fortified their swords with his charms. Many wars were fought, and the impact of charms made it easier for them to penetrate Islam. More so, as the new converts were allowed to continue their practice, they assumed it was permissible in Islam, unaware that it was only a strategy to gradually convert them. They embraced Islam, but the traditional practices were there to stay.

As time passed, it became increasingly challenging to completely cleanse the converts and separate them from their practices. Over a century later, the belief was revived in Sunday Igboho, a Yoruba man who attributed his victory against the Fulani herdsmen to the influence of charms.

I lived surrounded by charms throughout the 1950s, and they accompanied me as I entered the 1960s. I had many incisions on different parts of my body, made by herbalists and local Muslim charm makers. Those who took me to them were Christians. Most of those who visited the store of Iya Lekuleja, the herbalist, were Islamic converts, not pagans.

To this day, people believe in the efficacy of charms, and they manifest in bigger ways such that even boys in their twenties are using their girlfriend's underwear for ritual money. There is a widely held belief that prayers made to God, even though they are eventually answered, require time. And time is never on one's side! In other words, to get answers to your prayer, you have to be very patient, whereas charms, especially the *aajo* preferred by Muslims, provide a faster approach and accelerate results. *Aajo* is a form of ritual appeal to God so that He can shower you with favor. God is patient, but humans are impatient. Things could go entirely wrong before God's intervention, so one must stay steps ahead, and it is believed that the imam can accelerate the pace of the intervention.

We had millions of Sufis, sometimes unrecognizable, but often, you could never know who they were. Sufis believe that as long as what you are doing has the name of Allah and recitation from the Quran in it, it is not *shirk*, even if it is mixed with herbal leaves and concoctions. It's fascinating that millions of Yoruba Muslims are Sufis, allowing them to drink Islamic magical water with Aladura holy oil in a stomach inhabited by dangerous reptiles put there by sorcerers.

Most of the converts at Ijebu, Abeokuta, Owode, Ibadan, Osun, Lagos, and other parts of the southwest practiced Sufism. I know of the Tijjaniyah, Qadriyyah, Jam'iyyah, and many more who are seen as "liberal" Muslims because the society is such that Christians, "pagans," and Muslims cohabit and have good relationships. Many families, like my own, have members practicing different religions; my grandfather was a pastor, and his wife was a practicing Muslim. This makes it easy for the Yoruba Muslims to seamlessly blend different practices to create a unique form of Islam.

Our version of Islam gained success, and the differences between us were no more than worshipping God in different buildings. We even produced prominent politicians, mainly Muslims, who derived their power from potent Yoruba juju.

Who wasn't afraid of our former commissioner of local government, Busari Adelakun, an alhaji, who wore a tortoise underneath his flowing agbada? Live tortoise! He even wore it to the Friday Jumat service. No bullet could hit him. No machete could cut him. No axe could slice him into pieces. His successor as a warlord, Lamidi Adedibu, "one man equivalent to half the city," was an alhaji. His charms were so potent that he claimed to be able to leave Ibadan and travel to Sokoto without taking any vehicle or physical moment. He would stay in his room and issue a command, "Take me to Sokoto," and in an instant, he was there!

In most households, forefathers worshipped Yoruba pantheons like Ogun, Sango, Osun, and Esu in the presence of Christians and Muslims. These practices were seen as their cultural heritage and passed down through generations. Being a Muslim wasn't a barrier, as long as the practices aligned with their perception of what is ideal. You find alfas, alhajis, and alhajas partaking in Ifa, Ogun, and Oro festivals and similar traditions without hesitation, considering them integral to their existence, with one not conflicting with the other. Ojelabi, for instance, converted to Islam but continued practicing it alongside his masquerade.

I'm familiar with the various classes of alfa Sufis, what they consider the right/ideal charm, and what is extreme and forbidden. This means that there is a scale; some are very close to traditionalists, while others are farther removed from them. However, they all have their roots in Yoruba traditional practices.

Those who converted to Islam in later years at Ode Aje practiced Sufism and maintained a closer connection to traditionalism. During the masquerade festivals, these were the ones we could identify beneath the masquerade garb.

I witnessed one instance in Ode Aje involving a masquerade clan close to our house, where many of its members had converted to Islam. During the masquerade festival, one wondered if such a clan could still parade its masquerade, but to our amazement, the massive turnout and crowd indicated that the clan possibly had more converts than practitioners of the traditional Egungun religion.

Some alfas I know only use the tasbih. They firmly believe in calling the name of Allah, no matter how long it takes to get what is desired from him. They don't do any other thing but sit down and fervently call the name of Allah while reciting the Quran. These two practices are their only charms and weapons to fight the battles of life. For them, their patience is the essence of their charm, involving days, months, and years of consistent prayers. Consequently, impatient people and those who need fast answers don't go to them.

I remember visiting an alfa with my mother. He started his consultation for us by first asking us to pick one of the beads of the rosary and state the reason we had come. Taking the selected bead, he began to pray in Arabic for a while. As soon as he was done, he communicated the revelations and solutions to us. His remedies didn't involve herbs or concoctions; instead, they were centered solely on invoking the names of Allah and Quran recitations to be accompanied by fasting. He gave us some Arabic words to repeat a stipulated number of times during the fasting period—an undoubtedly challenging task.

Ya Lateef × 2,000 times
Ya Hafeez × 2,500 times
Ya Wahab × 1,500 times
La ilaha illallah × 3,000 times

As I voiced "Ya Lateef," I must count with my fingers until I reached 10. I had to make ten checks to get to 100. By the end, the loss in calories would likely be close to 1,000! I wondered if the imam magic man knew I had no faith or if he thought my arithmetic wasn't good enough to count the numbers. He emphasized that all these names worked together for the desired results, provided there was an unwavering faith in the power of prayers.

My church already told me there was power in prayer, which was why I kept seeing the Psalms as more magic than holy verses. The alfa told us he could join us in the prayer if we couldn't do it ourselves. It struck me that the *babalawos* and the pastors always follow the same technique: If you couldn't perform the task imposed on you, you could pay them to do it for you. It was a way to collect double payment—the first for the magic, the second for executing the tasks on your behalf!

The alfas were remarkably talented in their ability to draw from the ninety-nine names of Allah, and the meaning of each determined its appropriateness for distinct situations. Similarly, the divination tray does precisely the same, as the *babalawo* would look at the formation of the cowries and tell you the corresponding *odu* and verse, often longer than the Bible. The alfas also used *surahs* (chapters) from the Quran to combat evil forces, especially when the situation was similar to the one the Prophet faced when that particular surah was revealed to him.

Our myriad problems, such as financial difficulties, illness, bad luck, infertility, co-wife troubles, and witchcraft, prompted alfas to prescribe specific surahs. However, the efficacy varied; some surahs could work, and some may not if that problem didn't exist in Mecca and Medina. These alfas do not do *huntu* or other ritual permutations. They depended solely on fasting, along with Allah's names and his words. I often wondered how these words were different from the *odu ifa*, but to ask was to commit blasphemy!

If you believed that only the *babalawo* had the divination tray with sand, then you haven't encountered the Sufi alfas in Ibadan. They also receive their revelation and guidance from patterns in the sand on a flat object. The Dogons of Mali use the footprints of animals to interpret one's future, just as our alfas craft fingerprints with their fingers and tell you the interpretation. These methods involved invoking jinns through the sand (or recalling the jinns who live in the sand), posing questions, and receiving solutions to problems as delivered by the jinns. Yoruba towns were teeming with these jinns and the alfas who understood their language.

I doubt you would come across many people in my city who didn't patronize one alfa or another. I, too, sought their guidance to decide what course I should study in university after gaining admission to the top five best universities, offering five different disciplines, including law at the University of Lagos and public administration at Ahmadu Bello University.

We turned to an alfa when we were confused, whether it was deciding to embark on a journey, determining the right time to marry, or choosing a life partner when entangled in a relationship with multiple partners. The alfa would speak with the sand and see whether the journey would be hitch-free and profitable.

"Don't marry Mary as her womb has no fruits!"

"The jinn said Hidiat, the hunchback, is your best choice!"

The sand and the jinn, two voiceless entities, spoke to our interpreter.

As I discovered, a decision wasn't enough; there was a second stage involving supplications to do some *aajo* depending on the instructions received from the jinns.

"You must cook for all the kids in your area, the jinn has commanded."

"You must do something similar to the sacrifices that the *babalawo* asked you to make and place it at a road junction in the middle of the night."

Some directives were funny: "Be fully naked and recite this passage precisely at 1:00 a.m. Don't tamper with the script to avoid failure."

These alfas went beyond tasbih, chanting various names of Allah, reciting the Quran, and fasting. They incorporated additional things drawn from existing Yoruba practices and *aajo* to hasten the process. Many of these alfas come from families where these practices had been in place for generations, making it difficult to distinguish between Yoruba and Islamic elements. So when their forefathers became Muslims, they combined everything to become Yoruba Muslims.

Some Alfas used water, as the Aladura did. Like those who used sand, their power is in water. Within walking distance from our house in Ode Aje was the cult of water, Omi. The alfa did exactly what Omi cult members did. They could see everything hidden through the water and gave solutions based on what they saw. This was their special power. These solutions also included specific instructions on what to do or not do. Some alfas used mirrors, where individuals, upon looking into the mirror, could see the problems affecting them and the possible solutions.

There was Alfa Jarata, a class comprised of the first generation of alfas, also known as Alfa Oni Lawani, referring to those who wore heavy turbans. They were the closest to the traditionalists, given that when Islam was introduced in Yorubaland, traditional practices were not outright condemned. These alfas were often seen looking for lizards, frogs, and birds and visiting the people called *olori eku* to buy items for *aajo*. They frequented Ojaba, Oje, and Oranyan markets, renowned centers for herbs and different kinds of skulls.

Practicing what could be termed "hybrid Islam," they continued worshipping Ifa, Ogun, Sango, Egungun, and more. Because most people in Ibadan and other Yoruba towns understood how much power they wielded and the extent to which they could influence events and cause harm, these types of alfas and Muslims were dreaded. There was a sharp difference between such Muslims and the Ahlu Sunna.

For the Ahlu Sunna, as I fully understood them, the tenets of Islam must be strictly adhered to without any mixture or deviation. Charms are classified under *shirk*, indicating the act of placing other supernatural orders above Allah. As purists, the Ahlu Sunna were against any form of traditional practices and the use of charms. For them, relying on charms implied a lack of absolute trust in Allah and Islam, undermining the principle of total submission to the will of Almighty Allah.

The concept of charm in Islam is quite controversial, as the Ahlu Sunna and Sufis have divergent opinions on what constitutes *shirk*. From what I heard, the Ahlu Sunna view any practice beyond normal salat and fasting as extreme. If a religious practice is not documented to have been done by the Prophet or commanded by him and the Quran, it is *shirk*. To them, even sitting for an extended period and using the rosary is an innovation without a basis in Islam because the Prophet didn't use it. Hence, using the rosary, *huntu*, and the like was considered unacceptable to them.

I took *huntu* several times, a blackish or brownish liquid with the taste of ink. The alfa would write passages of the Quran on a tablet, wash it into a bowl, and then have you drink the water. If the purpose was to acquire more luck, you could collect it in a container, take it home, and spray it in your room or store.

I didn't recognize an Ahlu Sunna until a friend pointed out a distinctive feature of their trousers. It happened during Ramadan when I followed our Muslim neighbor at Ode Aje for *ashamu*, as we called it then, later learning its proper name was Tarawih. This prayer consisted of ten *rakkas* observed during Ramadan, immediately after the *isha*. I didn't know it took such a long time until I observed one at a mosque dominated by the Ahlu Sunna.

My first observation surprised me—their trousers were short, as if afraid to touch the ground. I found it amusing until I was told that it was sunna, an act not compulsory in Islam but considered voluntarily good and accepted. When I got home, I started cutting my long trousers, which I used to fold to make them shorter, ensuring they didn't go below my ankle. I wasn't a legitimate Ahlu Sunna, though!

In the complex interplay between traditional beliefs and Islamic teachings, a popular Yoruba proverb comes to mind: *Bi a ba ni a o ni s'oogun ika mo, eni maa je iwo o ni gbo*, meaning, "If we decide to stop making harmful charms, those that want to devour poison will not let us rest." This was the point that made Alhaji Agba bring his knowledge of the traditional medicine arts into his Islamic practice.

One incident happened to Wasiu's aunt in our presence. When she was still unmarried, there was a loutish boy who always catcalled her. She wasn't interested in a relationship with him and told him off several times, but he was undeterred. One day, following another rude rejection, he took a charmed ring and hit her with it, which made her start convulsing. The boy ran and left her for dead. Fortunately, she was taken to her father's house by some good Samaritans.

As soon as Alhaji Agba sighted his daughter, he knew how delicate the matter was and was left with two options: either begin making an antidote from his knowledge of Yoruba medicine or begin a prayer session according to his Islamic faith. The weight of guilt from his father's death hung heavy on his shoulders. He couldn't risk the life of his daughter when he knew how to save her, and his father's parting words rang in his ears again. Making an antidote for his daughter's safety didn't equate to worshipping another god; therefore, he made his decision on the spot. Swiftly, he gathered all the leaves and roots needed, ground and burned them, making an antidote that revived his daughter.

I asked Wasiu what happened next after Alhaji Agba's daughter became well, hoping he didn't do anything rash. I wasn't disappointed. Alhaji was a peace lover, but he did go to the boy's parents' home. He reported their son's actions and also threatened to use his charms to destroy their household if the boy ever crossed his daughter's path again. Aware of Alhaji Agba and what he was capable of, the boy kept to his lane, steering clear of any further mischief.

Wasiu recounted another instance where Alhaji Agba was pushed to the wall again when armed robbers attacked his household. The community was going to build a bigger mosque, and everyone had contributed money toward this cause. There was no bank in the community, so Alhaji Agba, recognized for his honesty, was entrusted with the money. All was well until one midnight when burglars invaded Alhaji Agba's house.

His children, including Wasiu's father, were all rounded up in the sitting room as Alhaji Agba sat stoically, clutching his tasbih. The robbers ransacked his room and took the money, but he never said a word till they finished and left. Immediately they left, the children and wives began to cry, realizing that their patriarch was in deep debt.

The community woke early that day and trooped to Alhaji Agba's house to console his household. They met his family, but Alhaji Agba himself was nowhere to be found. I asked Wasiu about his grandfather's whereabouts, and he said no one knew where he had gone. A wave of panic swept through the community, with some fearing he had gone to commit suicide. However, Alhaji Agba returned as quietly as he had left.

To everyone's amazement, the man they had come to console was now the one reassuring people and giving them hope that everything was under control. Some people wondered if he had gone senile, yet he sat with them and said nothing.

In a breathtaking turn of events, a miracle unfolded right before everyone.

The thieves returned, carrying the stolen money on their heads. They placed the money in a strange-looking basket, one side red and the other blue, with cowrie shells strung on top. When they got to Alhaji Agba's presence, they placed the basket and knelt at his feet. Alhaji Agba instructed them to take the bag inside and put the money exactly where they had found it. Everyone watched in awe as the thieves obediently carried out his order.

The "miracle" led to great excitement. How did this happen?! People argued among themselves, deliberating whether it was Alhaji Agba's prowess in Islamic medicine or his knowledge of Yoruba juju that helped him reclaim the money from the thieves. Remarkably, Alhaji Agba never commented on the matter, no matter how many times he was asked. The people formulated answers that suited them, keeping at the back of their minds that Alhaji Agba was spiritually a step ahead of the rest of them.

After that robbery attack on Alhaji Agba's household, stealing and robbery significantly reduced in the community. In Alhaji Agba's household they didn't witness such incidents anymore until another early morning when they were woken by loud bangs at the front door. Coincidentally, this disturbance occurred as he was preparing to go to the mosque for Fajr.

Upon hearing the noise, his children and grandchildren, including Wasiu, all trooped to Alhaji Agba's room to tell him someone was trying to break into their house. Unperturbed, he calmly informed them that he was going to the mosque. Understanding that attempting to stop him would be a futile effort, they let him go.

Wasiu said that they expected to hear Alhaji Agba struggle with whoever was outside the door; however, they didn't hear any noise, and neither did the intruders come in. Cautiously, they went outside to check what had happened. To their amazement, all of the five thieves had picked brooms and were sweeping the compound. The story traveled like wildfire to places more than twenty miles away. The thieves swept till Alhaji Agba's return. He brought out a short cane and whipped them one stroke each and then ordered them to leave.

Alhaji Agba's mystical nature left many perplexed, but the answer was staring at me. He was a man who found the middle point between Islam and the Yoruba religion, deploying traditional religion as a defensive measure and using Islam to guide the way he lived. Unfortunately, he died with his knowledge, leaving no successor to inherit his power.

From coexistence to intermarriage to sharing festivities and being joined at the hip with juju and tesbih to living with the *wudu* and the *mailaka*, Islam was part of Ibadan, and Ibadan was part of Islam. I was a part of both worlds. I could do ablution, even with palm oil. I could do the *wudu*, staying behind the man with the white gown leading us in prayer. I knew not to confuse *amin* with *amen*. I had vast knowledge about Mecca and Medina, the hajj, and its various rituals. I remember dreaming that, one day, I would perform the pilgrimage and become an alhaji.

A dream, I believe, is never too late, as long as death does not arrive before I undertake the pilgrimage, gaining the blessings and assurance of climbing the seven heavens without condemnation and raging fire.

FIG. 4. *Devotion* by Michael Efionayi. The Quran is the holy book of Islam, encompassing not just prayers but the teachings and guidance on the religion and the world in its entirety. Reading its English translation or in the original Arabic, it offers comprehensive insights into all aspects of life.

CHAPTER THREE

A Cane of Memory and the Joy of Pain

Alif-bā-tā-thā-jīm-hā-ḥā-khā-dāl-dhāl-rā-zāy-sīn-shīn
Sād-dhād-ṭaa-ḍā-'ayn ghayn-fā-qāf-kāf-lām-mīm-nūn-waw-yā

In 1963, my grandmother, a devout Muslim, struggled to manage my restlessness as a ten-year-old boy, so she enrolled me in a madrassa, a Quranic school. It worked like magic! Confined to a small stall, one becomes tamed, forfeits freedom, and throws one's restlessness out the window. Through rote learning and being forced to stay still, discipline takes root. Westerners, with their system, converted child discipline into child abuse in their textbooks, whereas those disciplined kids, when they migrated as adults, became highly sought-after factory workers.

In later years, I willingly returned to a madrassa in Ibadan to cure my restless disposition while I awaited admission to a university. My knowledge of the Quran expanded. In 1983, I went in search of Ilorin, a Muslim city, to learn Yoruba history. Not too long after, the madrassa became a prominent center.

In all my encounters with religion, be it Christianity, Islam, or Òrìṣà, there is a system of knowledge, and my engagement with their teachings is fraught with a barrage of tenets and structures. Consequently, there is an adequate provision for this knowledge to be transferred from one generation to the next, ensuring its continuity and sacrosanctity. This form of education has played out in different forms depending on the religion, but the utmost goal is the same: spirituality and piety.

The madrassa is the establishment that was put in place for Islamic education. In this context, I see Islamic education as all-encompassing because learning about the entirety of Islam as a religion is also a process of continuous knowledge pursuit. I'm also aware of the fact that Islam sees the pursuit of knowledge as an obligation, which is well spelled out not just in the Quran but also corroborated in the hadith:

> Anas ibn Malik reported: The Messenger of Allah, peace and blessings be upon him, said, "Seeking knowledge is an obligation upon every Muslim."

My journey into the city of Ilorin in 1983 began with a rough start but ended smoothly. We sped past thick bushes into the grasslands to the rough sandy roads and finally to the silky, tarred expressway. Ilorin, soft on the eyes, reflects a blend of Yoruba culture and Fulani cultures, evident from the stock of people in the society, their mode of dressing, language, and even architectural designs. The amalgamation of these cultures dates back to the early nineteenth century, when Afonja, a war general from the old Oyo Empire, was sent to conquer Ilorin. Instead, he betrayed his emperor, an Alaafin, declaring himself ruler of Ilorin. Later, he joined forces with the Fulani Muslim leader Alimi to fight the Oyo warriors who came to seek revenge.

Seeing people who embodied Fulani and Yoruba characteristics seamlessly speaking both languages was a remarkable sight. I had enough sightseeing at the bus park before I made my way to the cab stand for the journey to my final destination, my uncle's house.

It was a smooth ride; my head poked out of the window, and a cool breeze splashed on my face as I fed my eyes with the sights of the streets we zoomed through, even as my mind reflected on the city I was leaving behind.

In Ibadan, the presence of several Arabic Islamic schools was a testament to how Islam thrived in society. Among them were Imamsawwal School of Arabic and Islamic Studies, Al Alim Institute of Arabic and Islamic Studies, and Al Qurraa. Many of my Muslim friends and colleagues said that these schools were solely Islamic education in their original sense. This means that Muslims in Ibadan valued Islamic education enough to make sure their children acquired it in addition to Western education. The continued existence of these institutions over the years attests to the support they receive from families and investment in their children's education. I mean, if there were no students, such institutions would have folded up over the years.

I also conjectured that if the atmosphere were not friendly, or if the schools faced challenges in operating according to their Islamic principles or in actualizing their purpose due to hostility from either the government or non-Muslims, surviving in their existing forms would have been impossible. For instance, if it were an environment where legal registration posed problems, or where students, especially girls, were harassed in the streets and not allowed to dress the way they were supposed to, or where the stipulated rules and regulations were not suitable and convenient for the running of such schools, Islam would risk marginalization. In such cases, Arabic schools would not stand a chance, and even if created, parents would hesitate to enroll their children in such schools under such unsafe conditions.

In my experience, Islamic and Western education differ, yet they can be harmoniously incorporated to strike a balance. While the pure madrassa is strictly an institution for Islamic education, the other school allots time for Western education. In these Islamic-Western schools, both private and public, their goal is to nurture competent, sound, vast, and socially relevant students and to ensure that the ethical and moral teachings of Islam are not neglected. Students in such institutions are groomed to acquire both Western and Islamic knowledge, with the belief that this dual education will enable them to be a complete package of knowledge and morality. They are groomed with the conscience and awareness that the totality of their knowledge must be harnessed for the purpose of making society a better place in line with the rulings and principles of Islam.

Islamic education is different from Western education; it conforms to Islamic teachings, guidelines, principles, and rulings. In its real sense, this form of education involves training students to read the Quran and comprehend the laws binding humans as laid down by Allah and conveyed to humanity through his prophets. Since the Quran is written in Arabic, students delve into the additional task of learning how to read and write in Arabic. The core focus is on ethical, moral, and religious teachings, which are its primary objectives. The madrassa first teaches their pupils to read Arabic and then the Quran, with the development of writing skills following later.

For emphasis, the madrassa is not a full-blown institution but usually a subsidiary of a mosque, which is the most common form found in most streets, where children resume after school hours. This is the type of madrassa I attended for a short while in Ibadan, where I successfully memorized the Arabic alphabet from *alif* to *yā*.

Based on my knowledge of Islam, it's the total submission to the will of the Almighty Allah; everything must be done in compliance with the commandments of God—from dress and speech to practice, relationships, and attitudes. As a result, Muslims excel in Western-influenced areas like science, technology, and arts alongside Islamic culture. Today, several of these schools are scattered in the nooks and crannies of Ibadan. Children can have their education in Islamic schools from crèche through primary and secondary levels. Renowned for their standards, these schools often win many competitions with Christian schools. It's common to see school buses from these academic institutions traversing the streets of Ibadan to pick up their students.

These schools operate with considerable autonomy. Their female students cover up as expected, granting them freedom of movement in their chosen attire. These schools can be privately owned by a sole proprietor or established by groups of people or organizations, such as the Barakat Group of Schools, which was established over two decades ago and funded by an Arab association, and the Muslim Model College, established by the Muslim Student Society of Nigeria (MSSN) Ibadan, offering both day and boarding options.

The journey from Ibadan to Ilorin was a pleasant one and almost uneventful, except for when the driver stopped to refill his fuel tank and was accosted by a passenger who challenged him for wasting his time and setting him up to miss his brother's child-naming ceremony. Perhaps the situation would have gone unnoticed if the driver had not responded caustically, sparking a heated exchange with the passenger. Thankfully, other passengers intervened and calmed down the warring parties. The journey continued without further incident until I got to the garage where I hailed a cab to my uncle's house.

In Ilorin, Uncle Aminu welcomed me with open arms while his wife graciously took my bag and curtsied to greet me in the Yoruba way of showing respect. Islam forbids her from getting too close to a male who is not her husband, father, son, or brother; hence, she couldn't hug me as my uncle did. She walked ahead, and my uncle and I towed behind, trying to do a quick catch-up.

Having settled in Ilorin years earlier, Uncle Aminu met his wife, an Ilorin indigene, and they were blessed with a beautiful and intelligent daughter, Aisha, who enthusiastically ran into the house from school, gleefully interrupting my discussion with her father before her mother gently pulled her away. Moments later, the little girl reappeared, now in mufti wear and a *tira* (a textbook for Arabic study) in hand. After a quick check for any gifts I may have brought, she happily dashed away with some candies.

Aisha, my niece, never ceased to amuse me with her liveliness. Curious, I asked her father where she was headed, and he mentioned that she was headed to "macaranta alo" (Arabic school). I didn't quickly understand the significance. I understood that *macaranta* is the Hausa word for school, and Aisha had just returned from school, so I wondered why she would be going back to school again and what he meant by *alo*. Uncle Aminu noticed my confusion and seemed to be amused that something that basic could fly over my head.

The remarkable ability to translate Arabic into the native language for effective communication is always amazing. Those who undergo this learning become ambassadors of Islam and are regarded as scholars well versed in the laws and orders that bind society Islamically. By settling disputes and issuing orders, they become relevant and indispensable in matters concerning sharia and Islam. This is what Islamic education encompasses from the outset. However, with time and changes in the socioeconomic structure of our world, modifications occurred, and expansion of scope became necessary. Muslims had to start "westernizing" a bit of their products to fit into the rapidly evolving Western world. It's common to find many such schools in the northern part of Nigeria since Islam is the dominant religion there.

After mocking me with a laugh, Uncle Aminu enlightened me about two types of schools: *macaranta alo* and *macaranta boko*. A *macaranta alo*, he explained, is an Arabic school where students learn to read and write in Arabic. By the time they are ready to graduate, they can read the Quran and understand it, as well as other Arabic texts like the hadith. In contrast, a *macaranta boko* is a school for Western education, where students learn to read, write, and understand the English language. This is the school I was familiar with, but in Ilorin society, Arabic schools were equally important.

Further explanation from Uncle Aminu revealed that the small book, *tira*, that my niece had taken along with her to the Arabic school was equivalent to or even more advanced than the "Queen Primer" used in English schools. From the *tira*, they begin their Arabic education by first learning and memorizing the twenty-eight characters, known as *huruf al-abjadiyah*, from *alif* to *yā*. After that stage is mastered, students then progress to the next level, where they can start making sounds with single letters by adding diacritics to them. This stage enables the learners to form simple words, just as *a* + *s* = "as" in the English language. The process of word formulation continues for quite a while, with the students encouraged to create longer words and learn the spellings.

Upon completing this level, they can start reading short surahs from their *tira*, just like the "I go on" excerpts from the Queen Primer. They start with short surahs like Surat al-Fatiha, Surat al-Nas, Surat al-Falaq, Surat al-Ma'un, Surat al-fil, and progress through to Surat al-Baqarah while concurrently learning how to write these Arabic texts. Upon memorizing the Quran, the students partake in a graduation ceremony known as the *walimatul Qur'an*, signifying their proficiency in Quranic knowledge. However, their learning has not ended at this point; they still return to the *macaranta alo* and begin to learn Arabic words and also how to translate from Arabic to Yoruba.

Uncle Aminu's explanations were quite enlightening, but he also mentioned that there were even more standardized and less popular versions of the *macaranta alo*, known as madrassa, meaning a place of study. It's modeled on Western institutions but teaches only Arabic. These schools maintained strict disciplinary measures aimed at instilling good morals in their students and administered severe punishment, often in the form of strokes of the cane, for offenses such as truancy, lack of focus, and naughty behavior.

The duration of learning in these institutes spans ten years and is divided into three segments. The initial four years are spent in a beginner class, followed by three years in the intermediary or junior secondary class, and the final three years in the senior secondary class. Upon successful completion of the program, a certificate is issued to successful students, which can be used to secure admission to study Arabic at some universities in Nigeria.

After my uncle shared all these insights with me, he invited me to tag along with him to his daughter's Arabic school to witness firsthand how it operated. The school was just a spacious room adorned with benches and a big blackboard at the front. The youngest set of students, all of them about my niece's age, sat in the first three rows, clad in their house clothes. Another student, obviously a senior, stood teaching them the Arabic alphabet, which they learned by heart as they screamed each letter after their teacher.

An aisle separated the benches from the older students, who diligently copied Arabic texts from the board into their notebooks. Behind them, an even older set of students read from the Quran. Though the environment was rowdy, everyone seemed to understand the role they were to play, and they played it with dedication. In all that rowdiness, there was an unmistakable tranquility.

As we left the premises, I couldn't help but grin mischievously at Uncle Aminu. He understood the meaning of my grin and called me a little rascal, saying what I wanted was impossible for him at the moment because the only madrassa he knew was quite far away. But that wasn't enough to wipe the mischievous grin off my face.

Looking at me sternly, he groaned before saying, "Okay, I will take you to a better place."

When we got home, he explained that besides the *macaranta alo* and madrassa, there were a few *macaranta boko* (predominantly Western schools) that also teach Arabic. These schools had successfully integrated Arabic ways, knowledge, and morals into their curriculum. That was the kind of school my niece attended, and my uncle said we would take a tour of their facilities when we took her to school the next day. It sounded like music in my ears, and I couldn't wait for the next day to see how these people could seamlessly integrate Western and Middle Eastern education.

The following day, we were all ready, with me perhaps more prepared than the others, armed with my notecards and pen to take down every piece of information. The principal enthusiastically permitted us to tour his school, and he was more than happy to be our guide.

He led us to the Primary 5 class, and the students immediately stood up and welcomed us in a way I had never heard before, "Assalamu alaykum, warahmatullahi wa barakatuhu," the Arabic way of saying, "May the peace and blessings of Allah be with you."

My uncle and the principal replied, "Wa alaykum salam, wa rahmatullahi wa barakatuhu," which translates to "May the peace and blessings of Allah be upon you, too."

"Julus," their teacher said, and they all sat.

I stood there like a snowman, amazed, but all this did not move the older men I came with. I was utterly stunned. I had assumed the only subject taught in the school would be Arabic or related to it, so you can imagine my surprise when the teacher started to teach basic science, with the interaction in English.

We took our places at the back of the class, silently enjoying their lecture without interference or disruption. When the class ended, the teacher got a round of applause, after which he left with the phrase "Ma'a salam" and got a thunderous "Bi salam" in reply. I looked to the principal for an explanation. *Ma'a salam* means "Peace be with you," and the *Bi salam* means "In peace." This was a nice break from the norm. The class looked like an army base to me, and they were conversing in codes. I wanted so much to be part of their setup, but my age would not allow for that—I was too old for the class.

The next teacher came in, and from his attire, I guessed he was a devout Muslim. My assumption was correct as he wrote "ARABIC" in bold letters on the board. I expected to be deaf and dumb in the class as I didn't know advanced Arabic, but the lecture was done in English. I understood and enjoyed everything as he taught the students how to write in Arabic, construct words, and read them. Three sessions per week of this Arabic class would do my knowledge a lot of good. As the Arabic teacher finished and left, the mathematics teacher entered to start the next lesson.

We were offered snacks and drinks before another class started. The next teacher was a female who taught Home Economics. I wish I had attended this kind of school when I was younger. Although I had attended the informal madrassa in Ibadan at a younger age, I didn't really understand the nuances at that time. In fact, by the time I stopped attending, I could only read the *alif-bā-tā*, which is the basic Arabic alphabet, just like the ABC. This academic setup was like killing two birds with one stone.

After the Home Economics teacher left, another instructor came to teach *dīn* or *deen* (faith). Until that moment, I had never heard that word. *Deen* is taught to instill piety in the students, addressing issues like religion, ethics, and judgment. It was an enriching subject aimed at making the students upright citizens, and I gleaned valuable insights from it.

The students took a break after the class for food and refreshments, and the principal returned to his office, leaving my uncle and me. About thirty minutes later, classes resumed, and this time, the focus shifted to the Quran. The atmosphere became serene as the students brought out their copies of the Quran and read along with the teacher. Although I couldn't grasp the meaning of their words, their sonorous voices left a lasting impression on me, and I found myself giving a quiet round of applause when the lecture was over. The last subject of the day was hadith, the sayings and traditions of the Prophet Muhammad (PBUH). They are supplementary to the Quran and serve as a major form of guidance for Muslims. It was another beautiful lecture that ended at the stroke of 2:00 p.m., just in time for the Dhuhr (early afternoon prayer).

All students trooped from their classes onto an open field for the prayer. After their ablutions, each gender group converged at their designated area, supervised by teachers of their gender. My uncle joined them, but I stood aside to watch the proceedings. The prayer was well coordinated, with each movement synchronized harmoniously. The end of the prayer signaled the end of the workday, and we left for home with my niece.

As Uncle Aminu took me through the structure and administration of a pure madrassa, the Ifa learning system came to my mind. Ifa-Òrìṣà is a traditional spiritual discipline of the Yoruba people. This tradition has remained intact and expanded beyond the confines of Africa through the diaspora population of the Yoruba, with countless manifestations and variations.

Ifa-Òrìṣà was traditionally passed down orally by our forefathers. It's not uncommon to find my age mates, both at Ode Aje and Ibadan, who are well versed in Ifa-Òrìṣà knowledge, either passed down or taught to them by their fathers or by learning directly from an Ifa priest. Now that written educational materials are more readily available, the level of awareness of the learning system has increased. Just like the Islamic and Christian systems of knowledge, the Ifa learning system aims to cultivate good character. It's critical to have some sense of what a good character looks like from an Ifa-Òrìṣà point of view.

I was born into the lineage of Ifa devotees, which explains the origin of my last name, "Falola" ("Ifa is wealth"), but I didn't learn the practice. For us Yoruba, our language regularly finds its place in liturgical contexts or religious literature, often in condensed forms of knowledge communicated in simple sentences. For instance, making an elision is the process of merging words from a sentence in the field of linguistics. Consider the etymology of a word like *iwa-pele* or *iwa ope ile* (I came to welcome the earth). According to Yoruba tradition, a learner always bows to a teacher first. I was born to discover how

FIG. 5. *Ile Kewu* (madrassa) by Dr. Kazeem Ekeolu. The Mallim ("teacher") sits in front of his students, dictating and reading Arabic letters to them while pointing to the texts.

to live in harmony with the earth, which is encapsulated in the phrase *iwa ope ile,* meaning "to greet the earth." Embracing this responsibility for living in harmony with people and nonhumans that share our planet is part of living in harmony with the earth.

I'm familiar with the perspective of ancestor reverence, which implies that my purpose on earth is to learn from it and to leave it in a better shape than I found it. This notion is rooted in the concept of *atunwa*—meaning I come from the right in the elision, *otun iwa*—which serves as the foundation for this obligation. Coming from the right in Ifa-Òrìṣà signifies that I have undergone a bodily rebirth through the process of reincarnation. The Ifa-Òrìṣà moral precept to make the world a better place is based on the concept of *atunwa*, or rebirth. The guidelines for having a good character as a traditional worshipper and an Ifa-Òrìṣà knowledge seeker are straightforward to understand: always speak with honesty, don't pass judgment, don't assume anything, don't take anything personally, accept that you're always trying your best, never call somebody by their first name (except when you are older than the addressee), and always respect the taboo against gossip.

Many liturgical allusions to *iwa-pele* imply some principles for conduct that will raise our consciousness. *Ayanmo ni iwa-pele, iwa-pele ni ayanmo*, translated as "Fate is an excellent character" or "Good character is destiny," is an Ifa-Òrìṣà proverb I learned from Pasito in Ode Aje. The goal of every Ifa-Òrìṣà ritual is to align the person, the family, and the community with destiny in the form of good character since the Ifa-Òrìṣà spiritual discipline is predicated on the notion that good character is destiny. Before coming to Earth, we had the opportunity to pick our fate among incarnations, according to the Ifa-Òrìṣà scripture. It also teaches that destiny always manifests when one is in harmony with excellent character.

Uncle Aminu spoke about another familiar class of madrassa, *ile kewu zumura*, which was one of the first generations of madrassas in Yoruba societies. It operates as a form of apprenticeship where students live with the alfa, and there is no specific number of years or an official syllabus. Learning takes place at any time of the day, and students assist the teacher and his family with errands and chores and render all sorts of services. They are taught morals and discipline by the alfa, who doubles as their guardian. This is quite common with the sect they call "Oni Lawani." The children follow the teacher everywhere and only return to their families when the teacher feels they have learned enough.

This type of madrassa demands the most hardship and sacrifices, as students are in absolute service to the alfa and his family. Children whose parents believe they are obstinate and do not readily yield to corrections are often sent to this type of madrassa, which is always far from their homes. Some of the children who end up at such places are orphans who were taken there by family members after the loss of their parents to acquire Islamic morals, in-depth Quranic knowledge, and a deeper understanding of the religion. The alfas who run such madrassas do so as private endeavors, and they typically employ strict methods, including corporal punishment, to discipline erring students.

As Uncle Aminu pointed out, the last class of madrassa was the *ile kewu ratibi*. This was the one his daughter was attending after school when I was in

Ilorin and the type I later attended for academic purposes. This madrassa is a subsidiary of a mosque and usually operates for a few hours each day. The typical operating period is between 4:00 p.m. and 7:00 p.m. on Mondays, Tuesdays, and Wednesdays, with Thursdays reserved for non-mandatory prayer meetings and classes suspended. The last day of operation in the week is Saturday, when it opens between 10:00 a.m. and 2:00 p.m.

Our madrassa had only one alfa, but he had an assistant who had also learned from the same madrassa before graduating and celebrating his *walimatul Qur'an*. We called our alfa "Mallim," derived from the Arabic word muʿallim, meaning "teacher." The students were divided into different groups, with the group learning the Arabic alphabet being the lowest class. Promotion of students was based on performance. The older alfa took the higher classes, while his assistant took the lower class, sometimes delegating this duty to senior students. Our madrassa was under a shade close to the mosque. There was no provision for classrooms for each group/class. However, we knew our study mates and which corners to go to. Different groups could be learning simultaneously, especially as there were senior students available. The senior students, however, took turns teaching since only the alfa could teach them.

Uncle Aminu's description of this class of madrassa gave me more insight into why the madrassa was structured as it was. The main focus of this type of madrassa is Quranic recitation, which means there is no specific curriculum, as the ultimate goal is to be able to read and recite the Quran fluently. Students go from learning the alphabet and numerals, and then progress to simple strings of sounds and eventually reading the Quran fluently. In addition to these foundational skills, students are also introduced to basic concepts like the days of the week, the months of the year, nouns, verbs, simple etiquette in Islam, simple hadith, and Arabic songs.

After students have memorized the entire Quran and attained satisfactory proficiency in reading it, the big and final party, *walimatul Qur'an*, is held. Most students stop attending the madrassa after this party because that stage is believed to be the utmost goal. Before this big party, three other progress celebrations take place. One requires the students to bring packs of candies to the madrassa, the second requires the students to bring fruits, and the third is celebrated with any food of the alfa's choice. These celebrations are held on a low scale within the madrassa.

In our madrassa, *Mawlud Nabi* (the celebration of the birthday of Prophet Muhammad [SAW]) is another big event. Parents and people in the environment are invited. Lectures will be held, students will give performances, and there will be merriments. The alfa could deliver the lecture, or he may invite a notable Islamic scholar. The students are asked to present particular hadith of the Prophet (PBUH), which they would have been designated to memorize by the mu'allim. They give both the Arabic version and the Yoruba translation taught to them by the mu'allim. These could also be followed by a song and dance performance by the students, or a drama giving an account of a particular incident in the life of the Prophet, which could also be performed for learning, entertainment, and promotion of the madrassa.

During Ramadan, the alfa, with the students, goes to houses to give lectures. The alfa comes up with a roster to visit every different Muslim household within thirty days. They go to the family houses to give lectures on Islam, recite the Quran, and pray for the family. The family can, in turn, decide to provide meals (iftar), the meal specifically for breaking the fast during Ramadan, for the alfa and the students after the lecture. Our madrassa is free with no fee charges. There are no mandatory financial obligations for parents, yet some want to give the alfa monetary or material gifts and donations as a token of appreciation.

The madrassa is an Islamic community on its own. It's a community with a social framework whereby all members know their place and act according to the rules governing the system. These rules are based on the teachings of the Quran and the hadith of the Prophet (PBUH). The dress of the students and teachers is strictly in accordance with the prescription of Islam. The rule of dress goes beyond the classrooms and extends to the halls of residence. Whether it's the uniform or house clothes, females wear clothes that cover their full glory, with the hijab as their crown. The predominant language of communication is Arabic, except for students at the beginning level who are not yet proficient. The relationship is cordial yet puritanical. There are authorities at different levels to ensure that everything goes smoothly and that the madrassa exhibits governance, rules, and the harmonious coexistence of its members.

Some pure madrassas, by virtue of their size and functionality, have a working organizational structure and operate like a full-blown educational institution. From the administrative cadre to the academic cadre, there is a working system. A friend attended one such madrassa. The administrative structure is well organized, and the proprietor or founder of the madrassa is called the Mudir, usually an Islamic scholar who has been well trained in a madrassa, too. The Mudir is the highest-ranking administrative official since he owns the madrassa in most cases. The chairman and vice chairman are the next-ranking administrative officials, and they preside over board meetings, which are held to discuss the state of the madrassa and plan how the institution can make progress. Other issues that could warrant a board meeting are the examination schedule, PTA schedule, convocation, social events, and many more. The key purpose is to have all members of the staff together for deliberation and exchange of ideas for the betterment of the madrassa.

The "amir" is chosen from the young lecturers. Young lecturers are usually alumni of the madrassa who have been retained for employment. Appointed by the management, they are the link between the teachers and the students. They establish a curriculum and syllabi for the various classes and continuously write assessments and examinations. Students get promoted, demoted, retained in the same class, or even advised to withdraw. There are awards and prizes for outstanding students in as well as intra and inter-class competitions called *musabakoh* at intervals. Each academic year comprises three terms, each with an examination followed by vacation, which ranges between two weeks to two months, depending on the term.

Lectures are received Monday, Tuesday, Wednesday, Saturday, and Sunday, with the madrassa operating between 8:00 a.m. and 2:00 p.m. From 8:00 a.m. to 8:30 a.m., *al-sufuf* (assembly) takes place. Activities like words of admonition, recitation of the Quran, and announcements take place on the assembly ground. Classes commence by 8:30 a.m., and each is forty-five minutes. By 11:30 a.m., the timekeeper rings the bell for *istiroha*, which means break time, which lasts till noon, and the bell for *adukhur*, which means the end of the break, and students return to their classrooms. By 1:30 p.m., another bell is rung and the students move to the mosque for salat.

The collective name for the lecturers, all of whom are male, is *azatidha*, while the singular title for each is *ustadh*. All are graduates of a madrassa. Even though they have background knowledge of most of the courses taught, each of them has an area of specialization that informs the course they are employed to teach. The *jaduhal* timetable has times allotted for each *ustadh* to come to class and deliver their lecture.

Students belong to different classes, and they take notes that the teachers evaluate. They are given classes and assignments with a set deadline for submission. Male and female students receive lectures in the same classroom. Drawing from the rulings of the Quran, the school limits body-to-body contact between them. The school has dress codes to which the students must comply. The cap for the males and the hijab for the females is nonnegotiable. Some madrassas have hostels as a boarding option for students, with boarders called *ruwaq*.

Aminu told me *ibtida'i* is generated from the base word *bada'a*, which means "beginning" or "foundation," simply because students have no preliminary knowledge of Islam and how to recite the Quran. It corresponds to the primary level of Western education. Depending on the learning speed of a student, the number of years it takes to finish this level can range between two and four years. Some of the things learned at this level include but are not limited to the following. *Qoydah*, which means learning to read, is broken down into steps like learning the alphabet of Arabic and basic strings of sounds like two-letter words, three-letter words, etc. Some institutions call this subject *durusul lugha*.

Quran and Hizb have to do with Quran memorization. Students start with memorizing the basic short surahs of the Quran that have been compiled in the *tira* for their level. They proceed to basic nouns and verbs, including the Arabic terms for mother, father, friend, eat, dance, stand, sit, etc.

Kowaidul solat serves as a guide on how to observe salat in Islam, starting with how to perform ablution, answering questions such as: How many *rakkas* does each salat have? How many salats are there in a day? What time do they come in? What do you recite? What do you say when you bend and make your prostration? What do you do when you make a mistake in the salat? In addition to the practical aspects of prayer, students also learn short Arabic songs known as *adab*. They are like nursery rhymes, which serve as mnemonic aids and emphasize etiquette and the virtues of a good Muslim. These songs may also cover topics such as Ramadan and stories about any of the prophets.

There are other subjects like *sira*, "biography." So the subject is narrations of the birth, life, and death of prophets. As the classes advance, the stories of the companions of the prophets and their family members are introduced. *Tarikh* is a general history important to Islam. It's not as detailed as the *sira*. *Idaadi* is another level of class like the Junior Secondary School (JSS 1 to 3) of Western education, which takes three years in some madrassas and four years in others.

My friend told me that 90 percent of everyday alfa stops at this level. After passing the exams that test your knowledge of things taught at *ibtida'i*, the students proceed to the *awwal idaadi*. This is the first of the four years of *idaadi*. *Awwal* means "first" in Arabic. Due to curricula variations between madrassas, some begin to teach students *nahw* (grammar) and *sorfu* at this level, while others wait till the next class. This level includes general subjects from *ibtida'i*, along with additions such as *nahw*. This subject is the version of *qoydah* taught at *ibtida'i*, as it's one of the two breakdowns of the subject, including correct Arabic pronunciation.

In *ibtida'i*, you just need to have an idea of how a word is pronounced, but here you will be taught each sound and the rules governing its use and pronunciation. It's the phonetics of Arabic. For instance, at the primary level, the word "bird" can be pronounced as /bed/, and no comment will be passed, but once you are a student of phonetics, you will be taught the right description and pronunciation of the vowel. This subject equips students with the ability to correct themselves when reciting or speaking Arabic when they mispronounce a letter word. In the words of my informants, they are taught the "manuals" of each sound of Arabic.

The subject is offered throughout the years in the madrassa but gets more advanced and complex as the student progresses. It's a broad subject with diverse topics and aspects introduced to students at the appropriate time. Some examples of topics under this subject include *morfuati li asmohi,* which teaches everything about the use and pronunciation of the Arabic vowel *domoh. Masubati li asmohi* teaches everything about the use and pronunciation of the vowel *fathia.* This is the line above letters indicating the vowel *a. Mahfudati li asmohi*: this handles another vowel, *kesroh,* this is the line under letters representing the vowel *i.*

My friend even jokingly mocked those perceived as dullards. If you are not good in this subject as a student, they see you as *olodo,* which belittles your speaking and reading proficiency. *Nahw* is the grammar of Arabic and is the second breakdown of *qoydah* taught in *ibtida'i.* It teaches the tense, aspect, modality, case, etc. of Arabic. Here you are taught the base form of verbs and the way to express them in different tenses and aspects. Students also learn types of sentences, for instance, transitive sentences, imperative, requests, etc., as well as how to use nouns in different cases such as subject, object, and so on. All these will be different topics under *sorfu.*

Adab (ethics) songs learned at this stage are more advanced, complex, and longer. They delve deeper into more important aspects of life and preach detailed and ethical principles. Another subject is the Quran and *hizb,* which is an advancement from the one taught in *ibtida'i.* The 114 surahs of the Quran are divided into thirty different groups called *juz,* which are further divided into sixty *hizb.* These have varying lengths since these subjects span all through the years in the madrassa; the differences in each level will be the volume of *hizb* to be memorized. The *tafsir* (exegesis) subject is centered around the Quran as well but does not have to do with memorization. Rather, it's the careful study of the circumstances surrounding the revelation of each surah of the Quran, answering questions such as, Why the revelation? What is the surah teaching? How was it revealed to the Prophet? *Motalaha* as a subject is like literature. Different *tira* of narration written by Islamic scholars are studied. Also, Arabic literature is taught, and other general subjects are offered from *ibtida'i.*

Thania idaadi is the second year of *idaadi.* Some madrassas introduce *nahw* and *sorfu* at this level. Subjects offered at this level include the ones carried on from *ibtida'i* and *awwal idaadi,* such as *nahw.* As established, different classes have distinct *tira* for this subject, as it spans all the years of madrassa, with the syllabus as the differentiating factor. So while *nahw* of the first year will deal with an introduction to Arabic phonetics and simple sounds, this level looks at complex sounds and how sounds affect one another (phonology), for instance, how preceding sounds can affect the pronunciation of following sounds and vice versa. The variables of environment and context start setting in.

While year one *sorfu* introduces students to the basics of Arabic grammar, the *tira* for year two goes deeper into the complex nature and aspects of grammar, morphology, and syntax. *Figh* replaces the *qawa'idul salat ibtida'i*, going deeper into the rules governing salat. It teaches how to perform hajj, how to do sand ablution in the absence of water, how to perform salat on a corpse, how to join a congregational salat, how to make up for the salat missed after joining a congregational *salat*, and so on.

Ta'lim is the subject covering learning how to live as a Muslim. It's the replacement for *adab*. The word itself means "learning to be knowledgeable." All these precepts are learned in songs that encode the morals, etiquette, and rules of Islam. The songs are long and have deep content that arouses deep thought and is geared toward creating a positive influence in the lives of the students. *Ta'lim* could teach how to get closer to Allah, how to keep away from sins, how to treat parents and the elderly, how to judge a matter, and so on, as well as a return to others from previous classes.

Thalisa idaadi is the third year of *idaadi* with the certainty of general subjects from previous classes. New subjects are introduced, including knowledge of the world we are living in, countries where Islam is dominant, where it came from, iconic countries in Islam, and the knowledge of geography generally. *Hisab* is mathematics/arithmetic, which encompasses learning Arabic numerals and simple arithmetic system of equations. This year also teaches numerology, where each alphabet and number has a "spiritual implication" in Arabic, which knowledge helps with picking names for offspring and choosing a future partner.

Robia idaadi is the final year of *idaadi*. Since it's the final year, the students are given a project to submit, which will be graded and contribute to the overall grade at the time of graduation. A convocation ceremony called *aflah idaadi* is held for students completing this level, with certificates that specify that their grades range from excellent, very good, good, and fair. Most students do not proceed after this level. Some go into establishing *ile kewu ratibi*, becoming a cleric, learning a skill, or pursuing Western education. A student must finish this fourth year to be eligible for the certificate.

The higher level is *thanawi*, which is equivalent to the Senior Secondary (SS 1 to 3) of Western education schools. My friend told me that only about 7 percent of alfas finish this level. Only students who are determined to be deep-rooted Islamic scholars proceed to this level because parents want them to pursue Western education or skill acquisition. Most students from madrassas who merge Western education with the Islamic system of learning will be done

FIG. 6. Portrait of a young boy wearing a turban by Raji Babatunde Mohammed. Dressing complemented with a turban is not uncommon for Muslim men, especially clerics. A young boy wearing a turban shows his upbringing and the household. From the private collection of Omoba Yemisi Shyllon.

with Senior Secondary School (SS 3) and are faced with the quest of gaining admission to a tertiary institution.

Thanawi has three years, *awwal thanawi*, *thania thanawi*, and *thalisa thanawi*, which is the highest point in every madrassa. At this point, the student is, to a considerable extent, an independent Islamic scholar with great knowledge. The final *aflah* is done here, and a certificate is conferred, with few alfas reaching this level. The student also writes a project here, which project could be an Arabic song to appraise himself, a prominent figure, his madrassa, or an inspirational story addressing core Islamic issues.

There are not as many subjects studied at this level as in previous years because even though they are continuations, they are more complex. So a *tira* for a particular subject can have up to volume 15, with everything covered within three years. *Jami'a is* the equivalent of a university. There are no madrassas at this level in Nigeria. Graduates of *thanawi* travel to Saudi Arabia, Egypt, Iran, etc., for this purpose. Some of these pure madrassas are affiliated with the Arabic and Islamic studies departments of some tertiary institutions.

Madrassas have rules and regulations guiding the students and staff. After all, as the biblical saying goes, "A society without sin is one without rules." Some have them printed out as handbooks that are given to every student upon admission. In situations where a student or a staff has a complaint against them for investigation, interrogation, and appropriate punishment, *idaara* is the office where a defaulter meets with the panel for questioning. The panel comprises the Amir, the chairman, the vice chairman, and the Mudir.

Examples of bad conduct that could warrant facing the panel include examination malpractice; failure to do assignments or tasks given, such as memorization; nonpayment of obligatory fees; defying the rules guiding male and female relationships; flouting dressing rules; sexual harassment and rape; bullying and extortion; and fighting. After a thorough investigation and an accused person is found guilty, punishments that the panel can issue include flogging, a stern warning, suspension, a fine, rustication, demotion, repeating a level, or termination of one's job appointment for lecturers.

I remember attending a *walimatul Qur'an*, although I wasn't done and nowhere near being promoted. I had stopped going to the madrassa after I was punished for not fully memorizing some Arabic spellings. Before then, an incident happened that caused great fear in me and cemented my decision not to attend classes at the madrassa anymore.

As we sat in class on that particular day, somberly listening to Alfa as he reprimanded a student who had been absent for over a week, we heard a loud noise, and before we could make sense of it, a particular masquerade jumped into our madrassa, accompanied by his followers brandishing robust canes and looking ready to strike at the slightest provocation. Speaking in a mix of low and loud tones, the masquerade performed different stunts to instill fear in people.

Alfa and the rest of us took to our heels, forming small groups and running in different directions. Suddenly, the group I was with met a dead end in front of us, which meant that we would have to turn around and face the masquerade and his entourage. Bracing ourselves for the beating of our lives, we ran past the masquerade group. The Alfa threw away his cane and tasbih and ran even faster than some of us. But the masquerade must have had other plans as he never as much as took a glance at us. I didn't know how the story ended that day, but days later, I found out the reason for the masquerade's display.

It turned out that our alfa's wife had met the masquerade and his followers on the road and had disregarded them. While others were running away so as not to impede the masquerade's display, Alfa's wife hissed as she majestically walked past them. She even threatened them on her husband's behalf. An elderly alhaji had come out to appease the masquerade, and after he insisted that he must see Alfa and his wife and get an apology from them, Alfa came out of his hiding place and apologized on behalf of his wife, who was too afraid to face the wrath of the masquerade and his followers.

I have always put my madrassa experience into practice as a form of discipline, as the use of Arabic verses for admonitions, as drawing from multiple sources, and as a way of knowing.

CHAPTER FOUR

Lips of Angels

الله الله الله الله
يا إلهي والله
.الرحماني الرحيم
الملك القدوس
يا أفيزو يا صبر

Allah Allah Allah (Invocation of God's name)
O my God, and My Lord
The Most Merciful, The Most Compassionate
The Sovereign, The Holy
O Protector, O Patient One

My grandmother regularly attended *àsàlátù* on Sundays. It was an extension of our mosque congregation, so it was common for those who prayed in that mosque to attend *àsàlátù,* as it was the usual routine. I knew other women had a different *àsàlátù* they attended in the market. When I was younger, I didn't pay much attention to this practice, but as I grew older, I found it peculiar that there was an *àsàlátù* in the market and even Christians fellowshipped at the same location. The participants in these gatherings included market women who had their regular mosques or churches they attended, as well as the convenient ones in the markets.

One of the unique features of these arrangements was the designated day. Sunday is usually a day for rest, with people staying home to do chores, worship, and relax. It's a great day for *àsàlátù* and fellowships to thrive in residential areas because people had enough time to spare. However, Sunday is not a good day for *àsàlátù* and fellowships in the market because there would be a low turnout. Other days also weren't ideal because it wasn't an easy task to make market women leave their wares and spend time in *àsàlátù*.

I remember one of the market women saying Thursday was their *àsàlátù* day in the market. When I asked why, she said it was because the Lagos state government had designated that day for weekly environmental sanitation in the marketplaces from daybreak till 10 a.m.. So, the *àsàlátù* ran from that morning till the environmental sanitation period was over and market women could go back to their businesses.

I inquired further, since cleanliness is next to godliness, why did they abandon sanitation duties to attend to prayers, leaving their surroundings untidy? The Lagos environmental sanitation law prohibited all retail outlets from opening for business before 10:00 a.m. on Thursdays. Many market women would arrive early on Thursdays to clean their shops and avoid fines from government officials. After they were done, however, they were idle until 10:00 a.m., when they could officially open their stalls. This is why Thursday became the chosen day for *àsàlátù* in the market space, and there was always a large turnout of people who had two to three hours to spare before they started their business activities.

Another reason I found it intriguing that *àsàlátù* was held on Thursday in the market is the Yoruba belief that the dead come closer to us on Thursdays. I saw this as the Islamic adaptation of the Yoruba masquerade custom, which they call Thursday *Alamisi* (*al-Khamis*) (the day our ancestors come to visit us). It's the perfect day to pray and give out alms, both of which are regular activities in the *àsàlátù*.

Interestingly, there was a man who made a living off this *Alamisi* practice. He was like the Yoruba masquerade, only that he didn't come from heaven. From how he dressed, a turban on his head, and many tasbihs on his neck, there was no argument as to whether he was a Muslim or not. He came around on Thursdays and would dance around the market, claiming he was "Baba Oku" ("Father of the Dead") and could communicate with the dead. If you wanted to give anything to your departed loved ones, you would give it to Baba Oku, and he would give it to them on your behalf. He was literally the living collecting money on behalf of the dead! Our masquerades call themselves the dead, collecting money on their behalf; how Baba Oku and the masquerades transfer their earnings to heaven is what fiction or movie scriptwriters need to explore.

In Yoruba tradition, it's believed that giving offerings in memory of the dead ensures their well-being in the afterlife. This practice is rooted in the idea that the dead won't lack in the spirit world and will not go hungry wherever they are as long as you feed people or give alms in their name. It's akin to the ancient Egyptian pharaohs who built pyramids for themselves with provisions to consume in heaven. Islam also supports this idea, and Baba Oku cleverly exploited it to his advantage. He would collect money, food items, and things like soap and clothes, then return the following Thursday, bringing joyful reports from the ghosts he had been sent to and ready to collect new items.

Market women cared little about his activities but offered him what they had when they felt like giving. Years later, I learned that Baba Oku had passed away. I reflected on his activities and smiled at how he had manipulated the whole idea of *Alamisi* and the connection individuals have with their loved ones who are no more.

This brought to mind when the great Afrobeat maestro Fela Anikulapo-Kuti, tagged Christianity and Islam moneymaking organizations in one of his songs, singing, "These moneymaking organizations, dem come put we Africans in total confusion." He faced lots of verbal attacks from religious people who called him insane, delusional, and unholy. Fela's controversial personality only exacerbated the situation. Before his death from AIDS, Fela was known to be very promiscuous and a chain smoker of marijuana. I thought so too when I was younger, but my perspective changed as I got older and looked back to my younger years.

Reflecting on Fela's criticism of religion and remembering how *àsàlátù* operated, I could see a sense in his lyrical attacks. I mean, people already had places of worship in their residential areas, so why bring it to their workplace, too? What happens in salat prayers? Prayers for the congregation toward financial success, then numerous donations from the congregation, *fī sabī lil Lāh* this, *sadaqah* that. The interesting part is the special prayers and songs for those who bring higher donations, performed right there in the presence of the congregation.

Another is how awards and titles are bestowed on individuals while neglecting their spiritual devotion and prioritizing philanthropy. This means that those who consistently donate to the congregation are more likely to receive recognition and titles ahead of those with more knowledge of the religion and who practice it better. Maybe Fela wasn't entirely right, but he wasn't totally wrong either. Many of these *àsàlátù* give the "Iya Ad-deeni" (mother of religion) title to women of affluence who can barely pray, let alone lead a prayer session. Most of the time, they lack modest character and behavior, but a blind eye is turned to all of that.

One afternoon, as I stood in a shop where I had gone to buy bread for the household, I watched as the Muslim congregation conducted their prayer. Only this time, it wasn't their routine prayer. Dressed in white garments like angels, they sat in long rows on plain benches. The Òrìṣà people also wore white garments, but they held wooden images that represented their deities.

In this Muslim gathering, the men and women sat in different sections, mirroring the custom during the routine five daily salats in mosques. However, what stood out to me was that the number of women present at the meeting was about five times that of men, which was rarely so during the daily salat.

I was witnessing the *àsàlátù* gathering, where devout Muslims came in numbers to pray in honor of the Prophet Muhammad (PBUH). The Yoruba clerics have their saying, *Àsàlátù fún Anobi Múọ́mọ̀dú*, meaning, "Prayers upon the Prophet." Led by the group missioner, typically a male, the prayers were mainly in Arabic. The missioner would start the Arabic prayer, and the congregation would repeat after him a stipulated number of times before moving on to the next prayer point. They had a booklet with prayers listed, along with the number of times they were to be said and the proper procedures.

From where I stood, I could hear their slow *yā Hayyu yā Qayūm bi rahmatika, yā Hayyu yā Qayūm bi rahmatika*, translated as "O Living, O Self-Sustaining Sustainer! In Your mercy do I seek relief." As the congregation reached a point, the alfa continued to speak in Arabic while they stretched out their hands in silent supplications. I deduced he was doing a special prayer.

Following the alfa's lead, the congregation rose in unison, and a resonant *Ya ayyu ya qayummadhzta* filled the air as the prayers intensified. After reaching a specific number, the congregation went quiet again and spread their hands forth as the missioner did another special prayer before they took their seats and continued the prayer with a slow *Lā illāha illal Lāhu, lā illāha illal Lāhu*, taking the same form as the first prayer. They had alternating periods for the prayers, one to sit and do the prayers slowly and another for standing, where they fervently poured out their hearts to Allah.

At the end of the last prayer, the missioner gave a small pep talk, and bowls were passed between rows for *fī sabī lil Lāh* (donations). After that, the congregation started singing Yoruba songs, led by the missioner and heavily backed by the female members. Songs like *Gbogbo ohun ti a wi, l'Obu lí gbo, eleti gbaroye lalahura; Satia, sayin sii, ko maa ma je o pe*, meaning "All that we have said, the Lord has heard; Allah is the one with listening ears, sanction our requests, O Lord, don't make us wait too long."

Songs followed one after another, and one that particularly caught my attention was *Afeesu ba wa so omo wa, Afeesu ba wa so omo wa, s'ebi Iwo lo ní iso re lodo*. In that song, they called Allah *Hāfidh* (the Protector/Guardian), asking Him to protect their children because He is the One who has all protection with Him. This song is famous in Yoruba Muslim naming ceremonies. They continued with different songs in Yoruba, predominantly prayers, worship, and praises to Allah and the Prophet Muhammad (PBUH).

Assalātu fātiha, Assalātu
Wo Ola Muhammad se alekun ore wa
Assalātu fātiha, Assalātu
Salātu, wo Ola Muhammad se ore fun mi
Olorun ti gbe mi ga l'ola Muhammad se alekun ore
Muhammad ni ami rere l'aiye
Tori Muhammad se alekun ore
Emi ti ba Muhammad duro
E yon bo Anobi Muhammad
Baba Fatimo, omo Amina, omo Abdullahi
Adewale Anobi, olooto
Iyin rere lo je fun wa.

All the lines were praising the Prophet of Islam.

Until recently, when performances have become regular, the best time to enjoy Islamic songs was during Ramadan. The Nights of Majesty, when Islamic groups organized special prayers in the last ten days of Ramadan, was incomplete without songs of praise and prayers. For many, worship was a time to seek forgiveness and to make requests to Allah. Muslims from all over the world, including those in Ibadan, anticipated these nights, forfeiting their sleep to pray for the forgiveness of their sins.

Just as the Quran meticulously details the significance of the Night of Majesty, it also explains how powerful the nights of *Laylatul Qadr* are. The surah mentions that the Quran was revealed on the nights of *Laylatul Qadr*. These nights are deemed better than a thousand months because it's believed that during these nights, angels descend from heaven with approval from Allah to take people's prayers and supplications back to Allah. I remember my friend, Babatunde, claiming he had seen the angels on one of those nights as they descended with sacks and meticulously scrutinized people's prayers, throwing some into the sacks that hung on their shoulders and trampling some requests under their feet.

For the Muslims, on this night, humanity could have their destiny rewritten. People with bad luck can pray about it and have a turnaround of fate. Similarly, people can have their sins forgiven and erased if they pray with clean minds, with the intention to refrain from repeating past mistakes. Attending such prayer sessions during *Laylatul Qadr* holds great importance for Muslims everywhere.

FIG. 7. *A Band of Young Itinerant Entertainers* by Dr. Kazeem Ekeolu. Songs play a pivotal role in Islam, Christianity, and traditional religion in Nigerian communities. Beyond entertainment, music and songs serve various other purposes within these religious practices.

SURAH AL-QADR (THE MAJESTY)

إِنَّا أَنزَلْنَاهُ فِي لَيْلَةِ الْقَدْرِ
وَمَا أَدْرَاكَ مَا لَيْلَةُ الْقَدْرِ
لَيْلَةُ الْقَدْرِ خَيْرٌ مِنْ أَلْفِ شَهْرٍ
تَنَزَّلُ الْمَلَائِكَةُ وَالرُّوحُ فِيهَا بِإِذْنِ رَبِّهِمْ مِنْ كُلِّ أَمْرٍ
سَلَامٌ هِيَ حَتَّىٰ مَطْلَعِ الْفَجْرِ

Bismillaahi al-Rahmāni al-Rahīm
Innaa anzalnāhu fī Laylatil Qadr
Wa mā adrāka mā Laylatul Qadr
Laylatul Qadri khayrun min alfi shahr
Tanazzalul Malaa'ikatu war-rūhu fīha bi idhni Rabbihim min kulli amr
Salāmun hiya hattā matla'il fajr.

In the name of Allah, Most Gracious, Most Merciful.
We have indeed revealed this (Message) in the Night of Power:
And what will explain to thee what the night of power is?
The Night of Power is better than a thousand months.
Therein come down the angels and the Spirit by Allah's permission, on every errand:
Peace! . . . This until the rise of the morning! (Quran 97:1–5)

No one wanted to miss the *Laylatul Qadr*. Its spiritual significance mainly drew the adults, while the young people had various reasons for not wanting to miss it. After the iftar (food to break the fast) and the Isha (night prayer), the children would start preparing the mosque and its surroundings by spreading mats and arranging benches to be used. At the same time, we kept an eye out for designated spots for people who would share free food and those who came to sell food.

The perks that came with the *Laylatul Qadr* were enough to pique people's interest, but there were other things, especially for children. First, there was the gleeful feeling of being outside past midnight. With the mosques overflowing and spilling onto the streets, children would find themselves outside of the mosque, where there were fewer restrictions and more opportunities to play. The children who stayed inside the mosque during the *Laylatul Qadr* missed out on all the fun.

Second, there was always plenty of food, which was split into two categories. Those inside the mosque enjoyed this aspect more as people often shared free food, snacks, and drinks at the *Laylatul Qadr* to seek favor from Allah.

They would start handing the food out from inside the mosque, which meant that by the time they got outside the mosque, they would have just a little left to share or nothing at all. However, this didn't mean that those outside would not get to eat at all; it's just that they had to pay for the food. Some areas in Lagos had *Mai tea* (Hausa men who sell bread, fried eggs, tea, and noodles), and some women brought soft drinks, biscuits, puff-puff, doughnuts, and egg rolls to sell, making the *Laylatul Qadr* look somewhat like a Muslim carnival.

The month of Ramadan is a pious and enjoyable month for Muslims and society as a whole. Even though peace cannot be seen with the naked eye, its presence during this holy month is palpable. People strive to stay holy and engage in virtuous acts, leading to a noticeable decline in social vices like robbery, kidnappings, maiming, and fisticuffs, plus minimal usage of foul language on the streets. Even individuals typically known for unruly behavior exhibit improved conduct for thirty days, awaiting the end of Ramadan before resuming street fights.

Social establishments like pubs, clubs, and hotels record low turnouts of patronage. Everywhere is calm because those who are fasting are careful not to do things that would invalidate their fasts and those who aren't fasting exercise restraint to avoid compromising the fast of others and inviting the wrath of Allah upon themselves. Both young and old move around at will throughout the month of Ramadan. Late-night movements are always interesting because many people move around at odd hours for various reasons.

As a teenager, my friends and I walked about the streets at midnight with no adult to supervise us and only the moonlight to illuminate our paths. It made us feel grown up and in charge. No harm came to us whatsoever, even though we were roaming during ungodly hours. However, the peace and tranquility associated with *Laylatul Qadr* faded over time, or perhaps the rascals on the streets became more brazen. After several years of enjoying peaceful *Laylatul Qadr* in my neighborhood, I moved away, yet I continued to enjoy peaceful *Laylatul Qadr* in my new place. But one of my friends, Babatunde, didn't have such luck.

I received a shocking message one day that Babatunde had survived an attack at a *Laylatul Qadr* and had been hospitalized. I was surprised how that could have happened at a *Laylatul Qadr*. Did he get into a fight with someone? When I saw him in a stable condition, half of my fears disappeared, and we started to talk about what had happened to him. He said it played out like a movie.

The *Laylatul Qadr* was already slated to end by 3:00 a.m., but those who lived close by were leaving around 2:30 a.m. so they could fix themselves *sahur* to start the day's fast. Since his place wasn't too far away, Babatunde decided to leave too.

FIG. 8. *Musicians on Stage* by Dr. Kazeem Ekeolu. Yoruba Muslim music artists play live on stage and release recorded albums. Lyrics of these songs include Quranic verses, prayers, and praises. They do this for entertainment and spiritual purposes, and many have gained fame in this aspect.

Unknown to everyone who had plans to leave before daybreak, there were thugs in the area who also had plans for them. As they got far enough from the mosque to relatively dark areas with no streetlights, a group of boys appeared right in front of them, brandishing cutlasses and flashlights. Those in front were ordered to quietly surrender their valuables.

Babatunde and his neighbor thought they were lucky to be at the back of the lot. They turned around and ran away with a couple of other people. Unluckily for them, the thugs had planned out their operation. As they ran back toward the mosque, they were cut off by another group of armed thugs who had laid an ambush for them. This set of thugs didn't give orders but started raining heavy slaps on them for running from the first group of thugs. Some people, like my friend, got beaten with the flat sides of cutlasses before they were forcibly relieved of their valuables.

I felt pity for Babatunde, but his sudden laughter caught me by surprise. As he chuckled, he raised a hand to tell me to hold on while he composed himself. When he finally did, he pulled me closer and started talking in a mischievous whisper. He said the neighbor he was with was an "after-four," that is, cross-eyed, and he couldn't easily decipher where the slaps and beatings were coming from. The dramatic display when he was getting beaten elicited chuckles from Babatunde, even though he was getting beaten, too.

When they were asked to drop their belongings, including wristwatches, Babatunde's neighbor added an extra layer of confusion by pulling his watch, looking in a different direction, and then stretching the wristwatch in yet another direction. It was only by God's grace that Babatunde managed to stifle his laughter. The thug insisted that the neighbor make eye contact with him while handing over his valuables, but the cross-eyed fellow insisted that he was looking directly at him despite his gaze being elsewhere.

Babatunde found their argument amusing until they were going to start beating his neighbor again. He then explained to them that the guy was cross-eyed. Eventually, they let them go after my friend received a hot slap for not explaining his neighbor's condition to them early enough. Babatunde said he was sure his cross-eyed neighbor had said prayers at the *Laylatul Qadr*, praying for his fate to change, only to receive a beating that might have worsened his sight instead. We both burst into another round of laughter, and I couldn't help but feel relieved that the thugs hadn't beaten the sense of humor out of my friend.

Babatunde's story was amusing, but I felt pity for those who were attacked. How did that happen? *Laylatul Qadr*, nights when children roamed the streets without fear of harm, had now become an occasion where even adults couldn't walk freely. When I left Babatunde's ward, I also checked on his neighbor to sympathize with him before returning to Babatunde to notify him that I was leaving.

On my way out, I couldn't stop thinking of what happened to my friend. I had an epiphany that the world had changed from what I used to know, and people had become more desperate. Walking the streets at night was no longer safe, regardless of the occasion. Since then, I would either not attend the *Laylatul Qadr* or stay in the mosque till daybreak because, as the Yoruba say, *eni Olorun n so ko ma so ara e* (he whom God protects should also be careful). In an atmosphere of fear, it seems unlikely that angels would still visit us to take our petitions to Allah. The same lips that sang praises were now sour. Humans have changed the lips of angels to weapons of destruction.

Growing up in Ibadan among Muslims, Christians, and Òrìṣà devotees, I've come to realize the vital role music plays in human lives. It serves as a conduit for telling our history, a platform for political discourse, a source of merriment and celebration, praise, and motivation. Without the melodic songs, religion would become dull. Without those loud and boisterous songs, it would be difficult to capture the attention of children and teenagers alike. Without dance, there would be no gossip (and intrigue) about women and their big breasts and butts, and my friends and I would have been deprived of the joke of comparing our elders' voices to the croaks of toads. I wouldn't have been a fugitive, sneaking out of the house in the early hours of Ramadan to roam the streets, singing to wake people up to cook, eat, and pray before beginning the day's fast.

Throughout their history, the Yoruba people have nurtured a rich tapestry of musical genres, including *apala*, *juju*, *senwele*, and *rara*, serving as both spiritual and secular expressions of their culture. As the story goes, when Islam originally arrived, Yoruba Muslims were barred from singing songs of their ethnic origin, and the Islamic religion didn't provide them with any satisfying replacement. Instead, they were told to reach Allah in Arabic and to worship his angels with Arabic songs.

At some point, I believed that the only languages God understood were English and Arabic. But today, if I don't pray in Yoruba, I doubt if God will ever hear me. If God, as Christians told me, created me in his image, why would he want me to communicate with him in Latin?

What Muslims had was their five times daily prayer and devotional Arabic songs. Although these songs were musical, I didn't see anyone dancing to them, meaning that a chunk of the lifestyle of those who related music to worship was taken away. As a result, the Muslims had no choice but to be jealous of their Christian counterparts, who were still able to dance and sing as they liked. Every Sunday, the Christians could compose songs that aligned with the religion in their language and dance to their tune. When they returned home, they continued singing these songs while getting ideas for new ones.

I knew a woman in Ibadan who was called by a Muslim name (Iya Basit), and all her children also had Muslim names. But every Sunday, they dressed up for church. Bewildered, I asked Pasito, my grandfather, if they had converted to Christianity. He explained that they were yet to convert, but he reckoned it would happen soon as it seemed to be a common trend then. Pasito explained further how a Muslim woman would start going to church, then bring her children along, and eventually, the family either became bi-religious or the husband would also join the wagon to church.

Curious about this development, I questioned Pasito further. Why were Muslims converting to Christianity? Was it that the Christian God was more powerful than the Muslim God? Pasito laughed and told me that the reason people were jumping the Islam ship in favor of the Christian ship was far more petty. According to him, music had always been a big part of Yoruba culture; in fact, it could be seen as a dominant feature. The Yoruba people deploy music in many facets of their lives. In the worship of their gods, in the training of their children, in celebration, in mournful periods, and communication among themselves, the Yoruba incorporated music, and where there is music, dance is not far off.

After hearing several stories from her Christian neighbor and friend about various church activities, particularly Thanksgiving Sunday, when they got to wear their best outfit and had extra time to sing and dance, Iya Basit wanted to go to church to see for herself. Witnessing the vibrant atmosphere filled with drumming, songs, and women dancing to the rhythm, she felt a sense of liveliness and belonging and began to attend the church on Sundays, taking her children along. Gradually, they embraced the Christian faith, finding Islam boring and too restrictive.

Women who could warm their way into the minds of their husbands succeeded in persuading them to come to church, and those who couldn't end up with bi-religious families, leaving their children confused about the path to follow. As a result of this shift toward Christianity, the Muslim congregation started to decline. In an attempt to solve this, the *àsàlátù* was established, a replica of the Christian Sunday worship.

This new initiative mirrored many aspects of Christian worship, with the *àsàlátù* gathering being held on Sunday morning, as well as a sermon, prayer, monetary contribution toward the advancement of Islam, and most importantly, music and dance. The Muslims, however, adopted the Arabian drum, known as *bandiri* among Yoruba, instead of the Yoruba talking drums.

The exact moment when music became integrated into the Yoruba Muslim community is difficult to pinpoint, and we cannot rely entirely on oral stories, but the type of music that the community produced can be identified. This style of music, known as *were*, was propagated by Sikiru Ayinde Agbajelola, alias Barrister or Barry Wonder. Early in his career, Barrister pioneered a unique style of *were* that he used to awaken the Muslim community during Ramadan. He and his band would perform from house to house before sunrise to alert the Muslims that *sahur* was approaching.

Over time, Barrister evolved his sound and created a new popular style known as *fuji*. Unlike *were*, fuji was secular and not restricted to the Ramadan period. Fuji imbibed *were*, *senwele*, *aala*, *juju*, and many other styles of music. Due to his versatility, Barrister quickly made a name for himself, competing with heavyweights from other genres. Despite fuji being secular music, Barrister skillfully infused it with elements of Arabic or Yoruba songs aligned with Islam.

In the same song, Barrister seamlessly transitions between secular tunes and those aligned with Yoruba's traditional religion. One of my favorites was his album *Controversy and Precision*. Toward the end of the "Controversy" track, he starts to sing thus: *Wa lā sawta, yūthika, rabbika, fadharigah, gbogbo ohun t'Olohun Oba bun wa, alafia t'Olohun Oba bun wa, ẹmi gigun t'Olohun Oba bun wa, àsàlátù la ma fi se*. The Arabic line translates as "And your Lord is going to give you, and you will be satisfied," while the Yoruba line means, "Everything that God has given to us, the health that God has given to us, the long life that God has given to us, we will use all to worship."

On the second side of that album, Barrister opened with Yoruba lyrics that said, *E má digbo lu mi, mí o ṣ'ẹni a digbo lu ó. Ota labalaba ni mí ò, ẹ má digbo lu ẹgun mi ò. E má digbo lu ẹgun, labalaba to bá digbo lu ẹgun aṣọ rẹ̀ a fà yà ni ó*. This translates to, "Don't accost me; I am not one to be accosted. I am an enemy of the butterfly; don't accost me. I am a thorn; a butterfly who accosts the thorn will be shredded." The average listener would dance along to this song without a second thought, but for someone like me who knew more, I understood that Barrister had left Islam on side one of his albums and embraced occultic Yoruba music on side two. These particular words are commonly used by the occultists to sound a warning to anyone who tries to oppose them.

Indeed, one would have thought that since fuji has religious roots, it would maintain its core Islamic essence. However, as I've explained, Barrister, the progenitor of fuji music, was versatile and incorporated many things, not minding whether they aligned with Islam or not. In several of his songs, he maintained that fuji was birthed from *were*. For example, in one of his songs, "Fuji Garbage," he sang, *Wéré lo di fuji o, a fi n ji won l'oru ni, jọmọọ mi*, which translates to "*Were* transformed to fuji; we used it to wake people at midnight, comrades."

Aside from *were*, which was Islamically influenced, the Yoruba music industry emerged as a significant cultural force. This industry added entertainment to the life of Yoruba Muslims, propagated their religion, explained relatively obscure dogmas, gave them prayer points, and, most importantly, rivaled the Christian gospel songs. Muslim musicians favor *adhikr* or *dhikr* for most parts of their songs, with *dhikr* referring to a sequence of phrases or prayers said repeatedly in remembrance of Allah. This is one of the core reasons Muslim musicians are more likely to release their albums during the holy month of Ramadan, when the Muslim congregation strives to draw closer to Allah.

Anytime I walked the street and heard more than one new Islamic song, I knew that Ramadan was either approaching or already underway. The month itself gave publicity to the songs, especially those with captivating *dhikr* content. An example is the song by Opeyemi Jemila, a relative newcomer to the Islamic music industry who released *Kosida Baba Niyass*. The introduction to the first track on that album went thus: *idtha shita antayya, eh Abdul Qadir, baba na, Adkir ti ya o*, in which, for the larger part of that track, she essentially summoned people to do *dhikr*. It was all Arabic recitations after recitations. Those who are unfamiliar with the meaning or can't recite along simply bop their heads to the music. The song is truly epic, and it helped stamp Opeyemi's presence on the Islamic music scene.

Not all Yoruba Muslim songs feature much of *dhikr*. Some are based on happenings in society, allowing them to cross the borders into the Christian communities where they enjoy the song and receive its message. There are numerous examples of such songs, with my favorite artiste being the music of Kamaldeen Ayeloyun, known as Baba Ìyàwó, derived from his album where he sang about marriage. One memorable line from this album is *Igbeyawo o, igbeyawo o, igbeyawo o, igbeyawo o, oju mi o t'ẹyin mọ ó, ọ̀mọ́mi jẹẹjẹ, igbeyawo o*. This translates to repeating the word "marriage" four times before admonishing his child, who is getting married, to take it easy as she would no longer be under his watch.

Another favorite line from the song is *Bàbá ìyàwó ń sadura fún ọmọ rẹ, o n ke, ẹkùn ayọ ni bàbá ń sún*, meaning that "the bride's father is praying for his daughter, he's crying, but they are tears of joy." The line gained so much popularity that Baba Ìyàwó (bride's father) became his second name. The song itself was a common feature at the Yoruba weddings I attended during this period, whether Muslim or Christian.

There are other songs that transcend the boundaries of Muslim society and resonate with the Christian community. One such example is "Aiye L'oyun" in Kamal Deen's *Life Experience* album, where he sang about polygamy: *iyawo méjì ó dà, ìyàwó méjì ló dá, kí l'Olorun sọ nípa ẹ, ẹ sun mo bi ké wá gbó.*

FIG. 9. Sculptural representations of musicians by Adeola Balogun. Different local musical tools are used in Ilorin and different parts of northern Nigeria. From the private collection of Omoba Yemisi Shyllon. (*left*) A man playing a *goje*, a one-stringed instrument, and (*right*) a man playing an *algaita*, a woodwind instrument made of wood with a single reed, like a flute or an oboe. It is also used in various cultural and ceremonial music events, mostly in northern Nigeria.

Translated, this means "Polygamy is not good, polygamy is good, what has the Lord (Allah) said about it, come closer and listen." The line alone puts Yoruba people on alert as they try to listen to whatever it is that Kamaldeen's Lord has said about polygamy. In the markets and workplaces, that song is ever-present, becoming ingrained into people's subconsciousness from the countless number of times it's played on the radio or through other mediums in the community.

We also had Aminat Ajao, popularly known as Obi Rere (good parent). Her debut album was ground-shaking, earning her the alias and stamping her presence in the minds of Yoruba Muslims and Christians with her melodious *Mama ni mama mi, mama ni mama tí mo ní, òbí l'obi ti mo ní, ẹ má dàgbà d'arúgbó l'áyé; kò sì bo ti lè wù ké pe l'aye tó, ẹ ó ní f'ojú sunkún ọmọ, ẹ ó ní mo saare ọmọ l'ola Anọbi Muomoda*. She starts the song with praises for mothers and ends with prayers that they would not mourn their children by the grace of Prophet Muhammad (PBUH). The lyrics were enough to make Yoruba Christians put aside their reservations and listen to a Muslim song simply because of the universal message that resonated with many Yoruba people.

The Yoruba musical style often incorporates ornamentation and components of the Islamic modal scale, characterized by a half-tone and half-step cadential approach. I am familiar with some of the instruments that are combined to create these sounds, including the calabashes hammered with finger-worn iron rings, the *akuba* drum, little pairs of cymbals with bells, and the Yoruba Islamic melodies, which merged other traditional drums to create their sounds.

Most of my Muslim friends believe that music is permissible in Islam as there is no explicit prohibition against it in the Quran. When I was a child, we sang at the end of the day to wrap up at the madrassa, but we never discussed whether or not music was permissible. Babatunde, my friend, also informed me that music was played at the *nikkah* (wedding) of the daughter of Prophet Muhammad (PBUH). However, I am unsure if the Prophet listened to music when he was alive.

The call to prayer and the recitation of the Quran are considered the most permissible forms of music in Islam because they are believed to be the "purest" tones that Allah has created (*adhan*). Some Muslims approve of the playing of music during festivals like Eid Kabir and Eid Fitr, while Yoruba societies are more accepting of music during sermons (*khutbah*), known as *wáàsí* in Yoruba. Although the cantillation of the Quran is always described as recitation or reading, one can always detect melody and voice embellishment, which are musical elements, in its presentation.

Music encompasses various elements such as pitch, vibration, tonality, dynamics, and timbre, all of which are defined by the frequency of vibration and volume and determined by the amplitude of the sound. While these elements may be present in certain aspects of Islamic practices, such as the call to prayer, which is even more melodic, music is not formally recognized in the Islamic faith.

To prepare for the five daily prayers in the Muslim community's daily prayers, the *adhan* is called out five times a day, typically from the mosque. For each of these prayers—Subh, Zuhr, Asr, Maghrib, and Isha—the muazzin recites the *adhan* by chanting aloud from a raised platform or a tower in the mosque to draw the attention of the faithful. The *adhan* is delivered in a melodic and tonal style, incorporating musical aspects such as volume and dynamics to create a captivating and passionate call to prayer.

As stated earlier, Barrister was one of the foremost music artists who mixed Islamic connotations and Quranic recitation into their songs. In one of his albums, he asked for permission to sing in Islam: *Tira to ni ka ma lulu, e mu tira na wa o, Ka ma se sina, ka ma mu'ti, amo ta ba n se'hun re, ko ni ka ma lulu, ka f'ijo be o. Ka ma hu'wa 'baje l'Oluwa Oba wi o*, which translates thus: "The Quranic commandment that forbids music is clear for everyone to understand. God's prohibition on intoxication, immorality, and other wrongdoings is crystal obvious."

Other artists. like Wasiu Sideeq, in his song "Womise," noted that a Muslim must accept and adhere to all of Islam's teachings, avoid equating anything with the Almighty Allah, and have faith in the one and only God in order to enter heaven on the Day of Judgment:

Bowo fun Baba re pelu Mama ree
Respect your father and your mother
Beru Olorun ka le d'alujana, bo ba d'alaira
So that you may make paradise after departing this world.

In *Ola Fathia*, Hafsat Sideeq and Wasiu Sideeq provide a thorough study of the difficulties that those who didn't accept Islam before death would experience in the care of the angels while they were still in their graves. On side B, track 4, they sing thus:

E je k'omo yin kewu
Let your children learn the Quran
Kewu ni o ku wa ku bo d'orun
This is the only knowledge that will remain with us in heaven
Tori t'awon maleìka ba lo de,
For if angels should come down
Lati wa bere ise re
To come and inquire about the works that you did on earth.
Tani Anaìbi to o tele?
Which prophet did you follow?
Ewo ni tiìra tì o ke?
What scripture did you believe in?
To ba je eni ti ko ke Kurani laye
If you didn't follow the teachings of the Quran on earth

Awon maleìka yi o damu re
The angels will trouble you!

Apart from these, other melodic Arabic chants can be found in the songs of Yoruba Islamic musicians who have turned the ninety-nine names of Allah into melody to praise him and to plead with him to answer their prayers in accordance with these names. For example, Alhaji Ahmad Abolaji Akanni Alawiye in track 6 of the second side of *Sharia*, praises Allah thus:

La illaha illal Lah
There is no god but Allah
La illaha illal Lah
There is no god but Allah
E ba mi daruko Olorun to ga ju
Call out the names of God Who is the Highest God
La illaha illal Lah
There is no god but Allah
Al-Azim, the Almighty, the Strongest
Al-Rahman, the Compassionate
Al-Rahim, the Merciful
Al-Malik, the Master or the King
Al-Kabir, the Greatest
Al-Salam, the Giver of Peace.

Hafsat As-Sideeq and Wasiu Al-Sideeq, in the track "Olorun ma f'ara ni mi," sing about Allah as the Creator, All-Knowing, Merciful, and Compassionate God, and pray that he will show them mercy and protection:

Olorun ma f'ara ni mi
Permit nothing should trouble me
Oba ti n s'aanu eda
O God of mercy
Olorun ma f'ara ni mi laye
Have compassion on me
Olorun Allah ni mo ke si
It is the highest God that I call upon
Olorun Allah lo le se
He is the One who can do it
Oba nla to ju gbogbo Oba lo
The King that is greater than all kings

S'aanu mi Oba ti n s'aanu eda
Have mercy on me, the most merciful God
Olorun Allah ni mo ke si
For unto You I call
Loke ni, n'ile ni, lotun, pe l'osi
On the mountain and on the land, on the right or left.
N'iwaju ni ati lehin, ko s'iru Re o Oluwa
Before or after, there is none like Allah
Oun lo mo wa, Oun lo mo wa
He created us and knows us inside out
Oun lo s'eda wa
He created us
Muminiì, Mumina, gbe Olorun tobi
Muslim men and women praise Him.

Hafsat As-Sideeq in track 1, side B of *Iyaa Qur'an* also describes Allah as the God who is powerful enough to deliver those who put their trust in him. For he is the Creator of heaven and earth and the God of all seasons, times, situations, and circumstances:

Owo Olorun o kere lati gba ni la
God's hands aren't too short to deliver
Oju Olorun o kere lati s'aanu mi
His eyes aren't too small to see and have mercy on me
Allahu Latifu mo sa di o
I, therefore, hide in thee, the greatest King
Erongba mi je ko d'ayo
Let my plans be successful
Tori ko s'ohun kankan lehin Oluwa mi
For nothing can come out successfully without you
Gbogbo agbara ti'Re ni o
Oun l'Olorun gbogbo igba
He is the God of all seasons
Oun l'Olorun igba gbogbo
He is God of all times and in all situations and circumstances
O da orun, orun o subu
He created heaven and it didn't fall
O da okun, ki n gbe
He created the sea and it is never dry
Gba mi la o, l'ola Fathia Iya Qur'an
Save me in the name of Al-Fathia, mother of the Quran.

Also, Yoruba Muslim artists' songs demonstrate a clear comprehension of the Quranic teachings about angels, a realization that dawned on me through listening to some of their songs. Even though Babatunde had claimed to see angels on one of the nights of *Laylatul Qadr*, his description does not match what the holy book says they look like.

According to the Quran, angels are made of light, genderless and immortal, soar on wings, are visible only during specific missions, are capable of assuming various forms, can travel enormous distances quickly, and are so many that only God knows how many there are. Their duties include praising and adoring Allah (Quran 13:13, 14), supporting and protecting believers (Quran 8:9, 41:31), bringing blessings and greetings (Quran 33:43, 56), and acting as go-betweens for revelations (Quran 41:30, 2:97, 16:102).

Alhaji Wasiu Kayode As-Sideeq in *Toriola*, side B, track 1, warns that the two angels who are commanded to take records of our deeds are doing so; therefore, we must be very careful in whatever we do here on earth because of consequences in the afterlife:

Won n ko ise re s'ile
They are taking records of your deeds
Awon Angeli nko ise re s'ile o
Angels are keeping records of your deeds
Won mo ise re, won nko ise re s'ile o
They know your deeds and they're keeping records
Awon malaika mejeji won
The two angels commissioned to do so.

Remarkably, *waka*, *sakara*, *apala*, *awurebe*, *senwele*, and *dadakuada* are among the musical subgenres that share a connection to Islam, with *waka* notably closer in connection and historically proven to predate all of its contemporaries. *Waka* was performed vocally in a style similar to semi-religious music. A huge significance of the "Yorubanization" that has taken place in Islamic songs is that non-Muslim Yoruba now have an interest in these songs.

In Ibadan and other places in Yoruba territories, there has been a surge in plays based on Quranic stories in the Yoruba language as part of outdoor *kuthba* or *wáàsí* (sermon) programs by Islamic youths. Also, concerted efforts are made to interpret either the sermon or Quranic passages, with delivery in Arabic or interpretation in Yoruba by either the preacher himself or another versed person.

The chanter or interpreter occasionally delves into philosophical statements based on sociological data about the Yoruba people and their relationship with Islamic religious beliefs. Key subjects such as the role of the creator

(Allah), the benefits of worshipping him, and the rewards of participating in communal prayer sessions are emphasized. Interestingly, these discussions are similar to Yoruba chants like *rara*, *ijala*, and *iyere-ifa*, underscoring the interconnectedness of Islamic and Yoruba cultural expressions.

In social music genres like fuji, *sakara*, *waka*, and *apala*, most of the artists typically begin their concerts with solo chanting or call-and-response style introduction, which highlights certain musical elements like variation, repetition, retrograde, and retrograde inversion, the same way they are used in Yoruba poetry and music.

The album *Good News* (*Iroyin Ayo*) by Muri Salaudeen Thunder, Hajia Badiratu Olaniyan, and Zakari Muhammad, as well as *Oro Oluwa* (God's words) by Zakari Muhammad, teaches that the Quran is the word of God and is the good news in a world that is constantly full of bad news. Other works with titles, subtitles, and contents that are based on the Quran and specifically intended to teach the tenets of Islam include Alfa Lateef Oloto's *99 Names of Allah*, Wasiu Kayode Sadeeq's *Al-Janat*, and Fafsat As-Zideeq and El-Hadj Wasiu Kayode As-Sideeq's *Ola Fathia*, which use some of the social genres of Yoruba chants.

Muri Thunder's musical album *Good News* talks about the greatness of God and describes him as Self-Existent:

Mo tun ji l'oni, Oluwa mi
I wake up again today, my Lord
Oba mi, Oba nla
My King, the Great King
Oòba a mi to da duro
My King who is self-existent
Olukapa aiye pelu orun
He has control over this world and the heavens
Ko l'orogun ko bi'mo kan
He has no rival; He begets no child
Alamotan to m'ohun gbogbo
The All-knowing who is Omniscient
Paripari ola, Oga Agba
The end of all Greatness
Oba aterere kari aiye
The King that spreads (His canopy) to cover the whole earth
Apani jini Oba aiye
He who can kill and raise again; a Killer-Reviver, King
Mo ke pe O o Oluwa mi
I call on you, oh my Lord

Oba mi, Oba oro
My King, the King that rules the earth with the power of His
(invisible) Word
Orò lo fi da'le aye
You created the earth with Your Word
Oro lo fi d'ohun gbogbo
It is with sheer word that You created all things by a fiat.
Dakun ma je k'oro mi o su O
May you not be tired of me.

Wasiu Sadiq and Wasiu Alabi Pasuma also explore the divine attributes of Allah in *Salam Salam*. Within its verses, they affirm that Allah is worthy of holy praises:

Mimo Mimo Mimo l'Oluwa
Holy, Holy, Holy is the Lord
Allahu jala jala luhu
God is worthy of praises
Allahu Aziz Iwo l'ope to si
Almighty God, you are the One who is worthy of our praises.

Kayode Sadeeq states in his song "Egberun Meta" that Allah's names aren't just ninety-nine but three thousand. According to him, the first one thousand names are known only to the angels, the second thousand only to Allah's prophets, while the last thousand are divided into four parts, with three hundred in the Psalms, three hundred in the Gospels, and three hundred in the Torah (the Law). Out of the remaining hundred, only God knows one, while the remaining ninety-nine are in the Quran:

Allah, Allah ah..
Allah is the greatest
E pe Olorun tobi
Praise God, and say He is the greatest
E je ka konu Olorun yi
Let us fear Him and worship Him
Ko siju aanu wo wa o
Let us pray to Him to have mercy on us o
Tori pe egberun meta,
For it is unto three thousand parts
L'oruko Olorun pin si

That God's name is divided
Egberun alaakoko, o wa lodo awon malaika
The first one thousand are known only to the angels
Egberun lona ekeji, o wa lodo awon Anobi
The second one thousand are known to only His Prophets
Egberun kan to ku iyen pin sona merin
The last one thousand are divided into four parts:
Ogorun meta,o wa ninu Sabura
Three hundred are in the Psalms
Ogorun meta, lo wa ninu injila
Three hundred are in the Gospel
Ogorun meta, lo wa ninu Taoreta
Three hundred are in the Torah
Ogorun kan to ku, o din leyo
One out of the remaining hundred
Okan soso, Olorun lo fi n s'ola
It is known only to God
Mokandinlogorun iyoku, o wa ninu Kuriani o Qur'an
The remaining ninety-nine in the Quran
To ba tile n' igbagbo, problem to ba de, t'o ba fi won gb'sadura.
If you have faith and would pray with them in any situation
Won ni lati se patapata
You will surely be victorious.

In this song, Allah becomes unknowable! As humans, our knowledge of the spiritual or the Divine is limited, yet when musicians interweave Allah into Yoruba Islamic songs and extol his attributes, he takes on a tangible form. Without songs (especially devotional songs), there is no Islam. Without *ewe* (plant), there is no Òrìṣà. Without Christ, there is no Christianity. Songs have become as powerful as sermons. Angels do sing, but they use the lips of humans!

CHAPTER FIVE

Our Makkah and Madinah

On a fateful day with Alhaji in Ibadan,
At Ojaba Central Mosque,
A new dawn, a new epiphany arose
Where the Prophet's footsteps marked the way,
A guiding light, shining each day.

In the words of the Prophet, I discovered anew,
The essence of faith, noble and true,
From Adam's creation to Muhammad's call,
A testament to God's love for us all.

I saw the devotion in each believer's eyes,
Their prayers ascending like a thousand cries,
Seeking forgiveness, seeking divine grace,
Humbled by the majesty of sacred space.

I saw the calligraphy adorned with dazzling intricate designs,
Unveiling truths that words alone fail to define,
The mosque's architecture, a sight to behold,
A testament to the glory of stories untold.

Ojaba opened my eyes,
To a world where unity never dies,
Where faith and heritage intertwine.

After many decades on earth, I can boast of a plethora of experiences—some I learned and some I witnessed firsthand. There is a saying that threats are actually less impactful than seemingly innocent yet sinister deeds. It's similar to the Yoruba adage that says, *Odo ti a ba fi oju di, a ma gbe ni lọ!* (An underrated river might drown one!). Imagine a war veteran equipped with protective amulets against gunshot, machete, and mystical attacks, only to fall into a hornet's nest and be stung to death because he had no protection against hornets. The warrior is fully prepared with charms, enough not to suffer cuts from axes and daggers, even guns, but he loses his life to the stings of tiny creatures far inferior to objects he was fortified against.

To function as a Muslim, it's important to be less afraid of Saudi Arabia. If you see it as a threat to salvation, then face the nearby Ojaba, the power center. Ojaba is the epicenter of various social and even spiritual practices, where big cases are decided. It's the combination of the mosque and market with everything you need, the fusion of religion and politics, and the zone where the most concentrated charms are located. It's the zone of faith but also of deception, where genuine and fake imams coexist. Its landscape, in the oldest part of the city, represents history and chaos. This area is the history of the beginning of the city itself, with all the compounds of city heroes nearby, like the Mapo Hall, where the most visible of the colonial architecture is located, and the original largest market is still standing.

How did Islam get to Ibadan? You only need to go to Ojaba to unearth its history! How is Islamic power allocated? Go to Ojaba for an explanation! Who is the next governor? Collect gossip at Ojaba. Who can check the excesses of a local preacher? The boss at Ojaba!

Today, the different societies that exist in Ibadan are either from Ojaba or brought by settlers who came to Ibadan. Ojaba is the apex of the Islamic economy in Ibadan, as the majority of Islamic business outlets and activities are situated there. It's the place to go for a wide array of Islamic materials, including clothes, books, prayer items, foodstuffs, herbs, and medicinal items. The rich and thriving organizational and social structure of the Muslim community in Ibadan is an indisputable pointer to the autonomous status of Islam in the city.

The Central Mosque at Ojaba serves as the unifying hub for all other mosques in Ibadan. It's like the "mother" of all the other mosques. It's the domain of the chief imam of Ibadanland and the meeting point of the chief imam and other imams, as well as other important Islamic officials and dignitaries in the city. They meet to share updates on the running and state of other mosques and the state of Islam in Ibadan as a whole.

Accessible to Muslims from every corner of Ibadan due to its central location, Ojaba Central Mosque symbolizes a communal gathering place, welcoming everyone without restrictions. It's the cornerstone of the Muslim community in Ibadan, serving as a spiritual and social nexus for Muslims across the city. Numerous programs are organized for the benefit of the Muslims in the community and Ibadan at large.

The chief imam of Ibadanland oversees the Central Mosque and is in charge of Islamic activities in the city. Like every other institution, the Central

FIG. 10. *Oja Oba* by Dr. Kazeem Ekeolu. For those of us growing up in Ibadan, Oja Oba served as both a financial and religious center. The strategic proximity of the Central Mosque to the market provided a glimpse into the daily lives of the surrounding communities.

Mosque has its organizational pattern, with different officials and title holders appointed to see to the smooth running of the activities of the mosque. Among these officials are the alfas, who belong to one of two lines, either the Mogaji alfas or the Mogaji imams; the *mufasir*; and the council.

At Ojaba, the chief imam holds a revered position as the imam-in-council of Ibadanland. He is the general overseer of all the activities of the mosque. His supremacy also extends outside the Central Mosque, representing the embodiment of Islam for all Muslims within and outside Oyo State. His decisions are trusted and adhered to as the highest-ranking official and the number one in the Ibadan Muslim community.

Some of the duties of the chief imam include delegating duties and responsibilities to the alfas and the council, overseeing and vetoing the appointment of unit imams for other mosques, getting feedback from alfas and unit imams on the running and activities of their jurisdictions, settling disputes and misunderstanding involving Muslims, and monitoring the activities of the sharia court.

The Mogaji imams and Mogaji alfas are two distinct groups of officials comprising the prominent alfas of the Central Mosque. Each alfa belongs to one of the two groups. Those associated with the Mogaji alfas anchor open-air sermons commonly known as *wáàsí* in Yoruba; thus, they are referred to as *Oníwáàsí*. The alfas under the Mogaji imams are some sort of interpreters, working with the chief imam when he is giving a talk during an occasion by repeating what he says loudly and clearly. They are referred to as Ajanasi and assist the alfas under the Mogaji alfas during open-air sermons by reading required excerpts from the Quran and quoting the hadith of Prophet Muhammad (PBUH). In essence, they help to ensure effective communication with the audience.

There are also the *mufasir*, who are official anchors of *tafsir* (Quranic exegesis) during the month of Ramadan. Sometimes I'm unable to differentiate these alfas from the members of Mogaji alfas because their activities are usually both done in the open air. However, *tafsirs* and open-air sermons differ in their scope. *Tafsir* is the exegesis of the Quran (commentary and explaining the Quran, chapter by chapter, verse by verse), so it's common to hear Islamic scholars talk about the *tafsir* of a particular surah of the Quran.

An open-air sermon, on the other hand, is a discourse on a particular topic, such as marriage, inheritance, birth, children's upbringing, and education, among others, with references drawn from the Quran and the hadith of Prophet Muhammad (PBUH), as well as the examples and experiences of the *sahaba* (followers/companions of Prophet Muhammad), the *tābih* (the generation that learned from the *sahaba*) and the *tāabih tābihūn* (the generation that learned from the *tābih*).

As part of the structure of Ojaba Central Mosque, the council is made up of eleven members, including the chief imam. The functions and responsibilities of the chief imam are fixed and static; however, other members of the council are assigned other areas of responsibility as needs arise. Among these members, four officials are permanently appointed to oversee each of the four regular programs of the mosque, such as the *Mawlud Nabi* held in Rabiu Awwal, the third month of the lunar/Islamic calendar, which commemorates the birth month of Prophet Muhammad. These programs include prayer sessions, preaching, and festivities.

Another significant program is *Nisfu Sha'abān*, occurring midway through the month of Sha'abān, the eighth month of the lunar/Islamic calendar. During this time, a vigil is held at the Central Mosque, with fervent prayers and preaching. On Ashura, the tenth day of the month of Muharram, the first month of the Islamic calendar, it's customary for Muslims to fast. Prayer and preaching sessions, along with various other Islamic programs and activities, are usually organized on this day.

Furthermore, to mark Prophet Muhammad's journey to heaven to receive the salat, the fundamental Islamic act of worship (*ibadah*) is represented by the canonical prayers observed five times daily by Muslims. This journey, which started from the Prophet's mosque (Masjidil Nabī) in Medina, through the mosque in Jerusalem (Masjidil Qudūus) built by Prophet Sulayman (Solomon), isn't only spiritual but considered to have happened physically and is referred to as *Isra* and *Miraj*. To mark this memorable event, different activities are organized at the Central Mosque, including fasting, prayer sessions during the day, and preaching.

The officials who hold various positions are permanently in charge of the programs related to their roles. They maintain their positions till old age, at which point they may transfer their duties to another person, much like the kingship model in Yorubaland. Apart from old age, an exception to the permanence of these positions also happens when the officials receive a higher duty, such as becoming the *mufasir*, an *Oníwáàsí*, or the chief imam. In such instances of promotion, the incumbent official will be required to hand over the position to another member of the council.

At the Central Mosque, *da'wah* (preachings) occur fortnightly on Wednesdays, or Àlàrùba (Al-Arbiyai in Arabic), and Thursdays or Àlàmísì (Al-Khamis in Arabic), with ten alfas selected by the council to preside over these respective programs rotationally. Each alfa, after presiding over *da'wah* on their assigned day, awaits their next turn. This *da'wah*, as well as its rotation style, serves as a training ground for the alfas, preparing them to be competent ambassadors when they anchor events outside the Central Mosque and the Ojaba environs.

Another integral component of the Central Mosque was the sharia court, which operates according to Islamic sharia law. Sharia laws are codes of conduct based on the rulings of the Quran and the rulings of Islamic scholars (fatwas). *Sharia*, an Arabic term meaning "way" or "path," is believed to be the path laid down by Allah for true Muslims to follow. Therefore, it's the legal system of Islam that helps Muslims ensure they adhere to the rules, regulations, and guidance of Allah as stated in the Quran and corroborated by the hadith and sunna of Prophet Muhammad. It's important to note that the system, practices, and judgments of the sharia are different from those of the conventional Western jurisprudence system.

One of the renowned aspects of sharia law is its system of punishments. From my days in Ibadan, I knew that the punishment for theft under sharia was amputation, while offenses such as alcohol consumption or sexual activities before marriage were punishable by flogging. However, there was a lack of proper understanding of the sharia system among new converts in Ibadan, as well as among Muslims and non-Muslims in Ode Aje. This incomplete understanding can partly be attributed to the fear of the outcome of the court's ruling because some of these judgments were considered to be extreme.

The sharia court system at Ojaba was inaugurated on May 1, 2002, after which the court handled civil cases such as marriage, divorce, inheritance, land disputes, and environmental issues. As far as I was aware, the sharia court at Ojaba didn't settle criminal cases. The court was quite recognized at the state level, as some of its judgments, especially with regard to other divorces and disputes, get published in the newspapers. After the establishment of the sharia court in Ojaba, the chief imam announced that it was established for Muslims but that non-Muslims who had confidence in the court and were comfortable with its decisions were also welcome to use it, given the prevalence of interreligious marriage, transactions, and conflicts.

In several cases involving Muslims and Christians, sometimes it was the Christians who reported the cases to the sharia court because they believed the ruling would be impartial. The sharia court is under the jurisdiction of the chief imam at Ojaba, who oversees the affairs of the court as the number one member of the Muslim community in Ibadan and the highest-ranking official of the Central Mosque. He must be kept abreast of what goes on in the court, and no case can be resolved without his knowledge. He reserves the right to interfere and contribute to deliberations in collaboration with the presiding officers.

While the imam may not always be present at all the hearings of the court, his authority is always recognized and respected. The presiding officers in the sharia court are individuals who have studied Islamic and sharia law, both within and sometimes outside Nigeria. Only scholars well versed in Islamic and sharia law are permitted to preside and pass judgments.

In addition to their presence in trade and other activities at Ojaba, women play significant roles in the operations of the Central Mosque. Since the inception of the mosque, even when it was yet to be plastered and floored with cement, various offices have been saddled with distinct responsibilities. Women were in charge of diligently and painstakingly cleaning the mosque, making sure everything was organized and that the environment was beautified. They would painstakingly polish the clay flooring and walls of the mosque using local materials. This cleaning was done every day, not just on Fridays for Jumat service or special occasions, as prayer is observed every day in a mosque, and as a house of Allah, it must always be cleaned. Right from time, there has never been a day without an influx of people at the mosque for one reason or another.

For the purposes of differentiating functions and responsibilities of women at the Central Mosque, the overall head or highest-ranking official is called "Iya Adini," while all other female officials have their own designated titles. These officeholders no longer recognizably perform their conventional duties as they did in earlier times. Those who take these titles are high-class and important personalities, such as business magnates and others who are renowned as successful or educated. Their primary role in the Central Mosque is to support its programs and activities financially and through other crucial means within their capacities.

Furthermore, the involvement of youth and children in Ojaba Central Mosque activities is noteworthy. Although they have no association, they remain connected and function as a body, performing functions such as going around to collect *fisabililah* (donations) from members after prayers and during special gatherings when it's required. They also assist the women in cleaning and organizing the mosque and its environment, serve as menial volunteers, and run other necessary errands during programs and large prayers such as Jummah and Eid.

My childhood visits to Ojaba weren't the only times I recognized the mosque's significance and its organization, along with that of other smaller mosques in Ibadan. For many Muslims, Ojaba stands as the epicenter of Islam in Ibadan, sometimes regarded as the Mecca and Medina of Ibadanland. It's rare to find a Muslim of Ibadan heritage or current resident who doesn't recognize Ojaba as the city's Islamic hub, both historically and presently. Throughout my childhood and adolescence in Ibadan, I attended numerous events and programs at the mosque. Besides its prestigious status as the Central Mosque, Ojaba served as a marketplace for both Ibadan Muslims and the general population, owing to the bustling commerce activities that took place there.

With the number of Islamic business outlets I know in Ibadan and the atmosphere even at Ojaba, it can be said that the economy is Islam friendly. It would have been otherwise if Muslims couldn't freely own businesses whereby the goods and services are connected to Islam. In a place like Ibadan, which is a blend of Islam, Christianity, and traditional religion, the easy and common existence of such business outlets is a pointer to the fact that a friendly atmosphere for Islam operates.

Several Islamic centers are available, from book-publishing firms to dealers in Islamic clothing and attire. There are various types of Islamic clothing, such as abayas, hijabs, long skirts, *nikah* wear, and other Islamic materials, even at Ojaba. Some outlets are in large-scale shopping malls, while others are in small shops on the streets and markets scattered in various parts of Ibadan. An interesting aspect is that some business outlets even offer goods and services not restricted to Muslims, and we find non-Muslims patronizing them.

Based on experience and my encounters, I know Islam has been able to thrive in Ibadan because the Islamic social organization is a free one, comprising multiple societies with their different styles and modes of operation, each free in its own right and none dominating or oppressing another. Each has a leader or leaders but is still under the umbrella of the overall imam of Ibadanland to whom they listen in general fundamental matters such as festivity days, when to commence fasting, and so on. Also, peace and harmony are the order of the day, such that membership to more than one society is possible, and anyone can attend any program organized by any group regardless of membership. If Ojaba collapses, we have no Medina to run to for a new beginning and no Mecca to attend for a pilgrimage!

The penetration of Islam into Yorubaland, particularly in Ibadan, was an inevitable phenomenon, transcending any opposition. Like a Yoruba saying, *Aye o le pa kadara da, owo ago l'aye le fa s'eyin, eyi to je akosile a se*, destiny cannot be rewritten; it can only be delayed, but what has been destined to will be. Islam spread into some parts of Yorubaland when Usman dan Fodio and his soldiers of the Islamic faith came to Yorubaland in the nineteenth century, riding on horseback after conquering Hausaland, including Gobir, executing Yunfa, a prominent Hausa king, and laying the groundwork for one of Africa's largest empires (the Sokoto Caliphate).

Following the subjugation of the Hausa people, the Fulani jihadists seized control of some parts of Yorubaland. In 1823, they seized control of Ilorin (the northern part of the Oyo Empire), and the town became a sort of entry point into Yorubaland for the Fulani. They made it further into Yorubaland and sacked the Old Oyo Empire circa 1835–1836, and then tried to extend their control to Osogbo, another prominent Yoruba town.

In 1840, the Fulani were repelled by a joint Yoruba force at the Osogbo war, where Ibadan warriors and other contingencies from different Yoruba towns gathered together, put the Fulani jihadists on their heels, and "ate their captured horses." I don't really know if they ate the horses literally, but my grandfather said they did.

The altercations between Fulani jihadists and Yoruba warriors served as a conduit for the widespread penetration of Islam into Yorubaland. Despite other underrated methods of Islamic propagation, Islam also made its way into Yorubaland through trade and interrelations between the Yoruba and Fulani. They both looked harmless but accomplished what the jihad had failed to complete. They were the embers left after the Yoruba warriors extinguished the flame of the Fulani jihadists. The mixture of Yoruba and Fulani in Yorubaland, as in Ilorin, allowed for interrelationships that resulted in marriages, and many people of Yoruba origin converted to Islam, which became the dominant religion in the area.

Beyond the interrelations between the Yoruba people and the Fulani in Ilorin, there were extensive trade interactions between Ilorin, both Yoruba and Fulani, and the rest of Yorubaland. Ilorin people traded in other parts of Yorubaland just like people from other parts of Yorubaland traded in Ilorin. During these trade expeditions, people from Ilorin took the torch of Islam to other parts of Yorubaland, and those who came to Ilorin to trade were also persuaded to embrace the religion. A few people were won over, and, in turn, they also won a few people over to Islam, allowing Islam to spread across Yorubaland in a domino effect.

Several funny stories abound on how some people converted to Islam. One of my favorites is a romantic one, a real story about Ajani Olobi, a kola nut merchant from Ibadan, and the strategy he used to marry a second wife.

According to my grandfather, Ajani hailed from a rich and prominent masquerade-worshipping family in Ibadan and was a prosperous kola nut and bitter kola merchant with many farms and domestic staff. He frequented prominent markets to sell his goods, and the influx of Hausa and Fulani into Ilorin created a pot-of-soup market for Ajani. The Hausa had a great affinity for kola nuts, making Ajani's profits soar when he took his baskets of kola nuts to the market in Jebba, near Ilorin, to trade. Renowned for the high quality of his kola nuts and bitter kolas, Ajani sold his goods in bulk, enabling him to expand his wares quickly and make substantial profits. It also helped him make friends and gain popularity among the Fulani and Hausa retailers who patronized him.

Market day in Jebba was every five days to allow traders ample time to collect enough goods and also allow buyers to gather enough money. The market was always full and bustled with activities, and the competition between traders was fierce, with individuals vying to outsell one another. It was common to find over ten people who sold the same commodity within proximity. To attract customers, the traders employed different tactics. Some sold at cheaper prices, while some focused on displaying their wares more prominently. While some shouted to announce what they sold, some used extra nice gestures and personal charisma to attract potential buyers.

Another means of securing customers, which was kept secret, was the use of charms to entice people. According to my grandfather, these enchantments were not in any way harmful. They were made into soaps for baths, into water to be sprinkled on goods and stalls, or they could be made into small gourds to be buried at the entrance of one's stall. The charms were called *aworo* (crowd puller), and they do as their name implied—pull a crowd to the stall, leaving the task of persuading them to buy to the seller.

There was no need to ask my grandfather if Ajani possessed the *aworo* charms, as he had mentioned earlier that Ajani was from a masquerader clan. It was common sense to understand that he had such charms for his day-to-day activities. My thoughts on the matter were confirmed as my grandfather continued with Ajani's story. Before leaving home for Jebba market, he would go to his family gorge behind his house to worship his ancestors, eat concoctions, drink those that were in liquid potions, and lick the ones in powdery form. All of these were part of his preparation for a successful outing at the market, as well as ensuring his protection on his journey to and from Jebba.

However, as the saying goes, things that appear less harmful are often the ones that end up being the most destructive. Ajani protected himself against the perils of travel and his fellow traders but ended up getting defeated by love. With all preparations completed, Ajani entrusted his home to his wife and left for Jebba, accompanied by his apprentices and goods. Upon reaching his stall, he displayed his wares and sat in his shop, collecting and counting the proceeds of the goods sold by his apprentices, who diligently called people's attention to their shop and negotiated a bargain to meet Ajani's set price.

Everyone was in charge of his or her station, and Ajani only interfered when a bargain was beginning to drag on for too long, or disputes arose between his staff and customers. On one such occasion, Ajani had to interfere in a rift between his staff and a customer's assistant. His apprentice had disputed over a bargain, and the customer interfered in the matter, taking sides with her assistant, which resulted in a shouting match between the customer and Ajani's staff. To quell the matter, Ajani beckoned to the lady, Amina. As she approached, he couldn't help but notice her captivating beauty and her elegant attire. Ajani needed no one to tell him she was of a high-class family.

Ajani found himself quickly enchanted by Amina's beauty. In a spontaneous decision, he decided to impress her by holding their conversation in Fulfulde despite knowing only fragments of the language. To his surprise, she spoke in fluent Yoruba language before explaining that she was of mixed heritage, as her father was Fulani and her mother was Yoruba. Ajani sold his wares to her with lots of discounts and pleaded that she continue to patronize him. From that moment, he fell in love with her, and the fact that she spoke his language deepened his attraction to her.

Unable to shake thoughts of her out of his head, Ajani eagerly awaited the next market day. He packed gifts of Yoruba clothing for her and prayed to his ancestors for another encounter with her. True to his hopes, the lady came on the next market day. Ajani gave her the gifts and engaged her in conversation. Later, one of Ajani's friends in the market asked about his intentions toward the lady. Ajani expressed his desire to take the lady as his second wife. While Yoruba tradition allows lovers to court before marriage, Fulani and Hausa customs require you to seek the father's blessings first—a crucial step for securing the woman's hand in marriage.

In this context, the woman had reached marriageable age, and her beauty would inevitably attract numerous suitors to her father's compound. Upon learning this, Ajani gathered some gifts and made his way to Amina's father's house. He was given a warm welcome and a chance to state his intentions.

Ajani observed that Amina inherited her father's fair complexion, but her beauty clearly emanated from her mother. He calmly stated his purpose, that he had come to ask for Amina's hand in marriage. Amina's mother translated for her husband, who nodded in understanding. He then asked how many wives Ajani had, to which Ajani replied that he had one wife already and would love Amina to be his second wife, with her father's blessing. Through his wife, Amina's father asked Ajani about his business and financial status. Upon the mention of his name, Amina's parents recognized Ajani as a well-known supplier of kola nuts and bitter kolas in the area, which assured them that Ajani would have more than enough wealth to take proper care of their daughter without neglecting his first wife.

However, there was one problem stopping Ajani from marrying Amina as his second wife—her father wouldn't marry her off to an infidel (a non-Muslim). The verdict hit Ajani like a dagger! While Amina's family acknowledged Ajani's wealth and had no objections to her being a second wife due to their religious beliefs, his non-Muslim status proved to be the deal-breaker. They would rather let their daughter marry a Muslim who was less wealthy.

Devastated, Ajani explained his situation to his friend, who urged him to make up his mind as soon as possible because the next five days might be too late. When Ajani got home, he spent the next four days thinking about what to do and praying to his ancestors to help him win Amina's hand in marriage. In a desperate move, Ajani sought assistance from one of his relatives, who was skilled in charms-making, to help him make his pursuit of Amina easy.

On the fifth day, Ajani left for Jebba with his domestic staff, goods, and charms. Among the charms was *eyonu* (pacifier), believed to soften the hearts of those approached over anything and sway their judgments in favor of the bearer. Ajani intended to use this charm on Amina's father.

After setting up his store, he returned to Amina's father's compound bearing gifts and his charm. When he entered, four men were already seated, each of them with gifts of his own. He could tell from their appearances and the boxes of gifts that they were there for the same reason he was and that he had greater financial power, but being a non-Muslim put him at a disadvantage.

Ajani remembered his last meeting with Amina's father and his friend's warning. He looked at the four men seated, who all looked hopeful about the outcome of their visit. Ajani related the situation to his business, where preparation often determined success. He reasoned that just as he and his competing traders employed different means and charms to sell their goods, these men here must also have a joker up their sleeves. From his experience with charms, he understood that *ewe a ma sun ko* (charms could lose potency or be nullified). What if the charm that was meant to be his joker failed due to reasons he couldn't anticipate?

Realizing that relying on charms wasn't going to do the magic, as Amina's father's decision would be swift and final, Ajani sought a new joker that would swing the judgment in his favor. He walked up to Amina's mother and disclosed his decision to become a Muslim, also expressing his desire to marry Amina as soon as possible. Amina's mother went in to relay Ajani's message to her husband, who came out a moment later to ask his domestic staff to take the other suitors into the compound and entertain them.

Amina's parents sat with Ajani and questioned him about his readiness to embrace Islam. After Ajani confirmed his intent, they brought in an *alim*, who asked him to do the *Kalimatu shahadah* (the Islamic profession of faith), *ashhadu an lā illāha illal lāh, ashhadu anna Muhammada Rasūlul Lāhi* (there is no other God except Allah and Muhammad is his messenger). These words, made compulsory for new converts, symbolized a genuine commitment to Islam.

After celebrating his conversion to Islam, Amina's father gave his blessings to Ajani's union with his daughter. Ajani stayed with the family for the next few days so he could learn the basics of Islam and pick a Muslim name. Amina's father slaughtered a fat, healthy ram to celebrate his son-in-law's conversion to Islam, and Ajani was given the name Jabar, which means "to be mighty or giant." Now that Ajani had converted to Islam, he could have his *nikkah* marriage ceremony with Amina.

On getting back to Ibadan, Ajani dedicated himself to learning more about Islam, starting with the five pillars of Islam: *iman* (faith and belief in Allah as the one and only God), *salat* (the obligatory five daily prayers), *zakat* (annual obligatory charity given from one's wealth to help the poor, *sawm* (fasting during the holy month of Ramadan), and *hajj* (pilgrimage to Mecca for Muslims who have the means). Ajani was taught how to make ablutions and how to observe salat.

Immediately, Ajani felt confident in his newfound faith, so he invited his family to a feast at his house. After everyone was seated, he introduced Amina and told them about how he met her and how she became his second wife. The whole room erupted with joy, except for his first wife! When the initial excitement subsided, Ajani made further announcements, revealing his conversion to Islam and his change of name to Jabar. A deafening silence fell over the room, and gradually, members of his extended family started to leave without uttering a word, leaving Ajani with his wives and children.

Ajani reassured his first wife of his love, promising that she wouldn't be neglected. To prove this and demonstrate his unwavering love for her, he asked one of his domestic staff to bring in the various gifts he had bought for her. Despite the initial tension, Amina's good behavior and manners enabled the two women to peacefully cohabit, and with the ulama by his side, Ajani was able to easily adapt to the religion.

While Ajani's first wife and her children accepted his decision and resigned to fate, his extended family ostracized him for renouncing their religion. Ajani didn't take the matter to heart, but when his new wife gave birth to their first son, his relatives still wanted to have nothing to do with him and turned down his invites. Ajani had thought the newborn would help him reconcile with them, but he was wrong. As retribution, he ordered his domestic help to sack and burn the gorge where his family gods were kept in his backyard.

With the help of his ulama, Ajani strengthened his faith in Islam. His first wife also gradually integrated herself into the religion as a means of getting closer to him because she saw how he spent time performing salat with Amina. Ajani was glad when his first wife formally asked to become a Muslim. He threw a large party to rename her and their children.

For zakat that year, Ajani freed the head of his slaves who had become Muslim. The other slaves also followed the trend and started embracing Islam, hopeful that they would be set free someday, too, as an act of zakat. This attracted goodwill from Ajani, who gave them *sadaqah* (optional charity) either in cash or valuables or even by securing their freedom. Becoming Muslim was beneficial to the slaves as they were able to use the afternoon prayers of Dhuhr and Asr to get off work and rest. Additionally, they were given lighter workloads during Ramadan.

As Ajani's household gradually became Muslim, the influence of their new faith began to affect their community. Needy families in the community also started to make the switch to Islam. They secured jobs within Ajani's household and his other businesses, benefited from his yearly zakat, and enjoyed free meals during Ramadan. Ajani's prominence grew on the wings of Islam, and his popularity dwarfed that of his other wealthy extended family members, as more than a third of the community population was related to him.

Indeed, this is the story of just one man, as narrated to me by my grandfather. There would be several others who, in one way or another, got tangled with Islam and came back to Yorubaland to propagate it. The Yoruba people were able to displace the Fulani jihadists who brought Islam on horseback. They resisted the threat to the Yoruba religion, culture, and sovereignty, but still, Islam found its way into Yoruba communities through other harmless and underrated means.

As the saying goes, "The river people underrated eventually drowns them." Through these underrated "rivers," the Yoruba allowed Islam to penetrate their circles, establishing its presence through trade, marriage, education, and the pursuit of knowledge. Over time, some places became the base of Islam in Yoruba societies.

The introduction of Islam to Ibadan and some other Yoruba communities paved the way for diverse beliefs that could coexist alongside traditional fortifications for protection, healing, and other spiritual purposes. I witnessed this at Ode Aje, as the Iya Lekuleja store attracted alfas or other Muslims, some of whom were new converts who came to buy resources to prepare such charms alongside their Islamic praying culture and practices. This blend of traditional and Islamic elements wasn't so different in Ibadan and Ojaba. While many of these Muslims refrain from showcasing their traditional religion or want to align with or practice it around where they worship, most of them often turn to their traditional religion for healing or to seek protection in dire times.

Some of these charms are crafted from various materials, with the use of black soap being particularly common among those who adhere to traditional beliefs for cures and healing, even after converting to Islam. Individuals like Ajani Olobi continue to utilize mixed leaves added to black soap, believing it serves multiple purposes. *Ewuro* (bitter leaf), shea butter, and perfume are used to make a soap that Ajani believed would attract favor to people and elevate their status.

However, he emphasized the importance of adhering to precise usage and prescribed durations. For instance, some charms are to be used at least three times every week at the workplace, business outlets, meetings, presentations, or anywhere else. Some black soaps require burning an animal and mixing the soap with the ashes of the animal along with some leaves. Some are to be used in the afternoon, some at midnight.

Another potent soap was a mixture of *epo obo* and black soap for protection, which he believed would wave evil away and keep people safe from attacks by enemies. Also, a mixture of *ako okuta* and black soap for him to heal *akokoro* (toothache). This stone is crushed and mixed with soap, then rubbed on the palms early in the morning before speaking to anyone. The person would feel relief, and the ache would be gone.

I know some converts who still rely on what they refer to as *aajo* (underhanded self-help), which involves a combination of leaves and animals. A concoction is a good example of this practice. If a concoction is eaten without the proper motive, it will only serve as a nice meal, but if the person who eats it has faith, it can serve different purposes because it becomes whole in the stomach.

Different elements of fauna and flora, such as snails, catfish, goats, birds, snakes, and dried fish, are used together with leaves to serve various purposes. Due to my closeness to Iya Lekuleja and my subsequent meeting Baba Jimoh, a charm maker, I learned about some of these concoctions and their purposes.

For instance, at Iya Lekuleja place, I learned that a concoction for good sales/favor is prepared with a snail. If the person in need is a female, the snail will be cut into seven pieces, while the one for a male will be cut into nine pieces, the reason being that females have seven bones while males have nine! If this process isn't followed correctly and there is a shortage or excess in the pieces, the concoction is rendered invalid. A leaf called *afàmọ́'eni ko ni mo'ra*, pepper, palm oil, and salt are cooked with the snail. Iya Lekuleja told me that eating this concoction improves sales because people keep getting drawn to the person and patronizing him or her.

There is also a concoction for being financially self-sufficient, which is prepared with a bird called *ẹtù*. After killing the bird, its feathers are removed without soaking it in hot water; that is, they are removed dry immediately after it has been slaughtered. Baba Jimoh explained that every feather and hair peeled from the bird must be kept safe, with none missing. This concoction involves *huntu*, a surah of the Quran called *Al-Waqi'ah*, which is inscribed three times following the normal *huntu* process, which, in turn, serves as the cooking water for the bird.

When prepared, the concoction is eaten, and any leftover *huntu* can be drank after eating the bird. Afterward, the leftover bones, feathers, intestines, and hair, in fact, everything left of the bird that couldn't be eaten, is poured into the *ikoko* (pot) used for the preparation of the concoction and covered. A white cloth is used to sew a small bag that can contain the pot; the cleric then looks for *ile ikan* (a house built by termites), which will be broken and replaced by the bag containing the pot. If, by the following day, the termites have built another house around the bag containing the pot, the beneficiary will never go broke, as the person will start getting big monetary gifts from people around.

Concoctions like these demonstrate that these practices are traditional, with converts only brought into Islam. I observed that a *surah* of the Quran is always used in making some of these charms. Originally, the *surah* was used to make supplications to Allah when in need of blessing, and Prophet Muhammad (PBUH) stated that if it's recited frequently, one wouldn't suffer from lack. Muslims who engage in such practices justify them by replacing the incantations involved with this *surah*, thereby incorporating the Islamic faith.

According to Baba Jimoh, there is also a concoction for protection, which is prepared with *eyele* (domestic pigeon). The bird is slaughtered, and its blood is collected into a container. This blood is to be used for bathing at night before going to bed. The bird will be cut into sixteen pieces and cooked. A leaf called *oriji* is gotten, along with pepper, and cooked together. This concoction is eaten immediately after the bath, and the person must not go out again but go straight to bed. It's believed that enemies will never be able to hurt this person after this process.

For the Yoruba people, protection can be said to be one of the leading desires that push them to seek charms. They believe aspirations and plans can only be actualized if there is life. The Yoruba traditional system understands that there is more to life than meets the eye and that there are terrestrial and diabolical forces. They believe that there are witches, wizards, *ogbanje*s, and herbalists who specialize in evil. Yes, they exist. Iya Lekuleja taught me that trust is very expensive and that human beings are evil, so anybody at all can harm you. These fears push Yoruba people to resort to using things like *igbadi*, *onde*, rings, black soap, and concoctions, all in the quest to be fortified against evil powers.

Interestingly, Islam doesn't negate the possibility of such powers and, accordingly, has enough provisions for them in the Quran without resorting to traditional practices. The Quran has an abundance of *surahs* that are even more powerful than *igbadi*, *onde*, black soap, rings, or concoctions. Baba Jimoh explained that Tabatiyadah (Al-Masad) is a surah that Allah revealed to place a curse on a man and his wife during the time of Prophet Muhammad (PBUH). So, when recited often, God will protect one from enemies and curse them on our behalf.

I remember when I attended madrassa as a child; we were asked to sit with our legs folded and recite this *surah* seven times into the back of our palms, and then stand up and blow it into the air, believing the wind would carry it to our enemies and render them powerless. Such *surahs* are Suratul Nas and Suratul Falaq, both recommended by Prophet Muhammad (PBUH). Their essence is a supplication asking Allah for protection from the evils of man and jinn and from the evils that go about in darkness and the chants of envious people.

People hold the belief that Shaytan is very powerful and has many agents who engage in nefarious activities under the cover of night. But this power was bestowed upon him by Allah; therefore, Allah's power is supreme. So these *surahs* were revealed to Prophet Muhammad as a means of seeking Allah's protection over the possible powers of Shaytan and his agents.

Among these surahs are Suratul Inshirah and Suratul Fil, the combination of which is believed to serve as protection from illnesses such as pandemics. Each recitation of these surahs is seen as a shield for individuals. As Prophet Muhammad (PBUH) narrated, reciting Suratul Kahf on a Friday morning will safeguard one from evil attacks and enchantments until the next Friday morning. If this *surah* is recited every day with pure faith, such a person will always be protected from evil.

Aside from these *surahs*, Ayatal-Kurisiyyu is a very powerful verse extracted from the second *surah* of the Holy Quran. The Prophet narrated that those who recite it before going to bed will have two angels guarding them, and Shaytan or his forces will be unable to come near them while they sleep. Its protection goes beyond nighttime, as if frequently recited, evil attacks, accidents, ill luck, and other evil vices will be unable to reach the reciter.

Just as I learned about the potency of charms from Iya Lekuleja, the potency of these is proven by Muslims everywhere I've lived. I'm aware that in addition to Quran recitation, Prophet Muhammad (PBUH) laid down numerous supplications for Muslims. Every activity, whether eating, sleeping, entering the toilet, wearing clothes, leaving the house, or embarking on a journey, has its specific supplication to be made beforehand. In fact, even if one is unaware of these innumerable supplications, simply saying *Bismillahi* is enough to ensure Allah's protection and guidance.

CHAPTER SIX

Sir Sabo and *Conc Juju*

If Allah can paint the sky at dawn,
With colors of crimson and golden song,
If He can sculpt the mountains tall,
And shape the valleys, one and all.
Mysteries!

If Allah can design the universe vast,
With galaxies swirling, a cosmic contrast,
If He can place the stars in a perfect array,
Lighting the heavens, night and day.
Wonders!

If Allah can listen to every prayer,
No matter how whispered, no matter where,
If He can understand our deepest fears,
Wipe away our sorrows, dry our tears.
Miracles!

If Allah can forgive, with mercy so great,
Offering redemption, wiping sins' slate,
If He can guide us on the path that's right,
Illuminating darkness with His guiding light.

Then trust in Allah's power, strong and pure,
In His hands, all things find their cure,
For if Allah can create and command,
Surely, He can hold our lives in His hand.

Like many other religions, Islam is not only about the afterlife and receiving the mercy of Allah. It's more complex. For instance, adherents believe they must first live and then die before joining Prophet Muhammad (PBUH) in Al-Jannah.

Ironically, life itself is filled with many challenges, which causes humans to seek protection against destructive powers. Emotional balance is very important, as is the need to seek healing from doctors in the time of sickness.

Islam encompasses medicine and health issues, both in private and in public spheres, reflecting where and how it came from. In search of healing, individuals living in Ibadan could travel to Ilorin and even to Kano, looking for powerful marabouts who possess the power to see the future and who could heal them of their ailments.

A powerful imam with the most potent charms can reside in a house tucked away in a compound accessible only by legs. Incantations are in grades, from elementary to advanced, from post-advance to the most concentrated (aka conc!). Sabo, an Ibadan neighborhood of immigrants from northern Nigeria, Niger, Mali, Chad, and Burkina Faso, is renowned for its *conc juju*, next in efficacy to what Allah is capable of. The power of *conc juju* rests with the knights of power, the Sirs, before whom all men and women bow in deference. Whether true or not, one shouldn't underestimate Mr. Conc, especially in the early evening, lest they find themselves having dinner in heaven.

From my early childhood to the present time, I have always been fascinated by the concentration of potent charms in Sabo, a neighborhood created during the colonial period as a way of segregating "foreigners" from indigenes. To date, people living in Sabo are still considered "foreigners," although many were born there about the same time as me. Several generations reside there, and their first language is Yoruba, with some barely understanding Hausa. They have their own set of rules and regulations, and their chief, the *Seriki*, is so powerful that even the king of the city, the Olubadan of Ibadan, cannot always exercise control over him.

While Sabo is undeniably an epicenter of Islam, to me it is also the center of Islamic medicine. Here one finds a convergence of both scientific and unscientific practices, ranging from conventional bone mending and tonsil removal to the making of charms to kill one's enemy. Sabo is part of a regional network of charm workers, Sufi Muslims, clerics, marabouts, and the like.

These Sabo healers draw from various sources, which, in part, offer some insight into the spread of Islam in the region. To understand the spread of Islam, one can follow the journeys of missionaries, but the practices of marabouts and the potency of charms can also be explored to reach the same conclusion. My encounters with Islam not only relate to how and why Islam in Nigeria became intertwined with traditional religion but also underscore Africa's distinct cultures and traditions before they came under several foreign influences. In the northern region of Nigeria, the Hausa and Fulani embraced Islam before the

Yoruba. However, the Yoruba mixed Islam with their traditional religion, creating a distinctive pathway.

Islam gradually spread into the present-day southwestern part of Nigeria, partly from the present-day north, with Ilorin later becoming the frontrunner town for Islam among the Yoruba. It was the first Yoruba town the Fulani jihadists attacked and took over. The aftermath resulted in a community where Yoruba, Hausa, and Fulani lived together as neighbors. The cohabitation of these people facilitated the growth of Islam in the region, earning Ilorin respect among Yoruba Muslims. Some began to refer to Ilorin as a city of peace and a frontrunner for Islam, a religion of peace. I have heard them describe Ilorin as a town that is far from hell but close to Al-Jannah.

Besides the Fulani jihadists, there was also an influx of Muslim traders from Mali who, after becoming Muslims through their interactions with Berbers and Arabs, disseminated the religion to the northern and southwestern parts of Nigeria through the trans-Saharan trade. These Malians made the Yoruba give Islam the name *imole*, which is dissected as either *imo-lile*, translated as strict/hard knowledge, or pronounced as *imale*, which is translated as knowledge from Mali.

These stories, documented in established literature, highlight that Islam did not suddenly erupt in Yorubaland, nor did it come from a single channel or at a particular time. Instead, it crept in at different times through various channels. One noticeable thing during these periods of the coming of Islam was that the majority of the Yoruba population were predominantly worshippers. Òrìṣà worship held sway in the Yoruba communities, with belief in gods such as Sango, Esu, Obatala, Osun, and so on. To this day, not all Yoruba people are Muslims; some are Christians, while others have remained with their ancestral gods. Some have combined two of the three listed religions or even all three. The Yoruba appear to be natural polytheists!

When Malian Islam preaching traders and Fulani jihadists penetrated Yorubaland, they had to preach the new religion to Òrìṣà worshippers, some of whom had their spheres of influence. Many of the Òrìṣà worshippers had charms for attacks and defenses and were usually from warring families and, most likely, professional warriors. The *balogun* (war general) was selected from this type of family or clan. His personality was always that of a bloodthirsty brute. *Baloguns* were always hungry for war and challenges, and they never tolerated any disrespect.

Conversely, the other families comprised healers, who also had charms, although for healing sicknesses and diseases. In personality, some were said to be easygoing and friendly as they were more about peace and were custodians of health in the community. Among them, the highest rank is *Baba Agbomola* or *Iya Ewe*.

Cities are connected by religion and religious practices. Take, for instance, the story of Fijabi, who was a direct descendant of one of Afonja's lieutenants. According to oral tradition, Afonja was the Oyo general sent to capture Ilorin for the Alaafin. But he betrayed the Alaafin, settled in Ilorin, declared himself king, and later allied himself with Alimi (a Fulani Muslim scholar) against the Alaafin. Alimi and his Fulani Muslim followers later betrayed Afonja, and he lost his grip on power in Ilorin to them.

Fijabi is believed to be one of the great-grandsons of one of Afonja's lieutenants. His name, meaning "to be born with a fight," or metaphorically, "troubled birth" or "tempestuous delivery," is a popular name carried by warriors. So there is no denying the fact that Fijabi was from a warmongering bloodline. Well, generations have passed now, and his family have long put down their armor of war and replaced it with long-flowing white agbada whose front designs can be seen from a mile away, with a turban that would make even the Arabs jealous.

Afonja's lineage is now a well-respected Muslim family in Ilorin, and they happen to have a lot of *àṣe iri* or *asiri* (secrets / hidden knowledge / mystical secrets). Ilorin people are renowned for being custodians of many *asiri* from the Quran. This means that they are so prominent in the study of the Quran that they have found many secrets therein that have made them powerful. They know which *surah* to read to solve a particular problem or de-escalate a particular tension. They do things like pray for a stipulated number of days, write out verses of the Quran on a slate and make it into a drink, take a bath with it, or even mix it into food to solve physical or metaphysical issues.

Also, their knowledge of plants, roots, and animals can be processed into medicines and charms to serve a purpose. Some can even look into things like sand or water to correctly predict what those who came to them for consultation are going through, offering a variety of solutions tailored to their predicaments.

Fijabi was from the bloodline of warriors and was so named. His name depicted his character well. He was always angry and ready to fight, which made most of his mates stay out of his way and business to limit the risk of tango with him. Fijabi was said to have once beaten up someone for walking too slowly in front of him. He was such a troublemaker, but people believed he would eventually outgrow this behavior, as his father, whom the neighbors always reported Fijabi to, was worse than Fijabi when he was younger.

I couldn't imagine anyone being worse than Fijabi when it comes to unjustified anger. Even though I never met him nor had any personal encounter with him, those who did, like Uncle Aminu, had disturbing stories to tell. My uncle said it was in Fijabi's blood to fight since he descended from a lineage of fighters. I never understood all the analogies back then; all I knew was that Fijabi was a wicked person.

As time went by and Fijabi got more mature, the noise around him greatly reduced. He grew along with his temper and wore a calmer look, unlike in his younger days when he always had a scowl. Fijabi later enrolled in a madrassa, and after passing through years of training, he became a sophisticated alfa, swiftly rising through the ranks at such a great pace that the older alfas were jealous of him.

During the period Fijabi attained full knowledge of Islam, after passing through the stages of Islamic education, Yoruba communities were in a phase when newly graduated students sought to demonstrate their prowess in Islam through religious lectures and spiritual powers. There was stiff competition among them, and those who were not strong enough lost their life in mysterious manners.

Controversies trailed many organized lectures where more than one alfa was invited to deliver a speech. Some of them suddenly went dumb, started to vomit blood, or suddenly became dazed and started talking gibberish. It was customary for alfas to inquire about the venue of such events, and those who had been invited to an organized lecture or program either accepted or turned down the invitation after weighing the pros and cons.

By this time, Fijabi had built a new reputation, and those who had known him in the past had forgotten what kind of bully he was and now saw him as an easygoing alfa. Unlike Fijabi, some students went beyond the madrassa to learn the *asiri* and other activities for which the holy book can be used. Some of them, I believe, were descendants of the healers from the Yoruba religion because even their manners and modes of operation look alike.

They were the kinds of alfa you tell your problems to, and they help you find solutions. Some of them use sand in small trays to check for causes of mishaps and probable solutions. Having witnessed them in action before, I can say the patterns they make on their sand look like those of the Ifa worshippers. Some other alfas would investigate a bowl of water to check the reasons and remedies for misfortunes, which is a common practice among Osun worshippers. In Yoruba mythology, most Ifa and Osun worshippers are healers, so it's easy to understand where these alfas are coming from.

Aside from Yoruba Muslims in places like Ibadan, Iseyin, and Iwo, Hausa migrants who lived in different parts of Yoruba cities, known as Sabo Ngeri, were also rated high in spiritual and religious matters. The Hausa word *sabo* is a short form of Sabo Ngeri, meaning "New Town."

Sabo is the hub of Hausa commercial, social, and cultural activity in Ibadan. They prioritized their language even when interacting with other ethnic groups, maintaining very distinct dress, food, and rituals. We called everyone in Sabo Hausa although they could be Fulani, Tuaregs, or Malians. The community has evolved into a stereotypically homogenous one and has recently become more heterogeneous due to their accepting integration with other ethnicities.

Sabo is one of the many non-Ibadan communities in Ibadan that people were primarily drawn to because of the trading opportunities in the early eighteenth century. Many Sabo community members practice Islam, and the religion serves as a common cultural denominator, emphasizing their expanded ethnic identity. Sabo works for ill and well, whether for benevolent or malevolent purposes. It invites no one; individuals venture there of their own volition, often disguising themselves at night to avoid being seen. They navigate through one of the more than twenty hidden alleys that connect to major streets on four sides.

Even if you are caught as you make your way across the community, you alone know the marabout you are visiting, the juju man of your preference. Describing them by their beards is futile, as many have long beards, some short, and some so long that they reach the chest.

Don't worry about the language: Arabic is fine. Hausa is not a problem. The charm makers understand Yoruba as well. The interchange is wonderful! It can even extend beyond charms and divination, as rumors suggest that women seeking charms from the juju man may find themselves entangled in sexual encounters. Yes, a woman cleaned herself with water mixed with black ink intended for writing Arabic texts on tablets. As she left Sabo with her wrapper wet and stained with black, everyone knew she had sat on a shady bench!

The Hausa at Sabo are popularly sought after by Yoruba students who go to them to learn some *asiri*. They also serve as healers, using indigenous knowledge to heal and carry out other spiritual activities. From my experience and my knowledge of other activities aside from trade, I have come to realize that the Hausa exhibit some traits that are like those of newly converted Yoruba Muslims. I know it wasn't always simple for many different groups to coexist as outsiders, so I could deduce that they needed their haven where they could feel at home and protected.

Through their collective skills, labor, and other services, they gently contribute to the economy of their new environment, even in terms of spiritualities. They engage in spiritual and trado-medicinal activities for those who patronize them, offering services like healing, love charms, protection, prosperity charms, fast sales, and more.

Besides being safe, another pressing need for every human is good health. In Sabo, healing is done by reciting appropriate verses from the Quran, and

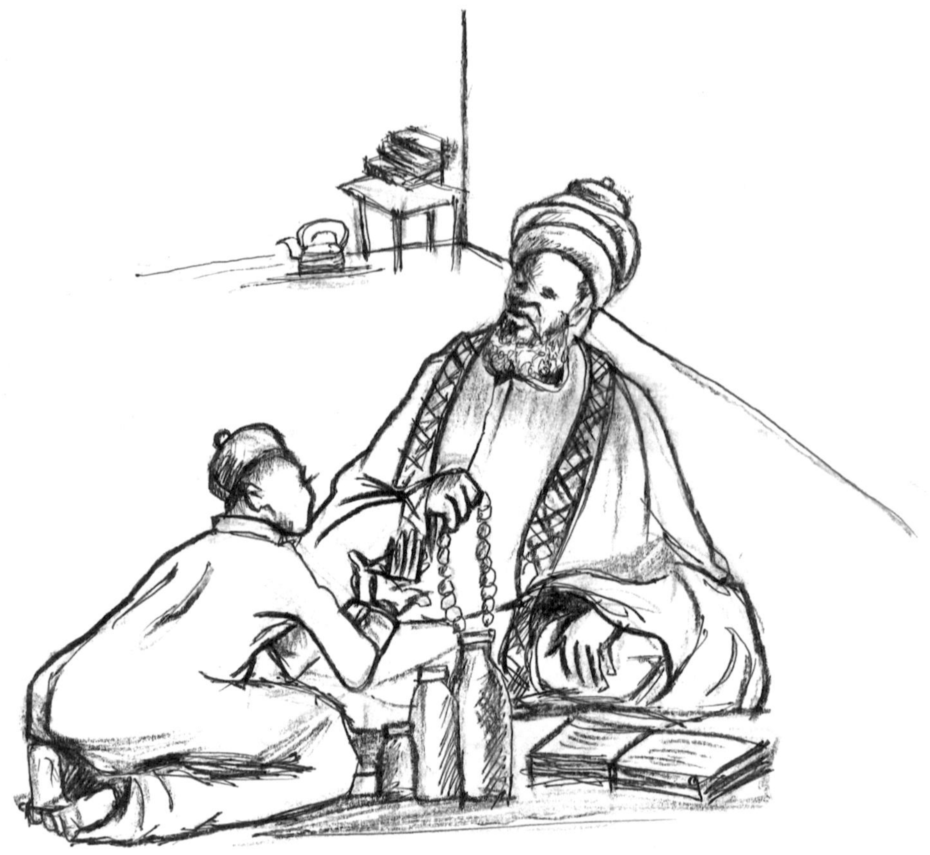

FIG. 11. *Sir Sabo and Customer* by Dr. Kazeem Ekeolu. The clerics at Sabo do more than just pray for their customers; they also offer consultations on their behalf, whether using tasbih, water, sand, or other elements; they are believed to have secret powers that others do not. According to their customers, these clerics possess unique abilities that set them apart.

adhkars (short prayers) are recommended by these spiritual men, who also use prophetic medicines. The first time I heard about these clerics who help "customers," as they called those who seek help from them, was the story of one of my neighbors in Ibadan some years ago.

Rasheed, a devout Muslim man in his late twenties, was desperate to win the heart of Aisha, a woman he deeply loved. Despite being from the same community and sharing similar values, Aisha remained indifferent to Rasheed's advances. Desperate for a solution, Rasheed learned about a cleric at Sabo named Sheikh Abdullah, who was known for his mystical abilities and unconventional practices. He was rumored to have mastered the art of crafting powerful love charms.

After days of persuasion from his colleagues, Rasheed visited Sheikh Abdullah's modest dwelling at Sabo, seeking help. The sheikh listened attentively to Rasheed's plea and agreed to create a custom love charm for him. However, he warned Rasheed about the consequences of using love charms, which he referred to as *conc juju*, cautioning him of unforeseen repercussions. But blinded by his love for Aisha, Rasheed was willing to take the risk.

The sheikh prepared a complex charm using rare herbs, incantations, some verses of the Quran, and a lock of Aisha's hair that Rasheed had secretly obtained. Rasheed was overjoyed as he received the love charm from Sheikh Abdullah. He followed the sheikh's instructions meticulously and soon noticed Aisha's behavior changing. She became more affectionate and responsive, leading Rasheed to believe that the charm was finally working.

As time passed, he started noticing other subtle changes in Aisha's personality. She became possessive and overly dependent on him, showing signs of obsession. Her behavior became erratic and unpredictable, and Rasheed began to feel suffocated in the relationship. It became so apparent that gossip went around the neighborhood that Rasheed had charmed Aisha to love him. However, this was not the only consequence, as Rasheed also started experiencing a series of unfortunate events in his life. He began to emit a foul odor from his body, causing everyone to despise him and leading to a falling out with his friends.

Disturbed by the unsettling events, Rasheed returned to Sheikh Abdullah for answers. The sheikh gravely disclosed that the love charm had backfired and had caused unintended consequences. He explained that love charms were not meant to interfere with free will and that tampering with someone's emotions could have severe repercussions in the spiritual realm.

Rasheed realized his mistake and pleaded with Sheikh Abdullah to undo the charm. The sheikh performed a ritual to reverse its effects, but it came at a heavy price. Rasheed had to offer something precious to him as a sacrifice to balance the spiritual scales. He gave up a cherished possession and was finally able to break the effects of the love charm. He apologized to Aisha for his misguided actions, and though she forgave him, their relationship was irreparably damaged.

They parted ways amicably, and Rasheed learned a valuable lesson about the dangers of tampering with spiritual forces. Realizing that true love cannot be forced or manipulated through charms or spells, he focused on self-improvement, seeking forgiveness and redemption, and embarked on a new journey of self-discovery and personal growth, guided by the teachings of his faith.

Sabo was not only a place to seek spiritual assistance from the clerics of Hausa descent, who are predominantly migrants, but also a hub for knowledge exchange. Many clerics who had learned widely from formal madrassas approached these spiritual men to learn charm-making, using unorthodox means to heal and conserve spiritual powers for protection. One such person was Adio, who surprisingly retained his *oruko oriki* (local name) after graduating from an Islamic institution and acquiring vast knowledge of Islam.

Adio's plan wasn't to learn how to mix juju or charms at Sabo after leaving the Madrasah, but the circumstances he found himself in pushed him to seek protection and a fast means to wealth. Moreover, as he experienced waves of wickedness and other scary occurrences at lectures he was invited to speak, he was compelled to seek immediate protection using charms mixed with Islamic teachings. He could have relied solely on Allah for protection, but he believed that even if the prayers would eventually be answered, it would take some time. Adio had seen colleagues killed by spiritual attacks and saw the need to seek additional protection beyond prayer.

He learned from the spiritual clerics in Sabo and became powerful, using various means, known as *aajo*, that transcended mere recitation of the Quran. One such means involved the use of *huntu*, in which the names of Allah, a Quranic verse or surah, and *adkhars* are inscribed on a board using a pen called *qalam*. This inscription is later washed out with water and put into a container. The ink is called the *tada* in Yoruba, and the board is referred to as *ọpọ́n ọlà*.

The writing materials used for this ritual are special and not accessible to everyone. The *tada* is a special writing material dating back to the days of Prophet Muhammad (PBUH), when it was used to write down Quranic verses on leaves for documentation, as there were no papers. This was the practice until proper writing began. The *ọpọ́n ọlà* is made from *igi ope* (palm trees), which cannot be grown by just anyone. Some Salafis and Ahlu Sunna members regard *huntu* as a *shirk* and an unnecessary innovation, but its practitioners justify its usage by saying that it's nothing but the words of Allah.

Adio did not stop in his quest to gain more knowledge beyond the ordinary. He sought greater dimensions, as he had more than enough knowledge of traditional medicines and procedures and went the way of the Muslim preachers with the purpose of learning their healing methods.

Before then, there had been several accounts and testimonies of how they performed extraordinary feats, including making barren women conceive. Adio consulted spirits and other supernatural bodies for help in his healing business. His worship of some of these bodies was a huge error, as his religion forbids worshipping any other god or being except Allah.

Islam provided Adio with some knowledge of a few healing practices, but the most important thing he did with the religion was to hide under its guise. Some healing procedures were mostly traditional, with just a little inspiration from Islam. To the outside world, he was an alfa; therefore, they never raised an eyebrow when he patronized herbalists' stalls to buy traditional items like black pots, calabashes, dried birds, chameleons, other reptiles, and so on.

Adio's belief in the Yoruba aphorism that *ìlera l'oògùn ọrọ̀* (health is wealth) compelled him to prioritize healing people of different ailments. Alongside his spiritual healing practices, he emphasized the importance of prayers, recognizing that the gift of good health is only given by Allah, who has dominion over everything in the human body, and that prayer could heal conditions inflicted by unseen powers.

Many of these prayers can be found in different books written by some of these clerics, and they are believed to cure any condition caused by evil attacks if the victim is a strong believer.

Among the *surahs* used for protection are Surah Nas and Suratul Falaq. I knew some of these *surahs* often prescribed by clerics like Adio, including Suratul Iklhas, Suratul Quraysh, Suratul Yasin, Fatiha, and the last two verses of Suratul Baqarah.

Ruqyah is performed if an individual is afflicted with ill health. The full verses of the *surahs* listed above are recited in the hearing of the patient. If the person is possessed by jinn, the jinn is commanded to leave by the power of these *surahs*. However, if no jinns are involved, the patient can be made to listen to the recordings of these *surahs* repeatedly for a week. Then, the *abbatul saddah* oil, over which prayers have been invoked seven times, is constantly applied to patients' forehead and the aching organs till they feel relief. Afterward, *adhkars*, recommended by Prophet Muhammad (PBUH) for healing, can be recited, and *insha Allah* (if God wills), healing will occur.

In cases where a Muslim woman is having difficulty conceiving after medical help has been sought, *Ruqyah* can also be performed. If the person has a strong faith, healing will occur. The person is encouraged to listen to the *Ruqyah* cassette thrice daily and recite some surahs morning and night—Suratul Mulk at bedtime, some *adhkars* recommended by Prophet Muhammad (PBUH)—seven or seventy times into the *abbatul saddah* oil, which would then be rubbed on the chest and forehead before sleeping.

When "customers" approached Adio seeking help with childbirth, he advised them to recite all the *Ruqyah* verses into a bottle of honey and take a teaspoonful every morning to be swallowed with the first saliva after waking up. Adio believed that following this practice diligently, along with abstaining from sins as much as possible, and following divine commands would increase the chances of conception for such an individual.

Adio further emphasized that there is a specific *dhikr*, recommended by Prophet Isah, that would guarantee safe delivery when recited by a woman during childbirth. The medical attendant should also silently recite Ayattul Kurisiyyu, along with other protective *surahs*. This practice is recommended because it is believed that once a woman goes into labor, Shaytan appears to make the labor difficult or to possess the child, and these recitations will keep the devil away.

Like many other Muslim clerics, Adio combined his knowledge of the Quran and *adhkars* with traditional health procedures to treat and cure mental illness, insomnia, difficulty in finding a spouse, and various other predicaments. Medicines like *abbatul saddiah*, black seed, and black seed oil are believed to have the power to cure any illness, including those that defy conventional medical intervention.

From the traditional methods and steps for solving spiritual issues and seeking protection, there is a clear line between charms rooted in Yoruba religion and Islamic means solely comprising verses from the Quran, the names of Allah, and *adhkars* recommended from the holy book, no matter how much they have been combined by those who use them together. Therefore, no matter the charms in which one may be invested, everything is dependent on the individual's judgment of what is acceptable in the religion.

While some Muslims conveniently align with Yoruba charms, others adhere strictly to prayers, and some blend Yoruba and Islamic content. For those who merge the two, after preparing the basics with materials for Yoruba charms, they recite Quranic verses over them to incorporate the "God factor." This indicates an awareness that they are not purely "Islamic" but also indigenous. Some Alfa Sufis even add Quranic verses to black soap. In some instances, after adding leaves to black soap to make soap for protection, they pour *huntu* made of *surahs* into it, believing that covering the indigenous items with religion will make it more effective.

Some clerics prepare concoctions for protection, healing, or whatever purpose, with *huntu* of *surahs* serving as cooking water. For example, a concoction prepared with guinea fowl and other ingredients may be cooked with the *huntu* of Suratul Waqia, a particular *surah* used to request blessings from Allah and Prophet Muhammad (PBUH) to ensure financial prosperity. The surah is inscribed seven times, with the *huntu* serving as the cooking water alongside other traditional due processes. If the *huntu* is in large quantity, the remaining portion is drunk as water after eating the concoction. Additionally, individuals may tie a small piece of paper with a *surah* of their choice around their arms, symbolizing the traditional *onde* and serving the same purposes as the *onde*.

Verses from the Quran can be used for protection, depending on usage and intention. These verses and *surahs* are very powerful and can serve numerous purposes, including protection, whether through consumption, bathing rituals, or other methods. A notable example is the story of a well-respected Muslim cleric named Sheikh Ibrahim at Ode Aje. He was popular in Ode Aje for his deep knowledge of Islamic teachings and his unwavering faith. He led daily prayers at the local mosque and was sought after for his guidance and counsel.

One day, a series of mysterious incidents befell the people of his community at Ode Aje. Crops withered, livestock fell ill, and the once-thriving market was plagued by misfortune. People whispered that evil spirits were at work, causing harm to the community. Concerned for his people, Sheikh Ibrahim decided to take action. He consulted the Quran and sought guidance from fellow scholars, but the cause of the misfortune remained elusive. In his quest for a solution, he remembered an old tradition passed down through generations in his family. This tradition involved the use of various means for protection, similar to those employed by masquerade worshippers who used local herbs, charms, and rituals to ward off evil spirits.

Despite being a devout Muslim, Sheikh Ibrahim remained open to the wisdom in his ancestors' practices, and he decided to give it a try. He sought the help of Baba Olumide, an elderly herbalist in Ibadan, who was known for his expertise in such cases. After consulting the Ifa oracle, Baba Olumide prepared a special concoction of herbs, roots, and animal parts, carefully following the rituals and incantations, and gave Sheikh Ibrahim an amulet, with the instruction to sprinkle the mixture around the outskirts of the community during a midnight ritual while holding the amulet for protection.

Even though he had some reservations about using Yoruba means for protection, Sheikh Ibrahim followed Baba Olumide's instructions diligently. He assured himself that his faith in Islam was unshakeable, and this was simply an additional measure to safeguard his community. The following morning, the people were amazed to discover that the misfortune that had plagued them seemed to have disappeared overnight. Crops were healthy again, livestock recovered, and the market was bustling with activity.

It would not be surprising if a typical Yoruba Muslim lacks a definitive answer regarding the permissibility of charms in Islam, nor would it be shocking for there to be disagreements as to which charms are allowed and which are not. This concept of "hybridism" has been with us since the very inception of Islam and has been passed down from generation to generation. Accordingly, the answers given will be based on experience, personal judgment, or the teachings of the scholars they follow. The challenge lies in the inability to separate religion, culture, and tradition, posing a foundational intellectual problem.

I recall a woman I spoke with telling me about how she had her husband under control, so much so that even though they separated long ago, he continued to shoulder the responsibilities of their two kids because she ensured he was unable to impregnate another woman. When they initially separated, she had run to her alfa, who advised her to be patient and gave her some verses to recite. However, she also went to the eldest member of her family, who still worshipped Ogun. The old man performed some traditional rituals, using her husband's name, and assured her he wouldn't have any other children and would eventually return to her.

According to the woman, if she had not taken that step, he would have remarried and started another family, and their getting back together would be almost impossible. In essence, she said that patience is not always the way and that one has to go the "extra mile" in addition to prayer. She justified her actions by saying she did not harm anyone and had to take that step to protect the future of her kids.

This perspective reflects how some Yoruba Muslims believe that there are aspects of charms in Islam that were inherited from Yoruba practices. But upon a closer examination of the Quran, I find the glaring answer that seeking power from other gods is not in line with Islamic principles. Muslims are to trust in Allah alone and follow only his commandments and the practices of his prophets. The stance of Ahlu Sunna emphasizes that Muslims are not allowed to place faith in any other entity or spirit besides Allah or be regarded as polytheists.

Surah Kafirun of the Quran says thus:

قُلْ يَا أَيُّهَا الْكَافِرُونَ
لَا أَعْبُدُ مَا تَعْبُدُونَ
وَلَا أَنتُمْ عَابِدُونَ مَا أَعْبُدُ
وَلَا أَنَا عَابِدٌ مَّا عَبَدتُّمْ
وَلَا أَنتُمْ عَابِدُونَ مَا أَعْبُدُ
لَكُمْ دِينُكُمْ وَلِيَ دِينِ

O, unbelievers!
I do not serve that which you serve,
Nor do you serve Him I serve:
Nor am I going to serve that which you serve,
Nor are you going to serve Him whom I serve:
So you shall have your religion, and I shall have mine.
(Quran 109:1–6)

Indeed, most typical Yoruba families have Òrìṣà religions that predate the establishment of Islam in their communities. However, Òrìṣà religions are meant to be sustained, as regarded by them. Islam commands believers to dedicate their worship to only Allah. The use of charms implies bringing *ìṣẹ̀ṣe* (tradition) into religion, and because it is believed that *ìṣẹ̀ṣe* produce faster results than ordinary prayers. Among Yoruba Muslims, there is a scale to the practice of charms, with some individuals maintaining closer ties to Òrìṣà practices than others. The choice, however, is often based on individual perceptions of right and wrong.

When news of Sheikh Ibrahim's use of indigenous means for protection spread in the community, some people were initially skeptical. But Sheikh Ibrahim explained that he had turned to Òrìṣà religion as a complementary measure, not as a replacement for his Islamic faith. He stressed his unwavering belief in the Quran and the teachings of Islam. From the amount of criticism Sheikh Ibrahim received from other Muslims and sheikhs, you would think those criticizing him did not also secretly use traditional assistance. The main reason for their outrage was because he openly sought traditional assistance for the plague while continuing to lead prayers at the mosque and provide guidance to his community in matters of the Islamic faith.

Despite the backlash, Sheikh Ibrahim maintained a respectful relationship with Baba Olumide, who had become his trusted adviser on matters related to *ìṣẹ̀ṣe*. Some people appreciated Sheikh Ibrahim's open-mindedness and his willingness to explore different avenues for protecting the community. He became a symbol of unity, bridging the gap between the two belief systems and promoting mutual respect within the community.

Regardless of religious affiliation, leading a fulfilled life is one of humans' most important needs, which include money, wealth, fame, power, and numerous other desires. This is why people seek *ose aanu* and *eyonu* (concoctions, perfumes, and creams with ingredients that attract favor). For Muslims, *surahs* and supplications that serve these purposes also exist, with believers trusting that by reciting them, they are communicating their desires to God and will receive what they ask. These *surahs* serve specific purposes once you believe in them. Suratul Nas is a *surah* for opening doors for blessing. *Nasr* means divine support, so it is used to seek help and favor from Allah, often recited alongside Quraysh and Salatul Fatiha.

A Muslim friend shared an experience where reciting Suratul Quraysh and Suratul Fatiha helped ease a dire situation he was in. He had an issue with DSS (a security operative of the government) and had to visit their office for interrogation. He was told to keep reciting these two *surahs* on his way to the DSS office so that, *insha Allah*, he would be welcomed warmly and the anger of the DSS officers would dissipate. My friend said he was really scared, as the phone conversations were frightening, but he did as he was told, and to his surprise, the issue was resolved quickly and without animosity from the officers. From that experience, he learned that these *surahs* work and that the key ingredient is faith and conviction that God will fulfill the wish.

According to my friend, Suratul Waqia and Suratul Mulk are good for seeking blessings from Allah, as *Mulk* translates to the God of dominion and wealth. Reciting these *surahs* a specific number of times, accompanied by *adhkars* for a specific number of days, is asking for wealth from Allah, and *insha Allah*, that request will be granted.

When my friend mentioned Suratul Qawthar, he was affirmative about the last verse in this *surah* as a great supplication against enemies. This verse was revealed when Prophet Muhammad (PBUH) lost a child on Sallah day, and his enemies wanted to mock him. Allah told him in the *surah* that he had provided abundance for him in paradise already. The last verse of this *surah* contains Allah's promise that those who seek to dishonor him will be shamed. So, if this verse is recited, it sends the evil arrow, plans, and plot of evildoers right back to them.

Yāsin is the heart of the Quran. It can be recited in different ways to make supplications to Allah. It is effective for healing, protection, and making a request when one is in dire need of anything from Allah. This *surah*, with over fifty verses, is usually read with specific instructions. *Allahumma salli ala Muhammad* is repeated after each verse, but for every verse that ends with *mubīn*, the reciter is to state his or her prayer point and pray about it before moving to the next verse. If this is done for seven days at the same time, the prayer will be answered, *insha Allah*. This prayer can be done after observing two *rakkas* of voluntary *salat nafilah*.

Suratul Ikhlas centers on the sovereignty of Allah and his power and can also be recited in different ways to offer supplications to him. One such way is preferably at midnight. This is seen as going the extra mile to show one's dependency on Allah, which he appreciates. The condition for this salat is to have just a single prayer point in one's intention.

Suratul Baqarah serves as light and guidance to Muslims. If it is recited by a newlywedded couple into their home, it is believed that evil jinns will not be able to penetrate their home. Similarly, Ayat Kurisiyyu does not only work for protection and healing; it can also be used to request anything from Allah. Muslims in need of a job, spouse, and long life can recite this *surah* numerous times with the addition of other *adhkars*, and Allah will grant their requests.

The list of beneficial *surahs* and their purposes is inexhaustible because there is no verse in the Holy Quran without a purpose. From experience, I must admit that the Quran is a powerful book. The Ilorin people have spent loads of their time delving deeply into the holy book, and they know quite a lot of things that many other Yoruba Muslims have little or no idea of. Some of the results they get, the processes they go through, and their methods of application all have too much similarity to those of the traditional religion.

Since many Muslims were once worshippers of some of the Yoruba gods, it isn't farfetched to claim that they have brought some of their old ways into the new religion and are reaping great rewards from their diversity. They have been able to propel themselves into prosperity under a new religion by using old religious methods.

Nevertheless, as believers go deeper in their faith in God and in serving him, they come to realize the benefits of the Holy Book and that it is enough as a charm. Some people not only grow in faith, but also become polytheists because of their quest for assistance and to find their place in the world.

On one of my trips to a market in Ibadan, I had an unforgettable experience that left me with amazing memories and gave me more insights into the seamless integration of Islam, Christianity, and traditional beliefs within the fabric of Yoruba life.

I was with a friend who had accompanied me to buy catfish from the market. As we waited for the catfish seller, who other market women said was on her way back from the major fish market, a young girl politely asked us to move our bench aside, explaining that it obstructed her mother's stall and that she needed to open for the day's business. I got up, and my friend promptly moved the bench to create space for the girl to proceed with her tasks.

The young girl's adeptness in opening and arranging her mother's goods showed that it was not foreign to her at all. However, her skill in setting up the shop was far inferior to the one she displayed in selling the goods. If I hadn't seen the girl sell to customers, I would have left the market with a lingering doubt about her ability to manage the shop in her mother's absence. More amazing was that she effortlessly managed both tasks simultaneously.

As she opened the shop, I was struck by the variety of commodities inside, and I thought that the girl would most likely have little knowledge of how to sell. It was a local herb stall, almost like Iya Lekuleja's, with different types of leaves and roots on display. There was a pen cage for live frogs, three cages that held a cat each, another for a bush rat, and one that housed two parrots. Small wooden male and female effigies hung from the ceiling, with calabashes of different sizes and feathers of different birds, heads, claws, and animal fur.

The catfish seller was not around yet, so I found myself absorbed in observing the surroundings. Eventually, the girl's mother arrived, and I could have gambled that she was an Osun worshipper and lost my money! She arrived like an angel in her white *buba* and *iro* (blouse and wrapper), her attire announcing her presence from afar. When she got closer to us, I could see that she was not an Osun worshipper, especially because she was holding a Muslim rosary in her hand. The other women greeted her in the Muslim way, *Salamalaykum, Alhaja* (Peace be upon you, Alhaja), to which she responded, *Walaykum salam* (Peace be upon you too).

During their exchange of greetings, I caught a glimmer of her golden tooth—a sign that she had been to Mecca. She also confirmed it when she called her daughter's name, Khadeejah, to ask her to bring a cup of water from inside the stall while also informing her that the *àsàlátù* took longer than usual.

Confirming that she was a Muslim made me wonder why and how a devout Muslim would be selling items that are directly linked to the traditional religion, and not just another religion, but one that has been tagged "idolatry." As if sensing my confusion regarding the crossover of religions, she bewildered me even more when a female Christian preacher stopped by her stall to pray for her, and she completed the trinity! She adjusted her scarf and replied, "Amin loruko Jesu" (Amen, in Jesus's name) to the preacher's prayer, and when they finished, she asked her daughter to bring money to give to the woman for the prayers. My head spun with the way this woman seamlessly integrated the three religions.

Noticing my intense focus on the woman, my friend informed me that she was a prominent figure in the market. She had a lot of customers due to her connections with big alfas, pastors, and traditionalists, who patronized her directly or by proxy by sending those who consulted them for spiritual help to her for the ingredients needed for potions or sacrifices. In return, she would give gifts to the pastors, alfas, and traditionalists and refer her customers in need of spiritual help to them.

Furthermore, my friend described the market as a battleground where the market women competed fiercely for dominance, both physically and metaphysically. It didn't matter whether they sold the same thing or different things or whether their stalls were close or far apart; they harmed one another over trivial things such as who sold more or who wore better clothes. They did *conc juju* for better and faster sales and sought protection from all three religions.

Embedded within these different religions are several mythologies and beliefs. People do not readily believe in anything unless it has proven itself worthy of their trust over time. To this end, can we dismiss the veracity of

African gods and the myths surrounding them? For them to have gained such followership and loyalty that transcended generations, there must have been some truth and efficacy surrounding their existence and activities. Africans have historically taken great pride in their gods and ritual worship, just as Islam comprises a blend of ideas and practices from diverse sources, validated by their tested truth and efficacy.

CHAPTER SEVEN

Alhaji Many, Alhaja Money

Whether Alhaji or Alhaja!
Money is involved,
Wealth matters, inherited or not,
It is given by Allah.
A tale of families, bonded by blood,
Divided by noise.
Plot of men, executed by Shaytan.
Flamboyant with riches, lose their faith
Roaming the streets with affluence
In their luxurious cars, neither here nor there
Meet an Alhaji with plenty Alhaja,
Or is it an Alhaja with numerous Alhaji
Allah is the judge, till kiyamo!

Growing up in a polygamous family was never boring. Just as I was brought up in one, the majority of my peers are also from polygamous homes. When they narrate their ordeals, while some are bittersweet, others are quite grave. There were always disputes over who got what and who was right or wrong during misunderstandings. Let's not even get started on the never-ending cycle of "Whose turn it is to do the chores?" among the wives. It felt like living in a constant state of sibling rivalry but multiplied by three (or a hundred on worse days). But there was never a shortage of people to blame when things went awry.

From childhood, I knew Muslim women who were stay-at-home mothers, dedicating themselves fully to domestic duties. A little peek into the lives of my Muslim friends and colleagues and one would quickly notice that their wives are relatively absent in public. My Muslim friends would always ring it like a bell in my ears: "Toyin, Islam is a religion aimed at reducing immorality to the barest minimum." Even when I want to believe them, the popular gist about the *eleha* at Ode Aje comes to my memory.

FIG. 12. *Alhaji and His Wives* by Dr. Kazeem Ekeolu. Polygamy is recognized in Islam and is also accepted in Yoruba culture. A man's ability to marry multiple wives and effectively manage his household gives him high regard among his peers.

At madrassa, in those days, we were taught that women are to be in purdah, that is, kept away from men who are not their immediate family members. This was achieved by restricting their movements to the household or having them wear a veil when in public. But amid these restrictions, the stories of how some *eleha* had slept with the young men in the community were a dime a dozen. Though I can't confirm whether the stories are true, they suggest that the women in purdah were not in chains. There were even rumors of men disguising themselves as women, wearing veils to gain access to these secluded women.

A short distance, and you'd see a woman in a veil. Enter a compound, and you'll see many women all covered up. I got used to seeing them, and even when their faces were hidden, I knew the identity of all those near our house, and I could call them by their names.

Veils come in two main types: the hijab mostly covers the head and leaves the face open. The length varies according to the wearer's preference, with the shorter one being the most common in Ode Aje and even in cities like Ibadan. These women proudly wear their veils, claiming they add to their beauty. To appear beautiful these days, women flaunt their hips and breasts, which are precisely the body parts veils were supposed to hide.

The second type is the niqab, which wasn't common in Ode Aje. It covers the face and only has openings for the eyes so the wearer can see. It's the type that the *eleha* use. Some of us regarded it as a mask because proper *eleha* cover even their faces. They are meant to be indoors most of the time, and even when they are outside, nobody recognizes them except for their immediate families and some friends. Their true identity is concealed unless you're familiar with their voices.

I've often wondered if these women find these veils comfortable, especially considering the Nigerian climate. Then I recall that the pioneers of the religion inhabit one of the driest zones in the world (the Middle East). Since they take this act of purdah more seriously than those from my region, I assume they must have no issues with it. Remarkably, not all Muslims in Nigeria or other parts of the world observe purdah, but it remains a common feature of Muslim women's clothing.

Weekends in Ibadan were often filled with different social events, especially marriage ceremonies–it was like there were new couples ready to tie the knot every other day. An important aspect of the life of Muslim women is the marriage rites, called *nikkah* in Arabic, which is translated as marriage in Islam and a contract between husband and wife.

During the sheikh's sermon at one of the *ahdul nikkah* (wedding ceremonies) I attended, he elaborated on the four stages of a legit *nikkah* in Islam. The first stage is called the *ijab wal qubul*, which translates to "offer and acceptance" in English. Here the suitor verbally expresses his intentions to the father of his prospective bride. This step holds significant importance, so the only men exempted are those who are hard of hearing and may have someone speak on their behalf.

After the verbal expression, the father-in-law takes the message to his daughter and relays her response, whether yes or no, to the prospective groom.

Importantly, the woman must not be forced to accept or reject the proposal. Alternatively, the woman may also begin the verbal expression process with her father, who will meet the family of the man his daughter is interested in. However, this practice is rare.

The next step is obtaining the consent of the parent or guardian, another vital step toward the *nikkah*. The father of the bride-to-be or anybody authorized by her father, such as her paternal grandfather, her father's paternal brother, her full-blood brother, or the ruler of her society or its imam. Failure to get the consent of one of these individuals makes the *nikkah* invalid.

By the time the sheikh got to the second step, the families of the couple had started to grumble. Regardless of the religion, I know my people love to party! For them, the sheikh had already taken too much time. While the sheikh aimed to impart knowledge to his listeners, they were eager to start the party proper. But since he held power at that moment, he ignored their grumbling and went on to talk about the last two stages of a legal *nikkah*—"witness" and the "payment of *dowar*" (bride gift).

The witness stage involves having a minimum of two witnesses present at the wedding to make it valid. According to Islamic tradition, any marriage held in seclusion is regarded as null and void. Paying the *dowar* is the last step of the *nikkah*, and the payment is demanded and received by the bride either before, during, or after the *nikkah* and must be paid for by the groom.

The bride has the liberty to request anything she desires from her groom, and he is obligated to meet her demands. In cases where the husband isn't buoyant enough, he may pay in installments, pay after the *nikkah*, or seek assistance from his brothers. However, he must not disclose to them that he is seeking help to pay the *dowar*. In the unfortunate event that a husband dies without paying the *dowar*, its equivalent will be removed from his property and given to his wife.

As I listened to the sheikh, I tried to imagine what the bride could ask for that would necessitate the groom to seek financial assistance and even pay in installments. I mean, the man could be entering the marriage already financially broke! I also imagined the bride being so kind and considerate that she would request a copy of the Quran as her *dowar*. I wondered if any man could be lucky enough to marry such a pious woman, a kind and considerate one who helps her fiancé by asking for what she believes is invaluable and does not cost too much.

At another *nikkah* I attended in Lagos, I noticed something new and different from the ceremonies in Ibadan. The clerics made it clear that other factors must be considered before a *nikkah* can take place. The oldest sheikh stressed the importance of religious compatibility between both parties to avoid a clash of religions in their home. He also emphasized that both parties must be free individuals; that is, a free man can't marry a slave or a prisoner and vice versa, though this is less relevant now with the abolition of slavery.

Additionally, he mentioned that the abilities and capabilities of the intending couple must match. The husband must be able to satisfy his wife sexually and capable of fulfilling her other needs, the absence of which can lead to a lot of troubles in the marriage if not handled well. As the sheikh continued, I observed that no mention was made of the need for couples to undergo a medical checkup before marriage. It made me realize how much attention we pay to religious matters and rely on prayers and spiritual practices to address issues that could be resolved through a simple medical diagnosis and treatment.

Islam is a religion with numerous rules and guidelines for all aspects of life. Islam takes care of all facets of human endeavors, with a laid-down step for everything. Just as there are guidelines toward *nikkah* for eligible women, so are there some categories of women who are not allowed to marry in Islam? Such categories are split into two: temporary and permanent prohibitions.

I learned this from a conversation I had with Qudus, my friend and neighbor when I lived in Ibadan, who had since become an alfa. Qudus was so notorious that he was punished one day by the elders in the community because he gathered young boys to mock *eleha*. He and the boys would sing songs of mockery when the *eleha* walked by, describing the woman as a masquerade.

One day, his parents became fed up and enrolled Qudus in a madrassa, where he stayed with the sheikh family and was later sent to Egypt to learn more about Islam. He became well versed in the religion, attaining a huge rank synonymous with that of a professor in academia.

As our conversation progressed, we talked about marriage, and that was when Qudus mentioned the story of the women who are temporarily prohibited from marriage. These women can't get married at a certain point in their lives, but there is an expiration date for the obstacle preventing them from getting married. For example, a man can't marry two blood sisters or half sisters at the same time, but he can marry the other sister if the first wife dies. Similarly, a widow must complete a waiting period (typically four months and ten days) before she can consider remarrying to ascertain that she isn't pregnant from her deceased husband.

Slaves or persons serving a jail term can't be married under Islamic laws until they are freed from their bondage. Additionally, for the temporary prohibition, a woman whom a man has divorced can't remarry him unless she marries another man and consummates the marriage at least once before the man willingly divorces her. Only then can she go back to her former husband, who must also copulate with her before they are allowed to legally remarry.

To my further surprise, my once notorious friend, now a respected sheikh, continued his story, now delving into the category of women who are permanently forbidden from marriage. According to him, this prohibition is either due to blood relationships or other special circumstances. Under the blood relationship, a Muslim man is permanently forbidden from marrying his mother, grandmother, daughter, granddaughter, sister, niece, or paternal or maternal aunt.

Also, a woman who got divorced due to adultery can't reconcile with her former husband, and a woman who served as a wet nurse to a widower is permanently forbidden to marry, which means the widower's sons can't marry the wet nurse's daughters and her sons cannot marry his daughters. Moreover, a Muslim man can't marry his wife's mother, his son's wife, his daughter, or his wife's granddaughter. One particular restriction, which contrasts with Yoruba culture, is that a Muslim man can't marry his father's wife. This is against the custom of many Yoruba groups, as Yoruba culture traditionally allows a man to inherit his father's wife after his father's demise.

However, despite the seemingly different rules for Muslim males and females, the Quran makes it clear that there are some equivalents in treatment:

> *And whoever does good deeds, whether male or female,*
> *and is a believer, they shall enter the garden,*
> *and they shall not be dealt with a jot unjustly.* (Quran 4:124)

The verse stipulates that men and women have equal rights and privileges regarding matters of faith, as both are permitted to attain favor and good reward from God. There is no distinction between actions and consequences for both genders. For two people joined together by marriage, the Quran 30:21 says, "he created mates for you from yourselves that you may find rest in them, and he put between you love and compassion."

My understanding of that *ayah* (verse) is that the relationship between a man and his wife should be founded on love and compassion, as they were created from and for each other. A couple should find solace and peace in their union; in other words, they should not be a source of worry to each other and shouldn't be married for any reason other than genuine love and compassion. Compassion entails being kind and caring toward our spouse, offering support in times of need, and being wholeheartedly committed to them.

Another Islamic injunction that I found very intriguing is concerning polygamy. This practice allows Muslim men to marry multiple wives, with certain conditions and limitations, as outlined in the Quran. The Holy Book stipulates that a man may marry up to four wives, but only if he can ensure equitable treatment and equal provision for each woman and her children.

FIG. 13. *Ṣalāt al-Janāzah* (funeral prayer) by Dr. Kazeem Ekeolu. Muslims perform the special prayer that accompanies an Islamic funeral, performed in congregation to seek forgiveness for the deceased and all dead Muslims.

However, I cannot guarantee that Yoruba tradition aligns with this principle.

Quran 4:20–21 says:

> *And if you wish to have (one) wife in place of another and you had given one of them a heap of gold, then take not from it anything; would you take it by slandering (her) and (doing her) manifest wrong?*
>
> *And how can you take it when one of you has already gone into the other and they have made with you a firm covenant?*

The "heap of gold" is metaphorical and represents money, houses, cars, businesses, or anything, whether material or otherwise, that brings ease for a woman, which a husband is obligated to provide. A man intending to marry another wife must ensure he has the means to provide for both of them. He can't shirk his responsibilities to his first wife because of his new wife.

A man can't slander or wrong his first wife simply because he wants to marry another wife. The love and compassion between them must remain intact, ensuring that all wives find peace and rest with him. This commitment to fairness and justice is important because any man who neglects any of his wives, fails to take proper care of them, or withdraws any form of love and compassion is in manifest error and will face chastisement from Allah.

The sunna of Prophet Muhammad (PBUH) regarding polygamy is that men should marry widows, divorcées, and slaves as second, third, or fourth wives to liberate them and provide them with the love, compassion, and maintenance that these women need. Of all the wives of the Prophet, Aisha, his second wife, was the only virgin he married. His first wife, Khadijah, was over twenty years older than he, and he worked under her, assisting with the running of her business until she saw the qualities she needed in a man in him, and they consummated their marriage. Prophet Muhammad's (PBUH) other wives included widows, divorcées, and slaves, whom he married so that they might have a "crown" and enjoy the love and compassion they needed.

Islam does not permit men to engage in unlawful sexual relationships. It says "marry," not have concubines. Marrying another wife extends beyond mere gratification. In Islam, the sexual bond between a man and his wife is regarded as a firm covenant that must not be betrayed. Islam strongly frowns at *zina* (fornication); no Muslim is to engage in any sexual activity unless he is lawfully licensed by marriage under the provisions of Islam. Therefore, Muslims who engage in illicit sexual relationships are not considered good ambassadors of Islam.

Through my interactions with various individuals and colleagues over the years, I've come to realize that insecurity sets in for Muslim women due to the possibility that a man can decide to marry another wife at any time. The Quran clearly states an important clause in Suratul An-Nisa verse 3, that if a man fears that he will not be just between two, three, or four wives, he should marry only one in order not to deviate from the right path. This raises the question of whether it's possible to be just or what exactly is being just. Being just entails emotional, psychological, financial, and every other form of commitment.

Indeed, many women willingly enter into marriages with married men whom they believe can provide them with happiness. It's also true that some polygamous families experience greater levels of happiness than monogamous ones. However, it's essential to acknowledge that there are polygamous households where women endure suffering. There is the misconception that women hold no value in Islam, but Prophet Muhammad (PBUH) had more than one wife, all of whom he cared for deeply, and they were the envy of the other women who lived in their era. Any man who enters into polygamy without being just to his wives is going to be doomed on judgment day.

I recollect a man popularly known as Baba Adini in Ode Aje. He was a wealthy merchant who invested his money in anything that would advance the course of Islam in the community. His magnificent house, encircled by high fences and two beautiful gates, as well as a long table that fed many in the area, both the relatively comfortable middle-class families and the indigent, were some of the signs that showcased his affluence.

Baba Adini spent most of his wealth on the propagation of Islam, and the frequent calling of his name after the Subh (dawn prayers) and Jummah prayers helped cement his name in the people's minds. One time, he single-handedly renovated the community's central mosque, financed the construction of tap water in the ablution quarters, replaced the mats with rugs, and donated new lamps to the mosque. These made the sheikh and alfas unanimously agree to bestow on him the title of the *Baba Adini* (father of religion) in acknowledgment of his selfless service to the Ummah.

The day Baba Adini received his title was filled with pomp and reverie as he spared no expense to satisfy all who attended. Amid the celebration, he announced his intention to take a new wife, to which the people had no objection. Given Baba Adini's wealthy status, the two wives would definitely have no issues getting whatever they needed. The people celebrated another milestone achieved by Baba Adini and sang his praises, calling him *okunrin mesan* (a real man).

But soon after Baba Adini married his second wife, the noise of fights between the two women started rocking the community. His wives were never at peace as they constantly fought for supremacy and his attention. Ironically, the only people who seemed to be at peace in the house were Baba Adini and his children from his first wife. He would laugh in the face of complaints and sympathy from outsiders regarding the discord in his household, reassuring them that things were going just as they should. His response often ended with the saying that it was normal for women to be at loggerheads because *obinrin ti ko jo wu, obe re ko le dun* (if a woman is not jealous, she will not make delicious meals)!

As the noise and sympathy from outsiders increased, Baba Adini made a decision that left everyone bewildered, including myself. He married another woman, making three wives. While the people found his action strange and believed he had just increased the heat in his home, it somehow paid off, as the noise from his wives reduced. Surprisingly, the first wife was happy about the new addition, believing that if the second wife were so special, their husband wouldn't have taken another wife. She allied with the third wife in a mentor-mentee sort of relationship, teaching her things about their husband and how to escape the mischief of the second wife.

Eventually, the people in the community began to see sense in Baba Adini's move and applauded his ingenuity in solving the troubles that had besieged his household; however, the majority of the women were against him. Those who praised Baba Adini did so because of the means he used to solve the brewing trouble. Some of them applauded him in his presence, and others just gossiped while working on the farm, in places of relaxation, or even at their palm wine joints.

During one of the drunken gossips at the palm wine joint, an intoxicated man gave his perspective on Baba Adini's actions, saying, "Baba Adini se ni omo ina laa n ran si ina," that is, "Baba Adini fought fire with fire." His drunken comrades bobbed their heads in agreement, with one of them remarking that no truer words had been spoken.

Three sayings encapsulate the reasons behind the breakdown of peace in Baba Adini's household. The first is that man is his own worst enemy; the second implies that giving a woman a taste of power can turn her into a tyrant; and the third, a new wife is always the apple of her husband's eye. Baba Adini lavished attention on his third wife, making himself his own worst enemy. The affection he showed her gave her a little power, which went into her head, and she became rude to her senior wives. Feeling on top of the world, she broke her alliance with the first wife and started to exhibit the behaviors that the first wife hated in the second wife. The new developments forced the first and second wives to become close so they could jointly tackle the third wife.

The two senior wives planned to reduce the affection Baba Adini had for his third wife. The first place they attacked was the kitchen because Baba Adini had delegated the preparation of his meals to his youngest wife alone, considering she was his favorite. At first, they would steal ingredients and utensils from the kitchen, leading to delays or substandard meals. It worked to an extent as Baba Adini started to complain about the third wife's cooking. The first and second wives were happy with their tricks, but even though their husbands nagged at the third wife, she still had him in her corner somehow. This pushed them to orchestrate a more severe attack to kill Baba Adini's love for the third wife.

On a particular day, when their husband had ulama visitors, the third wife had to make a larger meal than usual. Taking extra care, she ensured she had extra ingredients and utensils just in case the ones in the kitchen mysteriously disappeared as usual. After she finished cooking and confirmed everything was in order, she went to take a shower to freshen up before serving the guests. Immediately, her co-wives confirmed that she had started bathing; the first wife kept watch while the second wife quietly slipped into the kitchen to add salt to the soup.

In a scene reminiscent of a scripted drama, Baba Adini, his visitors, his children, and the first and second wives all simultaneously spat out their food as soon as they put a morsel of pounded yam immersed in sumptuous-looking vegetable soup into their mouths. Shocked by the unexpected saltiness, the third wife found herself at a loss for words, her fingers lingering at her mouth in disbelief. Baba Adini flew into a rage, repeatedly criticizing her for the disastrous meal she had prepared.

More noise erupted as the first and second wives took the chastisement off their husband's mouth, shouting at the top of their voices and accusing their co-wife of trying to kill their husband with overly salty food all because he had made her his favorite, and she thought she would inherit the larger share of his properties.

By the time the noise died down, the third wife had been reduced to tears. She couldn't comprehend what was happening because she was certain she had made a flawless dish and had even literally given herself a pat on the back before going in to clean herself up. But when her senior wives appeared with new meals for everyone to eat, she knew that she had been played. The new food that appeared almost immediately also made Baba Adini suspect that the salty food was a scheme by his older wives to discredit their rival, but he had no concrete evidence to back up his suspicion.

Seeing that Baba Adini seemed to have seen through their machinations, the first and second wives retreated into a temporary silence, discreetly planning their next move. They planned to attack their co-wife's personality and tarnish her image in such a way that their husband would be forced to send her packing. The best way to do this was by accusing her of adultery, as Islam frowns heavily on the act, and a husband must divorce and not remarry an unfaithful wife.

The two devious wives went to a mallam and brazenly leveled the accusation that the third wife had been seen in the custody of a young man, insinuating that she was involved in adultery. However, the mallam burst into laughter and asked if they were ready to receive eighty lashes of the whip. The mallam's question took aback the women until he explained to all those present how adultery is reported in Islam.

In Islam, leveling an accusation of adultery is no child's play, as it carries grievous consequences. Accusing a person of committing adultery requires not only witnessing the act firsthand but also the corroboration of three other people, none of whom must have prior knowledge of each other's discovery. Only then can an accusation be made, supported by the other three people who must share their account of the story.

In a case where there are not up to four people corroborating an allegation of adultery, all those who made the reports will receive eighty lashes of the whip as punishment, and their accusations will be considered false. Such measures are implemented to safeguard against destroying others' reputations at will using baseless accusations of adultery as a tool.

After his explanation, the Mallam asked the women again if they were still willing to level the allegations of adultery against their junior wife. Who would still want to go ahead and take eighty lashes? Their plans, having failed, the women returned home with their tails between their legs. Islam and its guidelines just saved a woman from her peers. Maybe the many rules and regulations in Islam are not bad after all; they have their advantages. Now caught in a quandary and not wanting to push their luck further to the extent of shooting themselves in the legs, the senior wives continued to engage in a relentless war of words with the third wife.

Baba Adini's house became ground zero for civil war. As the Yoruba proverb says, *b'omode ba subu, a wo iwaju, b'agba ba subu, a wo eyin wo*—when a child falls, he looks forward, but when an adult falls, he looks behind him to check what tripped him. Baba Adini had fallen and was now looking behind him, into his past, to seek a solution. His self-prescribed solution was to take on a fourth wife, with the hope that she would bring him solace and happiness amid the ongoing war among the other wives. It felt like a good plan to him, but the community was concerned for his well-being, fearing that he was compounding his woes.

Initially, a semblance of peace returned to his household; the first three wives sheathed their swords and began to monitor their new rival to know what kind of behaviors she would exhibit and to try to get her on their side. However, the third wife remained somewhat bitter that a new woman had taken over her cherished position, particularly after all the attacks she had endured from the older wives. She naturally resented the latest wife, but since she had betrayed the first wife earlier, she couldn't forge an alliance with her against the youngest wife. The only available ally she had in the house was the second wife, who shared her feelings about what it meant to lose the special spot.

As a newfound friendship blossomed between the second and third wives, the first wife felt a twinge of betrayal for the second time. Choosing to distance herself from the fourth wife, she remained neutral, portraying herself as a more mature woman since she was the eldest among them. Meanwhile, the second and third wives bonded to protect themselves from potential attacks from the first and fourth wives while also maintaining a readiness to attack both parties if necessary.

The fourth wife, having heard of the atrocities all the wives were capable of, came in battle-ready. With the first wife out of the competition for supremacy, the two-against-one battle started, and the second and third wives' energies were evenly matched by the fourth wife, who fought them pound for pound.

Baba Adini paid them no attention and would retreat to his private room whenever they started their quarrels. After a while, he noticed that the fights, even though they remained constant, now ended almost as soon as they started. Watching them out of his window one day, he noticed his first wife pacifying the other three women who were engaged in a war of insults and sending them to their rooms.

Impressed by her intervention, Baba Adini invited his first wife to his room for a private conversation. They reminisced about the good old days when she was the only woman in his life, and they had peace. Overwhelmed by remorse, Baba Adini apologized to her for ruining their beautiful relationship. After that night, he promised to right his wrongs and dedicate more of his time to her.

Predictably, this stopped the feud between the other wives, and they redirected their anger and frustration to their husband and the senior wife. The old couple cared less, focusing instead on building their broken relationship and fostering a cordial relationship among the children. Eventually, the other wives grew tired, and the three of them buried their hatchets, living peacefully under Baba Adini's patriarchal leadership and his first wife's matriarchal guidance.

Once again, Baba Adini's ingenuity in restoring peace within his household earned him accolades from the entire community, reaffirming his stature among those capable of navigating polygamy within the framework of Islamic teachings. In Islam, polygamy is permitted under specific conditions, with the provision that a man treats all his wives with fairness and equality. This includes providing emotional support, financial stability, and companionship to each wife equitably, without favoritism. Baba Adini's eventual ability to maintain harmony among his wives demonstrated his commitment to upholding these principles, winning him the affection and respect of the people around him.

However, several years later, I heard that Baba Adini's third wife left the marriage without a proper divorce. Feeling persistently threatened by the presence of those who had almost gotten her into trouble and not ready to share in their husband's seemingly equal love for all his wives, she left Ode Aje and moved to another part of Ibadan. Tales of her exploits in the city abounded, and she became known as Alhaja Money, engaging in acts that didn't match her religious title. She could afford all luxuries and indulged in moral laxities, such as drinking and fornicating.

Unfortunately, she wasn't the only one who engaged in such a lifestyle. Even today, one can find an "Alhaja Money" in many big cities, and their opulent lifestyles make it easy to notice them. Often separated from their husbands, these women seem to have transcended the traditional bounds of marriage. They are not ready to be "controlled" by a man, using their wealth to challenge patriarchal dominance. There are often rumors that they have eschewed marriage altogether and would rather pay young boys to keep their beds warm. This phenomenon reflects a growing trend of women rejecting traditional gender roles and asserting their independence in a male-dominated society.

In Islam, women are regarded as creations of Allah, just like men, and both of them are subject to restrictions and guidance, with none exempted from chastisement from Allah when they default. One of the most noticeable things about pious Muslim women in Nigeria is their devotion and adherence to the Islamic rules governing lifestyle, comportment, manner of dressing, and total obedience to religious laws. This includes a strong commitment to respecting male authority and embracing their roles as women in society.

After spending many years in Ode Aje with Baba Olopa, I experienced other cities and noticed that fewer restrictions were placed on women. Sometimes I attributed these loose restrictions to modernity and the influence of acculturation. I'm not trying to paint the rural areas as resistant to change but rather to highlight that the kind of polygamy practiced in the interior still places wives under the direct control and supervision of their husbands.

Aisha, for instance, had everything a woman could dream of. She was married to Alhaji Ibrahim, a wealthy businessman in Ibadan, and enjoyed a luxurious lifestyle. Her husband was loving and caring, but despite all her material blessings, Aisha had a deep longing in her heart that had remained unfulfilled. They had been married for five years, and she had been unable to conceive. She had sought medical help, *aajo* (traditional remedies), and even visited spiritual healers, but nothing seemed to work.

As time passed, Aisha's frustration became well known within the community. She felt as if she was living in a beautiful cage, unable to escape the emptiness consuming her, which turned into despair, and she became withdrawn and isolated. The more she tried to conceive, the more distant she felt from her husband, who appeared preoccupied with work and other interests.

As her struggle to conceive persisted and she became desperate for a solution, Aisha confided in her mother, who suggested that they visit an herbalist known for helping women with fertility issues. Aisha was hesitant at first, but her mother, a devotee of the Osun goddess, persuaded her to consult with Iya Osun, who was popular for her powerful herbal remedies that had helped many women conceive. After consulting the goddess, Iya Osun prescribed a special blend of herbs for Aisha, who was really hopeful that the herbs would work and that she'd finally fulfill her dream of becoming a mother.

However, when Ahaji Ibrahim learned of the visit, he was angry. He had always been skeptical of traditional medicine and saw it as a form of idolatry and associating partners with Allah (*shirk*). He refused to let Aisha take the herbs, and they got into a heated argument, leaving Aisha trapped between her desire to become a mother and her husband's unwillingness to try alternative treatments. She couldn't make decisions autonomously, as her husband's consent and approval were important.

This dynamic reflects broader societal norms and religious beliefs that often place women in subordinate roles to men. Surprisingly, the same Alhaji Ibrahim who had accused his wife of *shirk* was himself guilty of adultery. Not only had he impregnated their housemaid, but he also had several mistresses outside his marriage. This was a secret until one of the mistresses threatened to reveal herself and the child to his family. It was no empty threat as she eventually brought the child to Alhaji Ibrahim's house and announced him as the heir apparent.

Heartbroken and disillusioned by the hurt and betrayal she endured, Aisha took decisive action by filing for divorce and leaving her marital home. Upon relocating to Lagos, she made a firm resolve never to enter into another marriage. Instead, she faced her trading business and became a rich and popular Ankara merchant in Oke-Arin, Lagos. A few years later, she got pregnant with an alhaji whom she had met on one of her trips to hajj. The man was married and was not ready to take a second wife, so Aisha had her baby out of wedlock and became an "Alhaja Money."

Based on my experience and observations of various public lectures, programs, events, and activities within Muslim communities, it's evident that men predominantly assume leadership roles as leaders, spokespersons, lecturers, and teachers. This raises many questions as to why there are no women imams, muazzins, or even Quran scholars in Islamic societies.

Unlike their sisters in other religions, particularly Christianity, where women hold active leadership roles and positions as priests and founders, Muslim women are not regarded as qualified to lead prayers in the mosque or public praying grounds; instead, they are primarily assigned tasks such as cleaning and sweeping. But women in other faiths, including African traditional religion, hold significant leadership positions and actively participate in religious ceremonies such as leading processions to spiritual groves, shrines, or other places of worship, such as during the Osun-Osogbo festival.

Following the demise of a man or when he is incapacitated for work and provide for his family, the woman may be forced to go out to provide for her family while still wearing veils. It's common to see these women in the market hawking their wares on their head, sitting by the roadside or in stalls and shops just to make ends meet. Some choose to stay at home and engage in jobs like sewing or selling consumable foodstuff and other essentials, with the proceeds from the sale of these items used to take care of their family's needs.

I remember a wealthy polygamous Muslim family who lived in a large mansion in the heart of the bustling city of Ibadan. The patriarch of the family, Alhaji Malik, was a rich businessman who had amassed a great deal of wealth and property over the years. With three wives and ten children who all lived under the same roof, they shared the same amenities and enjoyed the opulent lifestyle provided by Alhaji Malik.

However, despite the family's fortune, not all the children were educated. Many of them expected to inherit their father's wealth, oblivious to the harsh reality that awaited them. The greatest shock of their life came when their father died, and his properties were divided. Only four of the children had attained a university education, while another four had learned different artisanal occupations. The remaining two were a nuisance in the community, eventually becoming thugs' lords and causing havoc wherever they went. Even before his death, Alhaji Malik made repeated attempts to make them change their ways and return home, but they turned deaf ears to his pleas.

The peace and harmony that once graced Alhaji Malik's household crashed with his sudden demise. He left behind a vast estate comprising several businesses, properties, and investments valued at millions of dollars. Immediately after he was laid to rest, his family, particularly his extended relatives, began to fight over their share of Alhaji Malik's properties, not caring about his wives, who had recently become widows.

Widowhood rites vary across religions and cultures, with each culture or tradition being observed and mandated for the woman. In Nigeria, different ethnic groups have their unique widowhood rites, with some mixed with relevant religious guidelines. For Muslim widows, the period of mourning or waiting is mandated for them due to several reasons.

Typically, this period may last three to four months if the woman is not pregnant. For any widow who is discovered to be pregnant at the time of her husband's death, the mourning period extends beyond the four months mandated for non-pregnant women. The pregnant widow must wait till she gives birth before she is permitted to conclude her mourning period. During this time, adornments such as fragrances, jewelry, makeup, or beauty products of any kind are strictly prohibited. Instead, the widow must simply dress to reflect her status as a widow, regardless of her wealth or social status.

One of the primary reasons for the mourning period observed by widows is to uphold the late man's honor and dignity. Any Muslim widow who attempts to engage in social activities soon after her husband's demise is met with reproach, not only because of the newfound responsibility thrust on her shoulders or the need to provide for her children or other dependent relatives in the home but also to honor her late husband.

However, adhering to this tradition can pose significant challenges, especially for a woman who has a full-time job. It's almost impossible for a career woman to stay away from work for the three to four months period required of her to mourn her husband. Moreover, the enforced isolation and seclusion may not be too beneficial for a grieving widow as these can exacerbate feelings of loneliness, despair, and psychological alienation. Such emotional turmoil may degenerate into physical and mental problems like detachment, hallucinations, illnesses, and emotional instability.

During this period of mourning, the place of the male gender is elevated, underscoring the patriarchal structure within the African society. The same stringent conditions expected of widows do not seem to apply to men who lose their wives. And even if widowers are expected to live a certain way after their wives' passing, it appears to be less serious and important compared to the expectations placed on women.

In contrast to the expectations placed on widows, Muslim men are often encouraged to remarry if they don't already have other wives, as it is believed that their needs must be tended to. Upon the death of a woman, the man is free from any obligations to the dead wife except taking care of the children, if they have any. A man is scarcely mandated to mourn his wife beyond the basic initial display of shock and sorrow at her passing.

In Alhaji Malik's household, however, the mandatory period of mourning was ignored by the women when his relatives stepped in to claim his property. His first wife, Alhaja Zainab, claimed that she was entitled to the largest share of the estate, citing her long-standing marriage to her husband and that she had borne him the most children. Fatimah, the second wife, argued that she deserved a larger share of the estate because she was Alhaji's favorite wife and was with him throughout his illness. At the same time, the third wife, Aisha, who had only been married to Malik for a few years, wanted an equal share alongside the others.

The children were also divided. Some of them took sides with their mothers, while some insisted on an equal distribution of the estate among the wives and children. The dispute became so heated that the family members began to hurl accusations and insults at one another, leading to resentment and malice.

As the dispute dragged on, the family's financial situation began to deteriorate. Alhaji Malik's businesses and properties were not being managed properly, which resulted in huge financial losses. Realizing that their disputes were tearing them apart and that they might no longer have anything to share from their patriarch's property, they sought the advice of a trusted Islamic scholar.

After hearing their case, the scholar reminded the family that Alhaji Malik had left behind a will that clearly outlined how his estate should be divided. According to the will, each wife was entitled to an equal share of what remained after a portion had been given to charity. Similarly, the children were to receive an equal share, with the remainder given out as *sadaqah*.

Though initially shocked by the outcome of the will, Alhaji Malik's wives and children eventually acknowledged his right to make such decisions, and with the guidance of the Islamic scholar, they were able to settle their disputes and divide the estate according to the late man's wishes. This conciliatory process not only brought closure to the internal strife within the family but also diffused tensions among Alhaji Malik's extended family members, who had initially been poised for conflict with the widows and children of their late brother.

As depicted in the Quran, the ideal Muslim wife must be submissive to her husband by doing what he wants and avoiding things he detests. She must seek his permission before making any major decisions and must keep him informed of all her plans. At the same time, she is in charge of managing the household and taking care of the family. Her husband is the sustainer and provider, ensuring her happiness and well-being. The Quran describes a woman as a delicate being and the other half of her husband, created from his ribs, and also cautions against being overly harsh or overly lenient with women.

Indeed, the rules of behavior for a Muslim woman are all well known. She must be chaste and reserve her affections solely for her husband while also embodying refinement and decency in her conduct. Ironically, it's not just the "Alhaja Moneys" of this world who are regarded as not being submissive to men. Many women, regardless of their social standing, may negate the virtues expected of an ideal Muslim wife, with some not even living with their husbands anymore.

I once worked as a secretary to one Alhaja Money in my family at a young age. This particular woman was in a relationship with different men, a fact I got to know because I helped her write letters to numerous men, and I read their replies to her, as she could neither read nor write. Very often, she would say, *mi o le ni obo n'idi k'ebi ma pa mi*, meaning, "I can't have a vagina and continue to endure hunger." It took a while before I could comprehend what she meant, but as I continued to help her write and read the letters, the truth gradually dawned on me.

Even before the advent of Islam in Yorubaland, the region had its intricate social system. When Islam came, its preachers didn't immediately condemn every existing Yoruba custom; instead, it gave room for "hybridizing." Consequently, a Yoruba Muslim household would have some representations of Yoruba culture in their way of life. What distinguishes one household from another is the extent to which the impact of culture and religion influence their way of life, which then shapes the differences in their interpretations of the rulings of the Quran and the justifications for their practices.

I didn't only read about some parts of Yoruba communities where women had limited or no rights, but I also witnessed how these women were relegated to the kitchen. Often, in the rural areas, girls weren't considered to require formal education or training like the male children did. However, times have evolved, and now girls can enjoy privileges once exclusively reserved for boys.

Patriarchal structures are deeply ingrained in traditional Yoruba marriages. Yoruba men exhibit some common characteristics for which Islam was not responsible. These characteristics stem from the long-existing sociocultural patterns rather than religious doctrines. For instance, marriage had its social structure, and polygamy was a common practice among Yoruba men long before the incursion of foreign religions into their society, although many didn't have the resources to engage in the practice.

The number of wives a man had was also a pointer to his social status, affluence and wealth, and perceived masculinity. This was common in Ode Aje, Ibadan, and visible in all Yoruba societies. Hardly would you find a titled man without two or more wives. The women were not seen as "other halves" but rather as possessions and means of procreation. As long as a man provided food, clothing, and shelter, his responsibilities were deemed fulfilled, and he could marry as many wives as possible.

Respect and submissiveness from women are highly valued in Yoruba society. Elders are expected to be respected, with women expected to kneel before them and men to prostrate when greeting or addressing them. Children and those who are middle-aged are not even expected to talk in the presence of their elders. Even when it's obvious that the elders are in the wrong, the younger ones should never challenge them. Staring right back at elders and meeting their gaze when being corrected or admonished is a grave offense, likened to stripping them naked and striking them with a rod.

These customs, among others, epitomize the cultural norms of Yoruba society and also operate within the structure of a marriage. Usually, husbands are older than their wives, and even in rare cases where they are of the same age group, the husband is still accorded the highest level of respect. He dominates the life of his wife, with expectations that she kneels before him as necessary.

His food should be timely, laundry should be done diligently, and his sexual needs must be met as he wants.

A woman is always to massage her husband's ego and never make him feel less of a man. In instances of disagreements, the wife usually ends up taking the blame and rendering apologies. She has no right to fight back or raise her voice at her husband, to say nothing of asserting her independence, as such actions would invite societal scorn and judgment in the neighborhood. Endurance, tolerance, and perseverance are qualities expected of women, while men are expected to assert control and dominance.

However, with the advent of education and globalization, women are increasingly finding their voices and asserting their rights within marriage and society, which, nonetheless, doesn't completely eradicate patriarchal beliefs and practices. While some women have embraced the transformative power of education, others remained bound by the rigid sociocultural norms of Yoruba tradition.

Remarkably, the issue of divorce is not exclusive to Islam. Although the Christian religion forbids polygamy, even when many of them are from polygamous families, Christian marriages also experience divorce. Some of the divorce cases among Christians are due to infidelity, along with issues of mistreatment and abuse by the husband. In Islam, a man may initiate divorce, but he is given two chances of reconciliation with his wife. For a Muslim woman, however, it's almost unheard of or inconceivable that she would ask for a divorce, as society frowns against a woman initiating such a decision. It's not the same for Christians, where a Christian woman can initiate divorce or separation from her husband.

Even though Islam doesn't condemn polygamy, Yoruba Muslim women often find it difficult to share their husbands with other women, which can lead to marital conflicts in the home. As a result of the permissive attitude toward men having many wives, women are pressured to accept the men's infidelity. More often than not, women are at the receiving end of their husbands' indiscretions because society, aided by religion, has given men the freedom to have as many women as they want, with crises occasionally erupting because of their unfaithfulness.

For women, divorce often becomes the last resort after several attempts to endure stifling and abusive marriages, whether in Islam or Christianity. The Yoruba culture puts a lot of pressure and responsibilities on the woman, with sayings like *obinrin so 'wa nu, o l'oun o l'ori oko*, which implies that a woman's bad character is often responsible for her inability to find a man who would marry her.

Society expects a woman to endure and hang on even in an abusive relationship. The Yoruba term *ilemosu* is a derogatory aspersion of a woman who returned to her parents after marriage. A woman might even be blackmailed into staying in an abusive relationship because of her children! Thus, among the Yoruba, divorce has serious consequences for the woman, as she may be tagged a divorcée and have trouble remarrying. Some of them do not even attempt to remarry because they want to enjoy the freedom that comes with not being accountable to any man.

Even when the man initiates the divorce, the woman often bears the brunt of the stigma associated with a failed marriage, which both sides should typically share. Women are traditionally considered the better caregivers of the two sexes because of several physical and psychological attributes unique to the female gender. This is one of the reasons society and culture place so much responsibility on women to be wives and mothers to care for their homes and families.

I've come to realize that women are often overworked and saddled with the overwhelming responsibilities of nurturing the children, cooking, cleaning, and maintaining the home. Men neglect these responsibilities, believing their sole duty is to provide financially for their family, which leads to the creation of gender-based roles in the home.

Additionally, there exists a societal preference for male children, so the birth of a boy is more celebrated than that of a girl. Several Muslim women have had to accept the arrival of a concubine into their homes because they could not produce a male child. This is not restricted to Islam, though, because society elevates the male child above the female child. When the new wife gives birth to a male child, the previous wife with female children may be neglected and made to fend for herself and her children.

Furthermore, gender disparities are evident in the raising of children. When chores are divided, the girls are pushed toward home management duties, while boys may either be given other tasks outside the home or allowed to play as they want.

This inequality extends to the distribution of inheritance among the children in Muslim homes in Yorubaland. Muslim women do not receive an equal division of the estate or property with male relatives. One explanation for this unequal treatment is that women remain responsible for their husbands, while men have greater responsibilities. Some even hold the notion that women are not entitled to any part of their father's estate as they have changed their last names to that of their husbands.

An Alhaja Money represents women who became rich through personal achievements or after they may have gotten a portion of their father's estates after his demise. Their financial independence enables them to sustain themselves without relying on a man, and their ego will not make them see marriage as a necessity.

There are many "Alhaja Moneys" who are divorcées and have amassed substantial wealth from previous marriages, successfully establishing themselves in their own right. Upon closer examination, one may find that behind every Alhaja Money are probably many alhajis as their fathers, husbands, or even concubines.

As mere mortals, we must patiently await the Day of Judgment to know those who will receive Allah's mercy. It's on that sacred day that the true essence of individuals' deeds and intentions will be revealed.

CHAPTER EIGHT

In the City of Double Conscience

For Afonja or Alimi?
Ask your conscience
The bond of culture
I heard it is of Garin Alimi; ask Alaafin
Ilorin mesu jamba?
Ilorin our Makkah
Where is your conscience?
I will tell my stories of a city
It could be of love or hatred
In Ilorin
I saw no masquerade, but angels in veils
I asked, why are they wearing masks?
I got a reply. Religion!
Is a masquerade not for religion?
I got a reply in a deep voice,
Ooooooooo, mo n je!
I asked Afonja, where is your conscience?
Are you for us or for the emirate?
Strings interlaced on the head in place of *bante*, where is your conscience?
A city far from hell, close to paradise
Your offspring are scattered between tribes; where is your conscience?
I got a reply! It is double!
A sounding *bata* of clashes, accompanied by *algaita* from the emirate
Where is your conscience?
I'm a traveler, walking down the path of memory lane
I am with my conscience!

Having traveled far and wide across Yorubaland, I've observed how multiple cultures align. Anyone familiar with Yoruba or Oyo history can likely tell you how Ilorin came to be. One prevailing narrative is that Islamic ideals became the cornerstone of Ilorin's supremacy and have continued to serve as the fundamental principles that bind the people together. Ilorin is the city of complicated stories. One event, ten different stories, and several variants to each story converge on the narrative that Ilorin was later inhabited by Yoruba, Fulani, and Hausa, with Islam as the predominant religion.

One prevalent version of the Ilorin story is that the Alaafin of the Old Oyo Empire sent his war general, Afonja, to conquer Ilorin for the crown of Oyo. However, when he reached Ilorin, Afonja betrayed the Alaafin, declaring himself king and launching attacks on some towns under Oyo's control with the support of Alimi, a Fulani scholar. Afonja chose not to attack Ilorin because it was his maternal hometown; instead, he enlisted Alimi's help to join him in waging a war against the Alaafin.

The end to these stories is that after Afonja betrayed the Alaafin, there was another round of betrayal between Afonja and Alimi, leading to Afonja's ousting and Islam gaining supremacy over the Òrìṣà religion in a Yoruba town. Ilorin became a melting pot for Yoruba, Hausa, and Fulani cultures, and they blended through marriage and acculturation that developed over generations of living together in the same space.

In Ilorin, people spoke different languages, but the majority understood Yoruba, often with interpreters available for those who didn't understand the language. However, Ilorin is not just about the diversity of languages but about the ambiguities in the meanings of words and sentences. Expressions like "I'm coming" may mean the person is leaving, while "I'm not hungry" might imply a desire to share a meal.

Ilorin is a city of double scripts, where you must relate gestures to the words—verbal affirmations may mask underlying negations through the subtle movement of the legs and eyes. Sayings like, "It's difficult to wake someone who is pretending to be asleep," "A crook can swear by the Quran," and "If you sold goods at Ilorin and you were not careful, you might collect your money in small rocks," all speak to the city's reputation for cunning and the importance of being vigilant and discerning in one's dealings.

In contemporary times, Ilorin has been a serene environment, our "Nigerian Mecca." Unlike in bustling cities like Lagos and Ibadan—no insults intended—you enjoy relative peace and safety in Ilorin. I enjoy winding down in Ilorin with my friends. One of the many cultural shocks in Ilorin is the Fulani-looking people who speak fluent Yoruba, or people whom you believe are Yoruba seamlessly speaking Fulfulde, or those whom you can't discern whether they are Yoruba or Fulani by their looks.

The lines between the different cultures have become so thin that they are almost invisible. I would give credit to interethnic marriages and Islam for this fusion. Even though the people did well relating to each other despite their different origins and had become bonded through marriage and religion, this didn't mean there were no sparks or tensions sometimes that threatened to pull them apart.

Following Sheikh Alimi's victory and the establishment of the Frontier Emirate of the Sokoto Caliphate, Ilorin became the home of diverse Yoruba groups and a growing multiethnic, multicultural, Islamic melting pot. As a result, Ijesa soldiers, who still possess the ancient title of *Ajiya Ijesa*, were entrusted with guarding the Emir of Ilorin's flanks during all of the conflicts the Ilorin people engaged in throughout the nineteenth century.

In the 1970s, during one of my visits to my uncle's place in Ilorin, we had to assist his wife in purchasing some foodstuff from the market. Everything was going smoothly, and we were haggling and making jokes with each other while the woman selling her goods to us made playful remarks about our "boss" (my uncle's wife) getting angry if we returned home late or didn't buy all she wanted.

However, our fun was unexpectedly cut short when a man stealthily walked into the crowd and attacked a Yoruba man with a dagger. We didn't see when he slashed him, but my uncle and I saw the gash on him and how blood gushed out of him. Before the man's body could hit the ground, his assailant tried to cut him again, but what appeared to be a thousand hands grabbed and disarmed him. We watched in horror as people around, both Yoruba and Fulani, rallied together to carry the victim to a hospital. It was a novel experience for me, as my memory of Ilorin was that of peace.

My uncle suggested that we head home with our foodstuffs, but I was determined to know the reason for such a cruel act in Ilorin. I told my uncle I would like to follow the crowd to where the man would be treated, hoping to pick up some gossip about the incident. But my uncle warned me not to go, explaining that if the victim of the attack died, a fight could break out between the Yoruba and Fulani. His explanation took me off guard a bit. Could interethnic clashes happen between people who are so closely bonded?

Seeing that I had made up my mind to know the beginning of the story from the end, my uncle warned me to be careful and very vigilant and to run home at the first sign of trouble. I hurried after the people, and we didn't walk for too long before the victim was taken into a house. I was surprised because I had assumed he was being taken to a clinic. Inside the house, the occupants quickly attended to him and started doing their best to save his life, while those of us who were sympathizers and gossip enthusiasts waited outside.

It didn't take long for people to start forming huddles, and the gossip began to seep out. I squeezed myself into one of the huddles that looked like the real thing, because why was I endangering my precious life if not for this gossip? The gossip peddler among us said Ali, who I later deduced was the assailant, overdid things and had a terrible temper because the person he had attacked was a family member of his ex-wife, her cousin who had come to visit.

I wondered why Ali would attack someone from his ex-wife's family without reason. As if the man behind me heard my silent question, he muttered that Ali definitely stabbed the guy out of jealousy, and he probably didn't even know he was his ex-wife's relative. Without still voicing my thoughts, my fellow gossip-monger continued his story, explaining to no one in particular how Ali never allowed any man near his wife, Adedoyin, when they were married, which was the primary reason for their divorce.

There were sighs and silent prayers for the wounded young man, and a few people asserted that Ali would be in so much trouble if the man died of the injuries. With that, the gossip huddle started to disperse, which should have been all for me, too, but I didn't follow them all the way to get half of the story. I followed the fellow who spoke about Ali and his wife. He looked like he knew more, but my problem was that he looked more Fulani than Yoruba. What if I tried to poke-nose, and he chose to defend his kinsman and harm me? "Life itself is a risk" was the statement I used to dispel the stern warning my uncle gave me before I left him. What he said proverbially was, *Má ru ẹrù ẹlẹ́rù kó fa tì ẹ dání*, an adage used to caution people like me from wading into things that do not concern them.

I followed my self-appointed informant to where he wanted to make some purchases. Standing behind him as if waiting for my turn, I expressed my sadness about the situation and hope for the wounded man's recovery. This man then bought a cigarette, which surprised me because he looked too Muslim to be a smoker. He casually slipped a stick between his lips with one hand while his other hand delved into the left pocket of his trousers. I had heard gists about how the Fulani people could be temperamental, especially when provoked, so I took a few steps back so I could give him a head start just in case he was about to bring out a dagger. To my relief, when his hand emerged, it was only holding a lighter for his cigarette.

After taking a long drag of his cigarette and exhaling smoke from his mouth and nostrils, he settled on a nearby bench. My first instinct was to sit beside him, but I wasn't sure of his stance with me, so I opted to stand instead. I subtly shifted to the side, allowing the shop owner to attend to her legitimate customers.

"Only God will help Ali because if that young man died, there would be trouble in the community."

"Alhamdulillah!" I yelled in my mind when the man on the bench spoke.

Time to get the full details! I asked the woman selling to give me a bottle of beer and asked my newfound friend if he would also like one.

Sitting together on the bench, holding a bottle of beer, he began the story from the prologue. Ali, a young Fulani chap, had captured the heart of Adedoyin, a beautiful Yoruba lady. While Adedoyin's mother supported the union, alluding to Ali's moral uprightness and perseverance, her husband fiercely resisted the union on cultural grounds. Eventually, he was overpowered by the combined efforts of his wife and daughter, and he reluctantly agreed to give his beautiful daughter out in marriage to a man not from his people.

Although the marriage started well, the joy of the newlyweds didn't take long to dissipate. Adedoyin thought that praying five times daily was all that made one a Muslim. She couldn't adjust to the many rules her husband was imposing on her, such as prayers to make before wearing clothes, before entering the toilet, and the special bath after sex. This was particularly annoying because her husband was notorious when it came to bedroom affairs, and she needed to take a bath each time before she could perform her next salat.

In addition, Adedoyin was required to wear the hijab at all times in public and was restricted from public places unless her husband was with her. Before long, her love for Ali faded out, and she felt cramped. She took her complaints to her father, who was happy that his daughter had seen the light. Adedoyin's father sent for Ali to speak to him about giving his daughter some freedom, even threatening that he would take his wife from him if she ever reported Ali again.

Upon returning home, Ali unleashed his anger on Adedoyin, beating her to a stupor and commanding that she was no longer permitted to leave the compound, warning her of further punishments if she disobeyed. A scared Adedoyin restricted herself to the compound as her husband had instructed. She suffered in silence and regretted not listening to her father.

The situation reached a breaking point when Ali married another wife, a Fulani lady. Adedoyin's father heard of the development but bided his time, not wanting to be tagged a home wrecker. However, fueled by the gossip from people around the young couple, he eventually sent his people to bring his daughter back home.

Ali showed up at his in-law's place the second day to get back his wife, only to be informed by her father that their marriage was over. As Adedoyin had expressed her desire to end her marriage and her father had concurred, the union between her and her husband was deemed nullified. Ali was amazed by the new development and refused to agree, saying that was not how divorce was done in Islam, but he was whisked away from his father-in-law's compound amid his protests and curses.

At this point, I looked down and saw that my newfound companion had downed four bottles of beer, with the fifth one halfway finished in his hand, while I struggled with my first bottle of beer. Silently, I prayed that I still had enough cash in my pocket to avoid any embarrassment from this stony-hearted woman I knew was listening to the story.

Continuing the story, my friend detailed how Ali's behavior spiraled out of control from the day he was whisked away from Adedoyin's house. He became a madman, spending his days obsessively tailing his ex-wife and attacking any man she was seen with, accusing him of trying to take his wife.

Despite several warnings and reports to the head of the Fulani in the community to get Ali to stay off Adedoyin and her people, his attacks continued, leading the Yoruba community to believe that the Fulani people were supporting their own. This thought was further strengthened by Ali's last two attacks, in which, after beating the men talking to his ex-wife, some Yoruba boys gathered and beat him to a pulp.

Following this incident, the somewhat nonfunctioning Fulani leadership swiftly engaged with Yoruba leaders to complain about the attack on Ali. This enraged the Yoruba youths, who questioned whether the Fulani were blind when Ali attacked innocent people with impunity.

My friend ended his story by saying that we should expect trouble from the Yoruba community, especially if the guy Ali had daggered died. According to him, a fight was yet to break out because the majority of the Yoruba youths were waiting at the place where their person was being treated. Moreover, the Fulani around whisked Ali away to safety before the Yoruba youth could get to him.

As I looked beside me, I noticed the shop owner had packed all her goods and was requesting payment from me. She confirmed the possibility of a fight breaking out and advised that anybody who valued their safety should be indoors by now. It dawned on me why my uncle didn't come along with me.

I reached into my pocket, relieved to find just enough money to pay for our drinks and transport me home. To my dismay, however, this woman didn't give me my change, adding the cost of the pack of cigarettes my strange friend had purchased to my bill. I looked back to ask if he could pay for his cigarettes, as I didn't offer to buy that for him, but he was gone by then.

Frustrated, I muttered to myself, "*Kai!* Is this why they call Ilorin people *Ilorin mesu jamba*? Because this man just did me *ijamba*." How would I get home?

As I started to find my way home, "Walk a little, run a little" was the mantra I applied before everywhere became dark. I found myself praying fervently for the wounded man to survive for my sake, perhaps even more than his family and friends who were with him. I was quite far from my uncle's place, had no money for transportation, and was unfamiliar with the neighborhood.

It was pitch dark, but I trudged on until I could recognize my uncle's house and knocked on the door, which was opened by the angry-looking older man who refused to be bribed by my mischievous smile. Even his wife gave me an apprehensive look when I entered. I was anxious to relay the story my informant had told me, eager to score a cheap point against my uncle as having access to updated information about Ali and his exploits.

Before I could start talking, however, my uncle informed me that the assaulted man was in a critical condition, with a slim chance of survival due to the severity of the injury. After this news broke out, enraged Yoruba youths targeted some Fulani households in that area, trying to locate those who aided Ali's escape. In the ensuing chaos, a few Fulani people were attacked, and their properties were destroyed.

"You are lucky to have made it back home safely. If the Fulani had started a reprisal attack, we would probably not be having this conversation," my uncle concluded and walked into his bedroom, leaving me in my terrified state.

I sat there thanking my stars and marveling at the rapid spread of news, especially bad news.

As anticipated, a fight broke out on the second day between Yoruba and Fulani youths. I sneaked out of the house to our neighbor's, whose two-story building, with the second floor at decking level, provided an elevated vantage point for observing the unfolding violence. There were other people there who, like myself, only wanted to witness the fight without participating.

On the streets, boys chased each other with broken bottles, machetes, daggers, and other sharp weapons. Some Yoruba boys wielded *bante*—a Yoruba-charmed weapon that can render anybody useless in one hit. The user just needs to beat you with it, and you slump, faint, lose your senses, or even worse, die.

We watched in horror as a Yoruba man casually knocked two Fulani boys out with his charm. Though I didn't support his actions, I admired his ingenuity in not inflicting bodily injury on his victims. As the court had no means to act on metaphysical weapons, he would probably spend less time in jail if caught, unlike the other boys. When he suddenly dropped to the floor, I thought he had mistakenly hit himself with his weapon, but upon closer observation, we saw a Fulani guy behind him, swinging something overhead just like the *bante* that the now fallen Yoruba man had had earlier.

I couldn't hold back my shock, which I expressed aloud. My neighbor explained to me that the Yoruba guy was hit with a *tira*, which are powerful words from the Quran made into a small sewn leather and used as a protective charm or for attacks. I stood there with my mouth opened—so, Muslims too, have their *jazz!*

Suddenly, we heard the sound of a police siren from down the road, and immediately the street became empty, leaving the fallen Yoruba man. A policeman stooped close to him, and I assumed he was trying to find out what had happened. After a few minutes, the policeman beckoned his colleague, who came to join him to lift the Yoruba man into the backseat of the police vehicle. Realizing that the show was over, we dispersed from the deck one after the other.

Afterward, we heard that the chief superintendent of police in charge of the area invited the Yoruba and Fulani leaders to a meeting and urged them to call their youths to order, warning that anybody caught disturbing the peace of the community would be arrested and severely dealt with.

A few days later, when it looked like some normalcy had returned, mostly because the man Ali attacked was responding to treatment, I left Ilorin before the police could profile me and arrest me as part of the Yoruba youths, causing havoc. At that time, I didn't know it would be one of the best decisions I ever made.

When I later asked my uncle about the aftermath of the incident, he disclosed that the situation got worse shortly after I left. Both the Yoruba and Fulani were still smarting from their loss of property and injuries sustained in the clashes sparked by the Ali incident when another conflict erupted.

A Yoruba man had fatally shot a cow belonging to a Fulani herder. The man had warned the herder several times about his cattle trespassing on his farmland and killing his crops, but the Fulani herder had turned a blind eye to the complaints. This time, however, the frustrations from the earlier clash fueled his anger, and instead of talking to the herder as usual, he picked up his *dane* gun and shot the cow. The furious herder approached the Yoruba man, who threatened to shoot him, too, if he didn't leave his farmland.

Seeking intervention, the herder took his complaints to the Fulani leaders, who met with the Yoruba leaders to settle the new crisis amicably. But because the Fulani had frustrated all efforts to locate Ali and make him pay for the life-threatening injury he inflicted on their person, the Yoruba elders turned them away, instead emphasizing that they should ensure their cattle didn't trespass into Yoruba-owned farmlands.

Returning home embarrassed but reluctant to initiate a fight, the Fulani herders asked their youths to release their cattle so they could roam freely.

The next day, chaos ensued as the streets and roads were filled with untended cattle. While killing one cow might not ignite a crisis, killing multiple animals would ultimately lead to a local war. Yoruba farmers found themselves powerless to stop the animals from encroaching on their farms, trampling on their crops, and destroying their lands.

Now totally helpless and frustrated, the Yoruba leaders approached the head of the Fulani and asked him to call their cattle to order. However, the Fulani leaders dismissed their concerns, claiming that the cows didn't understand Fulfulde, their variety of the Fulani language. Enraged by this direct insult, the Yoruba elders left without a word but with their next line of action clear to them. They announced within the Yoruba community that their people should remain indoors the following day and selected a few of them to hatch what I called a heinous plan.

Under the cover of darkness, the selected youths went to the Yoruba-owned farms and sprayed the crops with poison. Over the next two days, the Fulani continued to let their cattle roam freely and wreak havoc on the farms. Meanwhile, the Yoruba people remained in their homes and didn't make an appearance, giving the impression that the Fulani had gained the upper hand.

The Fulani knew they were in trouble on the fourth day when many of their cattle started to drop dead. They began quick and intense treatments for the surviving ones, sure that the Yoruba must have had something to do with it, but lacked concrete evidence to prove their case. To worsen their pain, they could not start a fight without risking police troubles, so they went to the police chief to file a report accusing the Yoruba of killing their cows.

In desperate need of a solution, before both parties took laws into their own hands and started another communal war, leaders of both groups were summoned to a meeting with the chief of police. In that meeting, the Yoruba leaders claimed innocence, stating that they had been hiding indoors since the Fulani unleashed their cattle upon them. They maintained that they were being falsely accused even though the Fulani had been troubling them, and they couldn't do anything because they couldn't fight cows, and they were heeding the police warning against fighting.

After hearing from both groups, the police dispersed them and urged them to maintain peace while they investigated the matter.

My conversation with my uncle must have lasted over an hour, and all I could deduce from the story was that these people had just fought a silent war between themselves, and the Yoruba had won with their natural cunning behavior. Realizing the severity of the situation my uncle had just described, I was happy that I left Ilorin when I did. With the imposed curfew and severe food scarcity caused by the destruction of farmlands and the death of cattle, I wouldn't have found it funny at all because I don't joke with food.

One of the fundamental characteristics of the Ilorin people is that they are deeply rooted in Islamic principles. Ilorin strikes me as an Islamic city, perhaps a place with two consciences! Its history of double conscience, whether rooted in "Garin Alimi" or "Ilorin Afonja," sheds light on why it operates under an emir-led Emirate Council. Within the Sokoto Caliphate, the Emir of Ilorin holds the eighth or ninth position in the north. When the people of Ilorin come together, they represent diverse ethnic backgrounds. Some have these facial markings indicating their ancestry, but they are all bound by Islam. I see Ilorin as crucial to the propagation of Islam and its philosophical system among the Yoruba. The Ilorin people are esteemed as leaders among Yoruba Muslims in the realms of both religion and Islamic education.

Growing up, I could relate to the idea that some Ilorin military triumphs during intra/interethnic wars, among other things, demonstrated a high level of proficiency in the Islamic esoteric sciences. I will not debate which of the two foreign religions first arrived in Yorubaland. Nevertheless, it's widely acknowledged that Islam arrived in Yorubaland before Christianity, but because the Yoruba people have a humanistic tendency to resist change, Islam faced fierce resistance. Islamic ideas were not novel to the populace, and even when Christianity arrived, its faithful actively pursued their efforts to convert the Yoruba. Islam's earlier entrance into the region was matched by Christianity's rapid growth (in terms of converts) within a short period, aided by the support of the British colonial government, which helped the missionaries influence a large number of people.

The development of Ilorin as a prominent Muslim city and a stronghold of Islamic learning was greatly influenced by the efforts of Islamic scholars, who have always been at the forefront of Islam. Ilorin's authorities focused on establishing the city as a Muslim state within the Sokoto Caliphate, eventually elevating it to the status of an emirate. To enhance the legitimacy of the city and its rulers as the guardians of Islam, they sponsored the settlement of scholars from Hausaland and Borno. Many of these experts lived there and started schools, making Ilorin the center of study for Muslims of Yoruba descent.

I know Ilorin came to be referred to as "Garin Alimi" or "the town of Alimi" and also as "Ilorin Afonja" or "Ilorin of Afonja," both names carrying unique historical significance and depicting this double conscience! Soon after, Shaykh Salih (Alimi), the Fulani nomadic Muslim teacher from the north, arrived in Ilorin. His successors quickly established an Islamic State in Ilorin and its surroundings.

Originally a military camp of the Oyo Empire, Ilorin's military power was a significant factor in the eventual collapse of the old Oyo Empire in the 1830s. This led to the displacement of large sections of the population and sparked decades of intra-Yoruba wars throughout the nineteenth century. Consequently, many survivors of the old Oyo Empire considered Ilorin an enemy and unsuccessfully tried to undermine its growing military and political influence, thus contributing to local conflict.

The dissemination of Islamic knowledge, which had previously been exclusively preserved for a few scholarly lineages, became more widespread and eventually systematized within the city. Even the youngest of their children were often well versed in memorizing the Quran.

Scholars who left Ilorin for other Muslim regions frequently returned with new teaching strategies, which were subsequently introduced throughout the Yoruba region. Islam remains the main identifier for most Ilorin people despite the diverse ethnic backgrounds within the population. During my sojourn to learn more and witness how Islam was practiced in Ilorin, I discovered the emergence of several pedagogical traditions that flourished there, brought in from other areas of the region by those scholars who had learned from other Islamic nations.

In my quest to understand some of these practices and not rely on the informal *ile kewu*, I interacted with students of such institutions to learn about their experiences and the structures of the institutions. The first one of them who became my friend was Quyyum, who shared his remarkable journey from aspiring to be a footballer to ending up in the formal madrassa. He said the last day he missed madrassa for joining a football training in the neighborhood was one of the days he'd never forget, as he was severely punished for it for weeks. Ilorin society is such that a child's refusal to acquire Islamic knowledge is often perceived as disobedience. Quyyum later became a highly revered Imam in Ilorin, fulfilling his parents' wishes, particularly his father's.

I also met Tajudeen in Ilorin after Quyyum. Even though they were from different backgrounds, their concepts of Islam were not different. I understand that different Islamic societies exist in Ilorin, just as in other places, but this does not affect what the people see as right or wrong; the Qur'an is the same as one.

Tajudeen was fondly called Taju because the Yoruba people have a way of shortening or localizing Islamic names. Even when you find some of these names funny, they hold deep significance for those who answer them. In Ibadan, when a lady tells you her name is Shakira, and you call her Shaki (internal organ), you should be ready to face whatever consequences that may arise. If she is not hot-tempered, you'd be lucky to get away with a stern warning not to ever shorten her name again.

Like Quyyum, Taju also attended the beginner *ile kewu*, but he didn't learn Islamic knowledge and Quranic memorization to the highest level. When he narrated his childhood days, he didn't hesitate to say he was a rogue; he was more interested in using religion as a tool for magic, voodoo, and other things unrelated to *ibadah* (the worship of Allah).

In Ilorin, it's widely believed that only a few households still practice the Yoruba Òrìṣà religion, worshipping deities like Sango, Esu, Obatala, Ogun, Yemoja, and Osun, among others. Even though these claims are not backed by empirical evidence, they hold some truth, possibly influenced by the double conscience and activities of the Fulani jihadist penetration into Ilorin to whitewash the worship of these Yoruba gods and goddesses. Some even claim that Ilorin has no Egungun (masquerade) tradition, using the phrase *esinsin ni eegun ile won*, meaning "house flies are their masquerades in Ilorin."

The development of Ilorin into a Muslim city underscores the significance of Islam as a unifying force among the Yoruba-Fulani people. In almost every community, no matter how small, you can find at least an *àsàlátù* group with young or older Muslims. Some have as their objective to assemble every week to pray, while some provide essential services to their Muslim brothers and sisters.

Individuals like Taju and Quyyum exemplify how Muslims in Ilorin prioritize giving their children Quranic education before any other education. For them, this is the first step in eradicating illiteracy, and they believe that children should be equipped with the knowledge of the Quran before pursuing any other form of education, including traditional Yoruba or Western education. The purpose of Quranic education is to teach children how to read the Quran, which allows them to observe their daily prayers and other religious rites to fulfill the purpose of creation as ordained by Allah.

The clerics who offer the kind of knowledge Taju sought do not showcase such knowledge for different reasons. Taju met some clerics in Ilorin who were moved by his passion and eagerness to learn. They took him under their wing and educated him about various Islamic principles and practices, which initially excited Taju. The rituals and prayers encouraged him, and he felt he was finally heading in the right direction, even though he knew that some of the teachings were not entirely in line with Islamic beliefs. The clerics instructed him on voodoo practices to attract wealth and fortune and demonstrated how to cast spells, perform rituals to invoke success and good or bad luck, and make amulets and talismans.

Taju confided in me that he was initially apprehensive about this occultic and magical knowledge because he was aware they were against the Islamic religion and beliefs. He didn't want to participate in anything that went against his Islamic beliefs, even though he wanted to be powerful, inasmuch as it worked for him. Taju knew that voodoo was often associated with dark magic and malicious intent; however, the clerics assured him that they were only teaching him how to use spiritual power for good and not evil. Ultimately, he continued to learn about voodoo until it became part of him. He didn't renounce Islam and only practiced these magical rituals among his Muslim peers when compelled to do so.

As often said, when the Devil gives a teaspoon of sugar, he will request a full-grown baby as reparation. By the time I met Taju, he was full of regrets for his past actions, so much so that I pitied him. Perhaps the religions that preach against malicious acts are right, after all. Jinns are created by God just as he created humans and animals and every other thing on the surface of the earth. However, while some jinns can be physically seen and interact with people, it takes extra spiritual knowledge and effort to encounter them. According to the holy books, these supernatural creatures possess the power to do both good and bad to people.

Taju's knowledge of these spiritual beings and their powers allowed him to see and interact with them. With the knowledge and power at his disposal, he enriched himself, and people in his immediate community were in awe of him. He could control some of these creatures to carry out any activity as he wished, and he sometimes used his power negatively, especially when offended. But this only lasted for some years as his misuse of the power eventually led to his downfall.

His doom began when he conflicted with one of the most respected clerics in his neighborhood over a plot of land belonging to the Muslim community to build a Mosalasi Adugbo to be named after the imam. Despite warnings, Taju never listened and went on a full, head-on battle with the cleric, not holding back on the voodoo to use against the cleric. But the voodoo backfired and came back to haunt him. Taju lost his child, wife, and all the wealth he had acquired. He was later banished from the community, and he found solace among the Fulani, whom I met some years later.

One might think the Yoruba culture is totally lost, considering how the Yoruba Muslims in Ilorin operate. Despite the jihad and the mixture with the Fulani, Hausa, and other northern groups that settled in Ilorin, the Yoruba descendants have relics of their own culture in the Muslim communities. The local Fulani group is often used to select the chief imams, also known as Fulani imams. Traditionally, there are two deputy major imams in the town—one serving the Yoruba community and the other serving the Hausa people. The Hausa imam, known as Imam Gambari, is ranked third, while the Yoruba imam, known as Imam Imale, is next in rank to the Imam Fulani.

The presence of numerous mosques dispersed across Ilorin is one of the religion's most notable characteristics. There are many locations, from the Central Mosque in the city's center to smaller neighborhood mosques, where

Muslims congregate to pray. Islam is widely practiced in Ilorin, permeating local culture and day-to-day life. Five times a day, the call to prayer resounds across the streets, reminding Muslims of their duties to Allah and fostering a sense of collective commitment. All the money given as offerings and those realized during special programs like the turbaning of Muslim leaders in the Central Mosque or at the Mosalasi Adugbo is used to support the mosque's projects.

Mosques in Ilorin are hubs of activity every day of the week. While adults congregate for prayer and religious study, children attend classes to learn Arabic and memorize verses from the Quran. Some mosques also offer social services to the neighborhood, such as giving out clothing and food to those in need. Every Friday, prayers at the Central Mosque draw sizable crowds, with devotees spilling out onto the nearby streets. During the sermons, the imam preaches from the Quran, urging Muslims to live in peace with people of other religions, in accordance with the teachings of the Holy Book, and by emulating the life of Prophet Muhammad (PBUH). After Jummah prayers, greetings and embraces are exchanged among friends and acquaintances.

Islam is more than just a collection of practices for Muslims in Ilorin. It's a way of life that influences the people's culture and traditions. Islam permeates every aspect of their daily life, even in their music, from the call to prayer that echoes throughout the city to the loving greetings and embraces exchanged among friends, acquaintances, and neighbors after Jummah prayers on Friday.

During the sacred month of Ramadan, Muslims fast from sunrise until dusk to purify their souls and get closer to Allah. In the evenings, families come together to break their fast with traditional foods and fruits, and the streets buzz with activity at night. Eid al-Fitr, a festive commemorating the end of the monthlong fasting, is celebrated on the final day of Ramadan. Families wear their best attire and go to the mosque for special prayers, followed by joyous get-togethers with friends and relations.

Regardless of whether you are Hausa, Nupe, or Yoruba in Ilorin, there are different opportunities to learn about Islam. The city is teeming with clerics, from the imam to alfas, *ladani*, Iya Sunnah, *eleha*, and students of Arabic schools. But Ilorin boasts of not just clerics; it's the home of Islamic songs in Yorubaland. Many Islamic music artists are from Ilorin, and they have different songs that praise the city of their origin. To date, one of their most popular songs is the one about Ilorin being a city far from hell but closer to paradise.

Ìlọrin ọmọ akéwú gbẹrú
Ọmọ akéwú ṣọlá lẹ̀bàá Ìlọrin
Àwọn ọmọ Ìlọrin wọn ò ṣẹbọ

Won ò ṣòògùn àmọ́ wọ́n ní kéwú
Ìlú tó tóbi tó gbáàyè tí kò léégún,
Ṣèbí ẹṣin leégún yín nílùú Ìlọrin
Ìlú tó jìnà síná
Àmọ́ ó súnmó àlùjánná bí àrẹ́ṣẹ̀ pa
Ìlọrin ìlu wérí-wérun, Ìlọrin ọmọ ọlá tódérin
Ọmọ àkukọja, Ọmọ afidà pa kèǹgbà
Ẹyin lọmọ atapín oníperin
Apín ata tọ́mọ ọlọ́mọ fi gbọ̀tín wọn,
Atoto òtó fira okùn idà ọmọ Àfọ̀njá
Tí wọ́n bá fibi su ló ń là ló ń lówó lọ́wọ́,
Olójú ẹni tó ń jẹ́ mèsúrú jàḿbá ara
Ìlọrin kìí fi oore san oore
Ìlú tó tóbi tó gbàyè tí kò léégún
Ọmọ akéwú gbẹrú
Ọmọ kéwú ṣọlá l'ẹ̀bàá Ìlọrin
Àwọn ọmọ Ìlọrin wọn ò ṣẹbọ wọn ò ṣòògùn
Àmọ́ wọ́n ní kéwú
Ìlú tó tóbi tó gbáàyè tí kò léégún,
Ṣèbí ẹṣin leégún yín nílùú Ìlọrin
Ìlú tó jìnà síná
Àmọ́ ó súnmọ́ àlìjánà bí àrẹ́ṣẹ̀ pa
Ìlọrin ìlú wérí wérun, Ìlọrin ọmọ ọlá tódérin
Ọmọ àkùkọjà ọmọ afidà pa keǹgbà
Ẹyin lọmọ àtàpín oníperin
Apín ata tọmọ ọlọ́mọ fi gbọ̀tin wọn,
Atótó òtó firà okùn idà ọmọ Àfọ̀njá
Tí wọ́n bá fibi su ló ń là ló ń lówó lọ́wọ́,
Ó lójú ẹni tó ń jẹ mèsúrú jàm̀bá ara
Ìlọrin kìí fi oore san oore
Ìlú tó tóbi tó gbáàyè tí kò léégún
Bẹ́ẹ̀ ni wọ́n lṍrin tiwọn lóde Ìlọrin
Ọmọ Àfọ̀njá láyà
Lópo alupirin, bí jagun ògbojà jagun
Àyàn ló bí èdè bí èdè jagun a là kàkà
Oníjà agbàgbé, oníjà asùnlọ,
Bo bá wá kẹ́ṣin dé jagun a binú gbà
Torí wọ́n n lọ *Ìlọrin àfọ̀njá ọmọ ùkùkù*
Ọmọ wérí wérun
Ìlọrin àfọ̀njá ẹnúdùnjuyọ̀

Ìlú tó jìnnà s'íná
Tó súnmọ́ àlùjáná bí àrẹ̀ṣẹ̀pa
Ìlú tóbi tó yẹn, wọ́n ò léégún rárá
Ẹṣin l'égúngún ilé baba wọn
Akéwúgbẹrú ni wọ́n
Aṣàdúrà gbore
Ají fi kálàmù da wọ́n lẹkun à ń ṣe kọ́ńdú
Wọn e lu lágbàdu
Kéwú ni wọ́n ń ké
Eégún wá búra
Bo bá dénú igbó rí
Pààkà wá búrá
Bó bá d'ìgbàlẹ̀
Èrò ìwàyí òpó wá búra
Bẹ́ò bá l'óbìrin
Ayídòpó láya ńlé ọmọ ègbìrìn ọ̀tẹ̀
Nílé òpó ọmọ láderin
Òpó kọrọbítí ajagun àjàsẹ̀
Òpó k'ájà ká r'Ọ̀yọ́ná
Abídesú ko jẹ́á wo ẹni tó l'ọba
Ọmọ òpó ò gbọ́ràn
Wọ́n pé ń kọjú ẹ̀ s'íná
Iná ò gbọ́ràn
Wọ́n pé ń kọjú ẹ̀ s'ómi
Omi ò gbọ́ràn
Wọ́n pé n fi pọntí *tó le*
Ọtí tó le ò gbọ́ràn
Wọ́n ní n f'ọ́mọ tó burú
Ọmọ wo wá ló le tíò gbọ́ràn
Àfọ̀njá ò gbọ́ràn
Ni wọ́n bá kọjú ọmọ poníléwá s'ógun
Ogun náà l'Àfọ̀njá lọ *tíò padà wá'nulé mọ́*
Tó fi lọ *tẹ ìlú Ìlọrin*
Ìlọrin Àfọ̀njá tí ń jẹ́ ẹnúdùnjuyọ̀.

Àyàn ló bí èdè bí èdè jagun a là kàkà
Jagun àródé ìjà kìí jagun ó tò là kàkà
Oníjà agbàgbé, oníjà asùnlọ,
Bó bá wá kẹ́ṣin dé jagun abínú gbà
Torí wọ́n ń lọ *Ìlọrin àfọ̀njá ọmọ ùkùkù*

Ọmọ wérí wérun
Ìlọrin Àfọ̀njá ẹnúdùnjuyọ̀
Ìlú tó jìnnà s'íná
Tó súnmọ́ àlújánà bí àrẹ́ṣẹ̀pa
Ìlú tóbi tó yẹn, wọn ò léégún rárá
Ẹṣin l'egúngún ilé baba wọn
Akéwúgbẹrú ni wọn
A ṣ'àdúrà gboore
Ajífi kálàmù dá wọn lẹ̀kun à ń ṣe kọ́ńdú
Wọn e lu lágbàdu
Kéwú ni wọ́n ń ké
Eégún wá búra
Bo bá dénú igbó rí
Pàákà wá búrá
Bó bá d'ìgbàlẹ̀
Èrò ìwàyí òpó wá búra
Bẹ́ò bá l'óbìrin
Ayídòpó láya ńlé ọmọ ègbìrìn ọ̀tẹ̀
Nílé òpó ọmọ láderin
Òpó kọrọbítí ajagun àjàsẹ̀
Òpó k'ájà ká r'Ọ̀yọ́ná
Abídesú ko jẹ́á wo ẹni tó l'ọba
Ọmọ òpó ò gbọ́ràn
Wọ́n pé ń kọjú ẹ̀ s'íná
Iná ò gbọ́ràn
Wọ́n pé ń kọjú ẹ̀ s'ómi
Omi ò gbọ́ràn
Wọ́n pé n fi pọntí *tó le*
Ọtí tó le ò gbọ́ràn
Wọ́n ní n f'ọ́mọ tó burú
Ọmọ wo wá ló le tíò gbọ́ràn
Àfọ̀njá ò gbọ́ràn
Ni wọ́n bá kọjú ọmọ ponílewá s'ógun
Ogun náà l'Àfọ̀njá lọ *tíò padà wá'nulé mọ́*
Tó fi lọ *tẹ ìlú Ìlọrin*
Ìlọrin Àfọ̀njá tí ń jẹ́ ẹnúdùnjuyọ̀.

CHAPTER NINE

Baba Agege Is Dead!

In Agege, where faith and culture beautifully abound,
There stands a cleric, wise and revered,
A beacon of light, to be admired and cheered.
Oh, Baba Agege of noble grace,
In your presence, hearts find solace and embrace
With deep knowledge, you guide the lost,
In your words, the seeds of wisdom are tossed, your voice rings clear,
With passion and conviction, you bring hope near,
Your sermons, like streams, flow with soothing ease . . .
Enlightening minds and stirring souls with a gentle breeze.
You teach the essence of love and peace
Embracing diversity, you quelled animosity
Respecting differences, your mission begun
Through the power of faith, you heal the wounded,
Providing comfort to those who feel excluded,
Your prayers transcend barriers, bridging divides,
In this bustling community, you're a tranquil guide.
With open arms, you welcome the weary and meek,
In your presence, strength and courage they seek,
Your compassion knows no bounds or creed,
You uplift the spirits of those in need,
your devotion shines bright,
Your gentle soul blossoms like a fragrant flower.

Lagos! *Eko wenjele* is a popular slang. I never quite understood the meaning of the *wenjele* added as a suffix, but it's part of the street lingo on the streets of Lagos. Lagos is popular for many things, and slang is one of its trademarks. They are coined at convenience and quickly become integrated into Lagosians' everyday language.

Beyond the vibrant slang culture, Lagos is that place where you acquire street wisdom, a place to become streetwise. My Ibadan people, in their *oriki* (praise poem), have been tagged master thieves who would win a theft case against the owner of the possession, but I believe that Lagos is more notorious than Ibadan. Daylight robbery and scams were not uncommon on the streets of Lagos in the past. Even the popular fuji musician, the late Dr. Sikiru Ayinde Barrister, in his album *Ọmọ̀ Nigeria*, where he praised different ethnicities in Nigeria, had this to say about Lagos: *Ẹni tó d'Eko tí ó bá gbọ́n, kí onitohun re Amerika ó, kò gba'be* lọ *sí Waṣintin, kò gba'bẹ̀ lọ̀ New York City ó, k'onitohun dá'rí* bọ *wá s'ile. Ṣaka lo dájú pé onitohun kò tún lè gbọn mọ ó*, which translates as "Anyone who comes to Lagos and still doesn't become wise would never be wise even if they leave Lagos and go to America, Washington, DC, or New York!"

Islam played a vital role in how Hausa traders succeeded in cross-country trade, leading to Agege's establishment as a commercial network. Also, Islam served as a unifying factor for the Hausa diaspora community, contributing to their prominence and attracting non-Hausa Muslim diaspora groups from northern Nigeria and other West African regions. These included the Ebira, Kanuri, Shuwa Arabs, and Nupe, as well as Ghanaians and Togolese Kotokoli, who settled in important Hausa settlements like Agege in Lagos.

This composition was what I met in 1966 when I first visited Agege. Subsequent Hausa communities established in Lagos and other Yoruba cities were composed of divergent diaspora communities of various ethnic groups from northern Nigeria and other West African countries, with Islam and the Hausa language as unifying elements among these diverse groups in the Hausa quarters in Agege.

Agege is one of the popular camps for Hausa long-distance traders, with commerce playing a major role in its establishment. The pioneer Hausa community members in Agege and subsequent Hausa migrants and settlers were attracted by the trade opportunities in the small Lagos town. Initially, Agege was associated with the kola nut trade, but later, the cattle trade became equally prominent due to the growing demand for meat by the rising Lagos population. The Agege railway station, market, and abattoir were the nucleus of various commercial activities, facilitating trade between the Yoruba and Gonja traders from Ghana.

My journey to Agege was driven by curiosity. I attempted to leave Ibadan to seek out Baba Agege, an Islamic cleric. It was an attempt to serve my curiosity, a search for knowledge beyond all I had seen of Islam in Ode Aje and Ibadan. But when I disclosed my intention to leave for Lagos, the first response I got was an exclamation of "Ha." For three valid reasons. The first was because I was young, the second was because of Lagos's infamous reputation, and the third was because I wasn't familiar with the city. Despite the obvious risks, I was determined to go on the perilous journey because of the prospect of gaining knowledge and the excitement of the adventures that waited.

The first advice I received was not to ask for directions from Lagosians. The reason is that when you ask for directions, they realize that you are a JJC (Johnny Just Come), and then they attempt to mischievously pull scams on you or extort you! I took all the advice to heart, and in order not to flout the first and most important advice not to ask for directions, I asked Abayomi, my friend, to give me a full description of how to get to my exact destination in Lagos. As a precautionary measure, I divided my money between my bag and my pocket, believing I couldn't possibly lose from both ends.

Before I set out on my journey, I prayed that Baba Agege had not gone on *khalwa*, pronounced in Yoruba as *alua*. *Alua* is prayer done by Muslim clerics in isolation. They stay locked in a room and pray for several days without distractions. This period of isolation could last for a month, two months, or more, so I needed to meet Baba Agege at home. If I arrived when he had just left for *alua*, I would have to return home and make another trip to Lagos when Baba Agege was back.

My arrival in Agege gave me a closer glimpse into the rich tapestry of ethnic and cultural diversity in Lagos. I saw the Nupe (Tapa) people roasting groundnuts, Fulani women hawking *fura de nunu* and *kunu*, Fulani men leading cattle from the streets to grazing areas, Hausa men selling fruits, vegetables, and medicines, some working as shoe cobblers, and some *almajiris* (beggars). Igbo men and women traded in foodstuffs and textiles alongside Yoruba locals. I also saw the Ebira, who crafted textiles with looms.

Truly, Lagos is a place where you look around till you lose your cap. After observing the hustle and bustle of the environment, I made sure not to fall into the trap of asking for directions, and I held my bag tight, mindful of the potential dangers lurking in the form of bag snatchers. There were stories of petty crimes in Lagos, and Agege was one of the hot zones and a haven for criminal contingencies. Despite these challenges, the Agege Muslim community played a crucial role in maintaining peace in the area by helping to forestall or minimize intra- and intergroup conflicts that could snowball into wider conflagrations.

Finding Baba Agege's residence wasn't a problem; the man was as popular as currency and held his community together religiously. Revered as the alfa of alfas, Baba Agege was a staunch and upright believer of the Islamic religion, churning out numerous students who went on to head mosques and congregations in the area.

In Agege, three religions existed. The traditionalists were quite popular (mostly masqueraders and Ogun worshippers), followed by the Christians and the Muslims. The traditionalists were predominantly Yoruba; the Christians were a mixture of Yoruba and Igbo people, while the Muslims were a mixture of the Hausa, Fulani, and Yoruba, which made them a bit more in number than the Christians.

Baba Agege could be regarded as the Amir (leader) of the Muslims of Yoruba, Fulani, and Hausa descent, and even though he had opposition, he rightfully deserved that rank. He was the oldest, very knowledgeable, and, most importantly, Yoruba. Though Lagos is often regarded, by strangers and visitors from other parts of Nigeria, as a no-man's land, I learned that Hausa-Yoruba clashes still occurred despite the trade interactions and the presence of Islam.

Despite the occasional clashes in the community, Baba Agege adeptly managed to hold everyone together and lead the Muslim population. The Muslim congregation in Agege distinguished itself from other religions in the area. You could see them troop to various mosques in an orderly manner to pray. Friday prayers were like festive occasions, with Muslim worshippers dressed in their finest attire and going to the Central Mosque to listen to Jummah sermons and pray. The crowd would overflow the humongous structure of the mosque, spilling out onto the streets till the Jummah prayers were over.

The Hausa and Fulani people had no problem praying behind Baba Agege as he led the Jummah prayer at the Central Mosque. He spoke fluent Hausa, so his lectures were rendered in Arabic, Yoruba, and Hausa languages, which facilitated unity among the diverse Muslim population. Although there were other central mosques for Jummah prayers in Agege, the mosque under Baba Agege's jurisdiction attracted the largest crowds, a testament to his leadership ability and how he fostered unity within the community.

Upon arriving at Baba Agege's house, I was greeted by the resounding echoes of Arabic recitations. The students were broken into squadrons like a military base. Some were reading the Arabic alphabet from the board under the guidance of a young-looking boy who displayed a remarkable command of the subject. In another group, students were reading from the *tira*, under the supervision of a young boy who was obviously above their age. Another group, led by an older guy, was reading the Quran, and others like him were reading the hadith.

From what I perceived, those reading from the board were beginners, and the young chap supervising them was the best student from the next class (the *tira* class). In the *tira* class, the learners were led by the best student from the Quran class. Those who have finished studying the Quran would go on to study the hadith, and the best student from the hadith class would oversee the studies of those in the Quran class.

Baba Agege was the overall head, meticulously tracking each student's progress through regular assessments. He determined the students who would move onto the next level and those who would remain at their current level. Also, he handpicked the smartest of them and made them supervisors of the level below them. His intelligence in structuring his school was the first thing that endeared him to me, among other things. For example, he didn't keep an unnecessary hold on his students. Once they completed their studies under his tutelage and fulfilled all requirements, they were free to pursue their path and even gather their followers.

Even though, naturally, they were still under Baba Agege due to his affluence and esteemed position, he rarely interfered in their affairs unless necessary, such as when disputes arose among alfas. He made some enemies as a result of this because once he stepped into a matter, the wrong party knew he had lost because there were no lies, no bribery, and Baba Agege would always be impartial in his judgment. He remained steadfast in upholding the principles of truth and justice, practicing what he preached without compromise.

Baba Agege never imposed an imam on a mosque even though he could do so and still be in his rights. Instead, he made recommendations based on the individual's character, knowledge, age, and ethnicities. He would not make a Hausa or Fulani imam recommendation on a mosque that has the Yoruba as the predominant stock of its congregation; in the same vein, he would not make a Yoruba imam recommendation for a mosque that the Fulani and Hausa dominate. He understood the importance of cultural sensitivity and ensured that his recommendations aligned with the demographic makeup of each congregation, fostering harmony and unity among the people.

Also, Baba Agege's humility was quite remarkable. But for his gray beard and the respect he commanded, he appeared an ordinary man. When I got to his place and confirmed his identity, I instinctively moved to prostrate in greeting, as per Yoruba tradition. But he stopped me halfway and explained that, as a Muslim, he could neither prostrate nor accept prostration from any human. This left me puzzled because, as a well-cultured Yoruba, you either prostrate or kneel to greet your elders. Moreover, the alfas from where I come from had no issues receiving this type of greetings from us.

Baba Agege saw the confusion on my face and calmly enlightened me that Allah is the only God who is worthy of receiving such a gesture of reverence and that mere humans should not bow to one another. I was amused by the humility in his explanation but was now confused as to how to greet him. As if he read through my mind, he smiled and said, "Asalam alaykum wa rahmatul Lahi, wa barakatuhu." I replied him saying, "Wa alaykum salam, wa rahmatul Lahi wa barakatuhu."

After I had settled, I expressed my purpose for seeking him out—findings and the pursuit of knowledge. Quickly, I added that even in our brief encounter, I had gleaned valuable insights from him. Baba Agege commended my courage and my thirst for knowledge and advised that I remain observant and receptive, as these were qualities essential for achieving my goals.

As it was time for the evening prayers, Baba Agege headed to the mosque with his students, and I tagged along to pray with them. Later, Baba Agege recited the Quran to a crowd of more than fifty people gathered in the compound, his voice resonating sonorously in the midst of the silence. At some point, Baba Agege said, "Sadaqal Lahul azīm," and a thunderous "Allahu Akbar" rented the air, bringing the Quranic recitation to an end. I later got to know that whenever the Quran was being recited, everyone around must maintain silence as a sign of respect and to get *laadah* (reward). I was shown where I'd stay throughout my visit. I instantly felt at home, like I had lived there all my life.

The next morning, Baba Agege's visitors, along with popular alfas, filled the compound. There was a rift between two alfas over who would become the imam of the mosque in their area following the death of the former imam. The disagreement had degenerated to the point where both alfas could no longer lead prayers in the mosque, leaving the mosque without an imam. Other alfas brought the matter to Baba Agege, who then invited the disputing parties.

Everyone gathered to hear Baba Agege's ruling on the matter. The first alfa, Alfa Shefiu, who was the older of the two, claimed the former imam had chosen him as his successor. Alfa Muideen, the second alfa, argued that the people had chosen him to lead them because Alfa Shefiu had a soiled reputation. After listening to both sides, Baba Agege called on one of his best students to recite the Quran while he contemplated the matter. Everybody maintained perfect silence with their eyes on Baba Agege, who sat chiefly on his chair with his eyes closed, and their ears tuned to the Quran reader.

The compound was quiet before, but when the Quranic recitation stopped, and Baba Agege opened his eyes, a profound stillness enveloped the gathering. Everyone eagerly awaited his judgment. Fixing his gaze on Alfa Shefiu and Alfa Muideen, Baba Agege pointed out that though Alfa Shefiu was older than Alfa Muideen, they had similar characteristics that qualified both to lead the mosque. However, only one person could be a leader, which automatically meant that the criteria to select who would become the lead alfa would have been based on individual character.

Baba Agege then asked the alfas to turn their back to the crowd while he randomly selected five individuals to attest to the character of both men. The first three chose Alfa Muideen, citing his exemplary behavior and clean records of morality, unlike Alfa Shefiu, who had deceitfully taken the fiancée of one of his subordinates and married her as his fourth wife. The fourth person also mentioned that Alfa Shefiu was harsh, short-tempered, and was known to fuss at the slightest provocation. He also hinted at the various accusations of kleptomania that had been levied against the alfa. The fifth witness didn't refute or support the misdeeds cited against Alfa Shefiu. For him, even though Alfa Shefiu had been accused of many crimes, he believed he should still be allowed to lead the mosque since the former imam had handpicked him.

After the fifth witness had spoken, Baba Agege asked Alfa Shefiu if he had any witnesses who could confirm that the late imam had truly handpicked him as successor. Answering affirmatively, Alfa Shefiu called them forward. Eight individuals lined up, but immediately Baba Agege announced that they would swear by the Quran and speak only the truth; six of them excused themselves and returned to their seats. The remaining two, after swearing, clarified that the late imam had not explicitly appointed Alfa Shefiu to lead the mosque but had only asked him to ensure the congregation's welfare.

With a loud sigh, Baba Agege asked the people to raise their hands if they supported Alfa Shefiu's leadership. A few hands went up. When asked for support for Alfa Muideen, the majority signaled their preference, filling the sky with their raised hands. For the final judgment on the matter, Baba Agege explained that the late imam couldn't have handpicked his successor, as that should be determined by the congregation or a committee appointed by them. Additionally, he pointed out that given Alfa Shefiu's moral character, which put him at a disadvantage, and the people's preference for his opponent, there was no need for further deliberation. Alfa Muideen was to be the imam of the mosque. The crowd erupted in joy and praise for Baba Agege, who then took Alfa Shefiu aside to speak to him.

Everybody departed peacefully, and there was no further dispute. In that one sitting, Baba Agege had settled an issue that had gone on for weeks. His generous influence, spanning administration, human relations, dispute resolution, and Islamic matters, taught me a lot and left a lasting impression on me.

After spending a few more days with Baba Agege, I returned to Ibadan, promising to return as soon as possible. Sadly, life's obligations and other commitments prevented me from making another trip to Lagos to see Baba Agege again. He had become a mentor to me, and as much as I would have loved to draw from his wisdom again, life denied me that for the next seventeen years.

In Agege, I learned about the division among Muslims within both the Yoruba and Hausa Muslim communities. Baba Agege explained how some societies initially comprised followers of the Qadiriyya and Tijjaniyah brotherhood. However, the Yoruba established some Islamic organizations, such as Anwar-ul-Islam, also known as the Ahmadiyya Movement of Nigeria, Ansar-ud-Deen Society, and Nasrul Lahil Fathi Society of Nigeria (NASFAT).

The Hausa Muslim community also witnessed the emergence of the

Jama'at ul Izalatul Bid'a wa Iqamatus Sunnah (popularly called Izala), which was established in 1978 in northern Nigeria and later penetrated the Hausa diaspora community in Agege. Izala was founded as a movement against negative innovations in Islam and orthodoxy. In Agege, as was the case in Northern Nigeria, Izala was fundamentally opposed to the religious practices of the Sufi scholars and customary practices that had been incorporated as part of Islam over centuries.

My Muslim friends often talked about some of these influential Muslim organizations, noting their spread and membership. While some had members drawn from across both the Yoruba and Hausa Muslims, others were predominantly Yoruba or Hausa. Anwar-ul-Deen, Ansar-ul-Deen, and NASFAT remained mostly Yoruba-based, while Izala was largely a Hausa Muslim organization, with few Yoruba Muslim elites among its members.

A particular friend further explained that the Sufi Muslim orders of Tijjaniyah and Qadiriyya had adherents from both the Yoruba and Hausa Muslim communities, but each operated in different camps, maintaining different mosques, *dhikr* circles, and schools. To the greater Yoruba Muslims, however, Islam has had an insignificant effect on the social structure. In places like Ibadan, Ilorin, and Lagos, many Yoruba people are now either Christian or Muslim, sometimes resulting in siblings belonging to different religions yet living together amicably.

Baba Agege knew my intentions to seek knowledge, and during our extensive conversations, he mentioned another environment he would like me to explore. As a Lagos native, he recounted that his grandfather was from Epe and stayed with the extended and polygamous family alongside his parents until they eventually relocated to the Lagos mainland. He asked if I could take a message to his younger sibling in Epe, who was a Muslim cleric like him. I couldn't refuse his request, especially considering the potential of gleaning from another wise alfa in Epe and learning about that environment.

Among the Lagos towns that witnessed the early adoption of Islam, Epe was at the forefront. Being a coastal town in Lagos played a significant role in the emergence and development of Islam there. Epe remains one of the highly Islamized towns in Lagos, owing to circumstances connected with the dynastic upheavals that enveloped the royal families in Lagos during the nineteenth century.

During my time in Epe, I got firsthand information about the growth of Islam in the area. Baba Agege's brother also had a madrassa, and I noticed the similarities in their styles and organization. However, I could see there were different neighboring groups in Epe, unlike in Agege. Baba Agege's brother was popularly known as "Baba Alfa," and even his wives addressed him as such, yes! He had three wives compared to Baba Agege, who had only one. I attributed this to the largeness of his compound, or maybe he was just a man with an affection for polygamy. While not all his wives dressed like *eleha*, they all wore the hijab as expected.

Baba Alfa attributed the spread of Islam partially to the activities of various Islamic pseudo-groups that populated the town, notably mentioning the Mahdi Movement, which had previously been established in Ijebu-Ode. With this, Epe became a major Islamic enclave in Lagos, so much so that strangers who were not Muslims had difficulty getting assistance from their local communities. There was a Christian minority residing along the shores of the lagoon, primarily consisting of fishermen. However, Islam was perceived as more than just a religion in Epe; it was a way of life that upheld the dignity of its adherents, and it gradually gained more prominence over Christianity.

During meetings, if a Muslim said the opening prayers, the closing prayers would be led by a Christian. Similarly, when a Christian organized an event such as a funeral or a naming ceremony where Muslims were invited, it was very likely that the Muslims would slaughter the animals to be killed for the occasion. Baba Alfa even mentioned how difficult it was to predict the extent to which religion would create a major cleavage in Yoruba society in the future.

Within the confines of Lagos, the early acceptance of Islam was possibly helped by economic considerations. As more people embraced the new religion, they began to enjoy more patronage and commercial assistance from Muslims in Epe. Prominent Muslim clerics like Baba Alfa's grandparents worked tirelessly to provide economic and moral assistance to villages with a significant proportion of Muslims. This act also extended assistance with respect to the building of mosques in such communities and the installation of imams. In Lagos, Muslim pseudo-groups like the Ahmadiyya Muslim Mission, Ansar-Ud-Deen, and Zumuratul Islamiyah became more popular, and their establishments in places like Epe and Agege served as a boost for the development and growth of Islam.

Baba Alfa told me things were now different. Before the spread of Islam in Epe, people who were mainly Eko and Ijebu Yoruba practiced their respective traditional religions as it was in other Yoruba communities. The coming of Islam into Epe gave rise to the embrace of a foreign religion whose growth was surprising to the indigenous people. Baba Alfa pointed out that the growth and development of Islam, which started on a good note of peaceful coexistence, couldn't be sustained for long.

An interreligious rivalry occurred a year before I visited Epe, which threatened the existence of some Epe communities. The incident happened between the Ijebu and Eko communities that made up Epe. During the preliminary

FIG. 14. *Baba Agege Portrait* by Dr. Kazeem Ekeolu. As a religious leader, Baba Agege embodies the high regard of the ulama, who serve both religious and advisory roles in their communities, within and outside the mosque.

stages of Islam in Lagos, trading was one avenue through which Islam was propagated and promoted in Lagos and the entire Yoruba land. Arab traders, engaged in selling kola nuts and other farm produce like onions, moved to the coast of Lagos to trade in various markets. This facilitated the spread of Islamic doctrines and ideologies to other trading merchants.

Islam appealed to the people in Epe and other communities in Lagos as the religion rarely preached against the various Yoruba cultural practices. Unlike Christianity, which was seen as a religion against all aspects of Yoruba culture, Islam supported existing cultural norms such as dressing and polygamy. This made it easier for converts to embrace Islam as it didn't place them in a precarious situation of losing their cultural identity.

For instance, Yoruba's mode of dressing aligned perfectly with that of the forebears of the Islamic religion on its shores. Even the use of amulets was also a part of the Yoruba's people culture that populated Epe and other communities in Lagos. Baba Alfa himself believed in the potency of amulets and that they protect the wearer against negative forces. This is because some of the clerics who dominated the community in which Baba Alfa grew up upheld the values of amulets as a means of security against negative spiritual forces. However, some of these mutual tolerances have been used in the present day to portray the Islamic religion in a manner that is not ideal.

In Epe and its environs, the proliferation of various pseudo-associations made the Islamic religion appealing to the Yoruba in Lagos, particularly due to the nondenominational construct of the religion. Baba Alfa explained how groups like that will affect Islam in the future. As in Agege, salat prayers in Epe brought all Muslims together under one roof, be it a Sunni practicing Muslim or a Shiite, unlike Christianity, where adherents are divided along denominational lines and affirm their allegiance to a particular denomination. The disadvantage is that a Catholic Christian, for instance, would not feel inclined to worship in any other denomination on a Sunday, preferring to go as far as possible to find a Catholic church. Such does not apply to Islam, as the religion fosters inclusivity across sects and groups.

Prayers (salat) bring together all Islamic sects or pseudo-groups, such as the Tijjaniyah, Ansar-Ud-Deen, Nawair-Ud-Deen, Ahmadiyya, and a host of others, without any form of segregation or division. Up till today, it continues to be a pride of the religion. During the early stages of Islamic propagation in Lagos, various Islamic scholars engaged in public lectures to garner more appeal from potential converts.

Baba Alfa attested to the fact that the best way to get more converts was to embark on public lectures so that the teachings could be transmitted to a larger crowd. Islamic scholars embarked on what is generally referred to as *wassi* to disseminate Islamic teachings to the people. While the crowd pulled from such public lectures was relatively small, the numbers often increased during Ramadan, when Muslims were more attuned to attending such lectures. During such public lectures, the public is given the opportunity to ask questions about various aspects of Islam and its conformity with the cultural norms of society. The large gatherings lend credence to the continual growth of the religion.

Visiting Baba Agege and Baba Alfa wasn't the only experience I had of the values, modes, and rhetoric of Islam in Lagos. Although I didn't visit Baba Agege until several years later and didn't return to Baba Alfa in Epe, I've visited Lagos countless times after those years as a lecturer and researcher and for events and other important occasions. One of the striking observations I made regarding Islam's influence in Lagos is its integration into the existing monarchical structure that had been regarded as an authority long before the advent of the colonial government. Islam perfectly infused itself into the existing cultural contents in Lagos, indicating the seeming tolerance of the indigenous Lagosians to foreign concepts and ideologies.

The evolution of Islamic titles in Lagos stemmed from the need to honor deserving members of the faith for their support and significant contributions to the propagation of the religion within their communities. From the *olori ebi* (head of the family) to the *baales* (compound heads), the sociopolitical strata of Lagos were strategically structured before the coming of Islam. Islamic title holders aren't only perceived as religious leaders and sociocultural authorities. They organize and oversee social ceremonies like marriages and burials, ensuring adherence to Islamic principles and practices.

Titles are typically conferred on deserving individuals in either of two ways. The first method is through heredity, where certain titles are confined to a particular family or set of families within the community. Hereditary titles carry more weight and responsibility as the paramount ruler, such as the *oba* selected from families with such titles. This practice isn't exclusive to Lagos alone but is prevalent throughout Yoruba societies. The second method involves giving honorary titles to individuals, irrespective of their origin or family background, based on their various contributions to the development of the community.

Honorary titles are bestowed based on individual achievements within society as an avenue for non-indigenes to be honored for the different ways they have contributed to the growth and development of their host communities in Lagos. The most prominent among such titles is the *Baba Adinni* (the patron) of the Islamic religion in Lagos, which is conferred on individuals with respectable standing in the community. As the head of all other titleholders, Baba Adini's authority is limited to nonreligious issues.

As the Islamic community in Lagos grew, a need arose to increase the number of honorary titles available. One such popular title introduced into the Muslim structure in Lagos is the *Balogun Mùsùlùmí,* which was bestowed upon individuals deemed influential and faithful to the Islamic leadership and the congregation. The Balogun Mùsùlùmí's title was modeled after the traditional *balogun* title in Yorubaland, which was conferred on the strongest warrior.

From the Islamic point of view, the Balogun Mùsùlùmí is a warrior in his own right because he provides the materials and funds needed for the successful propagation of the religion within his community. Occupants of this esteemed position automatically garner respect from the traditional ruler of the community and other smaller authorities. Typically, the Balogun Mùsùlùmí is chosen from the pool of rich men within the community, as his influence must correlate with his financial capability. Such an individual is expected to use his wealth to cater to the mosque's numerous programs and activities.

Notably, Islamic titles are not exclusively reserved for men, as appropriate titles are also conferred on women according to their involvement and contributions to the activities within the mosque and the community. Wives of Muslim faithful formed themselves into a group known as *àsàlátù,* initially an all-exclusive female affair comprising praise singers but later evolving into structured entities as their numbers increased. These groups eventually became organized under the umbrella term *Egbe Alasalatu,* with the title *Iya Sunnah* dedicated to the head of the group. Iya Sunnah has the power to appoint leaders to smaller units within the *àsàlátù* as its membership grows.

Another noteworthy female title that gained prominence during the growth of Islam in Lagos is the *Iya Adinni,* modeled after the male equivalent, Baba Adinni. While the latter serves as the patron of the religion, the former assumes the role of the matron of the religion in the community. Some other prominent Islamic titles introduced by the Islamic movements in Lagos include *Majeobaje Adinni,* who holds the position of the preserver of the Islamic faith, and *Durosooto Adinni,* perceived as the trustworthy upholder of the Islamic faith in Lagos.

The Islamic institution in Lagos has become an inherent part of the sociocultural and religious landscape, with its members regularly conferred honorary titles for their contributions to the development of their society. The Lagos Muslim society continues to make significant strides, rallying together to champion various initiatives aimed at societal development. To recognize remarkable individuals who have contributed significantly to the advancement of Islam within Lagos society, leaders of the Islamic faith instituted a highly valued reward system in the form of highly esteemed chieftaincy titles, serving as a token of appreciation for their dedication and efforts.

Without the establishment of such profound reward systems, it might have been quite impossible for Islam to experience the degree of involvement and dedication shown by various individuals for the propagation of the religion. Importantly, the conferment of Islamic titles isn't an attempt to disrupt or downgrade the status of traditional chieftains that exist within the monarchical structures; rather, they complement traditional authority on society-building and peaceful coexistence among diverse religious organizations in Lagos.

According to Baba Agege, the development of Islam in Lagos has faced challenges since its inception, many of which are not unique to the region. While the initial difficulties encountered during the early stages came from leadership tussles and issues related to factionalism, new and emerging factors have added complexity to these challenges. As I observed during a case brought before Baba Agege when I visited him, the introduction of Islam to the southwestern part of Nigeria has spurred the practice of syncretism among the Muslim faithful. The early integration of Islam into the Yoruba culture in Lagos made it difficult for some Muslims to totally do away with the cultural values of their ethnic group. For instance, quite a number of Muslims in Lagos still participate in traditional festivals, such as the Eyo festival, despite its stark contradiction to the fundamental teachings of Islam.

In Ode Aje, Agege, and Epe, while some regard participation in such festivals as harmless, the veneration of deities preceding these festivals is clearly against the tenets of Islam. Syncretism is prevalent among Muslims in Lagos because it is believed that Islam doesn't frown against it. This syncretistic tendency extends beyond participation in traditional festivals to using amulets and protective charms that aren't always from Islamic sources. Additionally, some Islamic clerics incorporate herbalism into Islam to create potent charms and medicines for various ailments and challenges. Everyone conversant with the bustling and boisterous nature of living and working in Lagos will understand some reasons for this act.

In recent years, I've noticed a growing level of nonchalance exhibited by the later generations of Muslims in Lagos, which is impacting the development of the religion in Lagos. Islam emphasizes the importance of religious knowledge, typically acquired through the requisite Arabic and Quranic studies under designated scholars. Despite the awareness of the importance placed on these studies, however, it's common to find some Muslims who do not adhere to this tenet for a variety of reasons.

I know some Muslim parents prioritize Western education, making it quite hard for their wards to take up Arabic lessons. Some others do not agree with the punitive measures meted out by Islamic scholars who still uphold the age-old system of flogging defaulting children. A lot of times, these practices have been compared to what is available in Christianity. From my experience, Christian children are always happy to attend Sunday school because the church provides various incentives to draw in children, while Muslim children are coerced into Arabic teaching. There are numerous cases of Islamic teachers going from house to house to forcefully take Muslim children from their parents for Islamic studies.

Over the years, I've witnessed the changes in the values and portrayal of Islam in Agege and Epe. I also see the global misconception of Islam as a promoter of terrorism fueled by the actions of a few extremists who hide under the pretext of religion to perpetrate acts of terrorism, with a spillover effect in places like Lagos. This perception is born out of the fact that various terrorist organizations around the world often hide behind the cloak of Islam to perpetrate heinous crimes. While Lagos has not experienced terrorist activities, suspicion toward Muslims has hindered the steady growth of the religion in Lagos. People are becoming less interested in Islamic propagation in order not to be perceived as potential terrorists.

Nevertheless, I observed that the Muslim community is a factor to reckon with in Agege's power dynamics. Most of the traditional rulers (*oba* and *baale* inclusive) are Muslims, and those who hold titles like Asiwaju of the Muslim Community also hold significant political positions. While religion doesn't feature overtly in the politics of many Yoruba communities, the Christian community in Agege is equally involved in power politics.

After over three decades, I had the opportunity to return to Lagos. I was there to represent an organization but couldn't pass up the chance to visit my old mentor. I imagined Baba Agege must be very old now, having advanced further in age since the last time I saw him. I bought provisions and medicines as gifts, hoping he would still recognize or remember me. This time, I drove into Agege in my car.

It was still a bustling community as ever; however, there were noticeable differences. For instance, the presence of thugs seemed more pronounced compared to my first visit. Thugs of Yoruba and Hausa descent lurked around smoking weed and accosting private vehicles, forcibly extorting fees from them for using a government-tarred road! It didn't stop with the males; the females were also among them, smoking hemp and selling alcoholic beverages and other illicit substances. They dressed scantily, and the way they carried themselves among the males drove home the point that they were harlots.

I pondered over the changes in the area. Yes, there were thugs during my earlier visit, but they were not this many and definitely not this daring. They soon stopped my car, and one of them knocked on my side glass with a big wrap of weed hanging from the corner of his mouth, asking me for "owo ile" (money for using the road). To avoid trouble, I quickly handed him two crisp five-hundred naira notes. He stomped his foot and threw me a salute before he signaled to his gang to clear the road, saying, "Je ko pass, o nice!"

As I drove past, I looked to my left and saw the guy who had just extorted me in the shop of a scantily dressed lady. He brazenly slapped her behind, and she didn't make a fuss as he exchanged the money I had just given him for three small bags of what I suspected to be marijuana. Shaking my head in disgust, I zoomed off to Baba Agege's house, which, though it still looked like it did years ago, now sported a fresh coat of paint.

Happy to be there, I quickly packed all the gifts I had bought and hurried inside. Some students met me at the door and took the bags from me, leading me to where Baba Agege conducted his teachings. I expected to see an older man on the chair, but I met a relatively young man who was a split image of Baba Agege. My first thought would have been that Baba hadn't aged a day since the last time I saw him, but even then, he was older than the person I was looking at. I approached the young man, offered my greetings, and inquired of Baba Agege. With a solemn shake of his head, he informed me Baba had died some years back, and he was Baba's son and successor. He led me to where Baba was buried. I looked at the old sage's grave in reflection.

Recalling how Agege was as I had encountered it many years ago, I wondered how many of those boys and girls were from Muslim families. I looked at Baba's son and remembered Panadol's famous advert: *If e no be Panadol, he no fit be like Panadol.* (Panadol is a brand of paracetamol). Indeed, there can be no replacement for Baba Agege, and his demise left a void in the Muslim community in Agege.

Baba Agege is dead!
In somber tones I sing this dirge,
A lament for an old scholar,
Whose wisdom once guided his people,
Now stilled forever, I fear.
Years have flown, like fleeting birds in the sky,
Since last our paths did cross,
Yet the memory of his learned mind and gentle soul were never lost.
A sanctuary of knowledge and truth, a place where brilliance shone.
With trembling steps, I sought his abode, hoping to bask once more,
In the presence of the venerable sage, who had shaped Esin Imale.
His desk, once strewn with parchment scrolls, lay empty, cold, and bare,
The inkwell dried, quills silenced forever, a silence too heavy to bear.
Where his wise eyes once kindled with light,

Now darkness veiled the room,
And the hallowed shelves, filled with treasures vast,
Echoed an empty gloom.
With a heavy heart and tear-filled eyes,
I whispered my final farewell,
To whom my gratitude will forever swell.
His legacy lives on in countless minds, his teachings etched in time,
And though I mourn his mortal loss,
His spirit shall forever chime.
So let us raise our voices high,
And bid farewell to the old scholar grand,
A guardian of wisdom, now among the stars,
Resting in a celestial land.
Legacy endure through ages untold,
Inspiring minds anew,
For the mark he left upon our souls,
In reverence, we shall forever strew.
May your grave be blessed with endless grace,

CHAPTER TEN

Slaughtering the Living Elephant

If Allah can listen to every prayer,
No matter how whispered, no matter where,
If He can understand our deepest fears,
Wipe away our sorrows, dry our tears,

If Allah can forgive, with mercy so great,
Offering redemption, wiping sins' slate,
If He can guide us on the path that's right,
Illuminating darkness with His guiding light,

Then trust in Allah's power, strong and pure,
In His hands, all things find their cure,
For if Allah can create and command,
Surely, He can hold our lives in His hand.

In my encounters with Muslims, I've observed that some of them engage in hybrid religious practices, particularly among those from my region of the Islamic world. As a child, I understood that those who introduced Islam to Yorubaland didn't force the Yoruba people to abandon their cultural practices and religion. Instead, they allowed them to convert slowly, with the conviction that Islam, as a religion of peace, would eventually justify their change.

As a result, many of them continued with their indigenous beliefs while also practicing the new faith. It wasn't surprising to see Kabiru lashing people with canes as he followed the masquerade procession through Ode Aje. This wasn't done to punish passersby but as a customary show by the masqueraders. Kabiru could participate in the Egungun (masquerade) festivals during the day, then return home to pray the Maghrib and Isha salat at night. The Yoruba people are accustomed to worshipping multiple deities simultaneously. They can worship Esu, the god of the crossroad, during the day and turn to Ogun, the god of iron, at midnight, reflecting their flexibility and adaptability to different spiritual beliefs and practices.

A maxim I've come to adopt, based on my life's experiences and encounters with different people in different places, is that "fire grows stronger by consuming everything in its path, yet when it has consumed it all, it weakens and eventually burns itself to death." When I think deeply about Islam, I draw parallels between the religion and fire. While Islam has overcome many obstacles and held sway, right here, in front of my eyes, I see internal strife within the religion and a gradual self-defeat.

You wake up to the news of terrorism, and immediately, it's linked to Islam. True or not, I can't tell you, as it's a secret I must not disclose. Even though most of these stories are from the Middle East, including the Boko Haram in West Africa's neighboring countries, they have serious effects on every other Muslim all over the world. As the Yoruba will say, *Oro to ba Aboyade, gbogbo oloya lo n se* (Whatever crisis befalls the *Oya* priestess concerns all her followers).

We watched the 9/11 attack in the United States, where four planes were hijacked—two of which crashed into the World Trade Center. The casualties were more than what hundreds of people could count, and the property destroyed was worth more than we can imagine. That attack was claimed by Al-Qaeda, a Muslim terrorist bloc led by Osama bin Laden. It became a wake-up call to put Muslims and other persons on red alert. After that incident, there was a story about some people who refused to be on the same flight with five Muslims with full beards, canceling their flight out of fear. The wicked activities of these groups were so notorious that one would think that this is the essence of Islam.

As Islam has its origin intertwined with wars and battles, it has made it more difficult to defend its followers. Indeed, how does one defend Islam when the media is full of proclaimed Muslim terrorists, mostly with full beards, with their hostages, as well as suicide bombers who cover themselves with long hijabs to conceal their IED devices to wreak havoc in densely populated places? The atrocities of the Al-Qaeda terrorist sect were shown across all media platforms, followed in later years by the emergence of ISIS.

Due to global advances, almost everyone now has access to a phone and the internet, which distorts the popular perceptions of Islam. Who else has access to the internet? Certainly, the terrorists. If I want to ruin my day or have nightmares, I only have to search the internet for ISIS news. There are internet videos of terrorists handing letters to a few of their victims to read before they are shot while in shackles. Hostages are also tossed from the top of buildings.

Even the most heartless of individuals would be horrified by the inhumane techniques these terrorists come up with to kill people.

Terrorism has hit my home country, and we grapple with multiple terrorist groups—from Boko Haram, which translates as "Western education is forbidden," to ISWAP and others. They have continued to hold the country in fear, unleashing their terror mostly in the northern part of Nigeria. At one point, they held several local governments in Borno State hostage and declared it a state under their control, with the impact of their actions reverberating throughout the country.

Some people have started to doubt their relationship with their Muslim friends, especially those who seem to find justification for what these evil people do in the name of religion. Visit the newspaper stands at Challenge bus stop in Ibadan, Yaba, and Sango in Ilorin, and you'll find mammoth crowds of men who may not patronize the vendors but will read headlines and have heated discussions and arguments centered around these atrocities, with facts, fables, and conspiracy theories.

These terrorists have wreaked a lot of havoc in the northern part of the country for so long, perpetuating attacks like arson, shootings, and kidnappings. Most of these atrocities didn't really gain widespread popularity in the country until after the daredevil abduction of almost three hundred girls from the Government Girls Secondary School in Chibok, Borno State, in 2014. During one of my vacations to Nigeria that year, I rushed to a newspaper stand one morning to hear what people were saying and to see what was in the papers. At the stand, various theories circulated among the crowd. One individual said that Boko Haram was being funded by Hausa Muslims who wanted to Islamize the country. Another said it was the Hausa people trying to sabotage Jonathan Goodluck's administration so that a Hausa president would emerge in the next elections. According to the third man, the Hausa didn't want their children to be schooled in the Western way, which led them to abduct the Chibok girls—many of whom were preparing to write their final West Africa Examination Council examinations to gain entrances to universities.

From the surface, none of their arguments seemed logical, yet there are fragments of truth in every rumor and conspiracy theory. The arguments stopped abruptly when a bearded man, holding a *tasbih* (Muslim rosary) and a black polythene bag, joined our group. We weren't immediately aware of his presence until we saw the newspaper vendor slowly retreating from his stand, leaving it unattended. That was when some of us looked back and saw him moving toward us. Unplanned, we all became mute and started to disperse one after the other. After all, this is how suicide bombers are said to operate—blend into crowds before detonating their bomb to the scream of "Allahu Akbar."

None of us waited to find out whether he was a suicide bomber or not, but when I passed by the stand the next day, it was still standing, and people were there, as usual, to read newspapers and share their thoughts. I chuckled at my paranoia. My newspaper-reading comrades and I had wrongly profiled the man, but you can't blame us. In that tense moment, fear had overridden reason.

I witnessed a similar case of erroneous profiling at a conference I attended. A man had arrived with a bulging backpack and, at the entrance to the conference hall, the security personnel rudely stopped him and told him to turn back without providing any explanation. They led him many meters away from the building before they asked him to unload his backpack. He did, and all he had in the bag were clothes and books. He was one of the presenters at the conference. Throughout the embarrassing search, the man remained remarkably calm. However, when one of the security guards casually joked that he looked like a Boko Haram member, the young man immediately lost his cool. The conference organizers intervened to prevent full-blown chaos and resolve the situation.

Muslims faced different challenges during this period, with their woes compounded by different sects said to be "jihadists" proclaiming their terrorist acts as a form of religious warfare—jihad. In this war, they flout numerous Islamic principles, torturing people, raping girls and women without shame or pity, and killing people in such horrific ways that even animals can't be subjected to.

My heart trembled as I watched online videos of Boko Haram members wielding knives and severing their hostages' heads. Another video showed one of the kidnapped Chibok girls buried to her neck while standing in a pit the size of a man. Stones were thrown at her head from a distance until life painfully left her body. I couldn't watch that video to the end! All these horrifying killings were carried out while they chanted "Allahu Akbar." At one point, hearing "Allahu Akbar," even if it was coming from a mosque, would send chills down my spine.

Our Alfas advised against killing one animal in front of another one. They emphasize that when slaughtering an animal, the knife must be very sharp to quickly slice through the animal and provide a swift death. Also, the animal's eyes must be covered, so it won't know when you are ready to carry out the task. These are some of the ideals that we have come to identify with Islam, which is why we refer to it as a religion of peace and define Muslims as overwhelmingly decent and peaceful. But these terrorists, who act like they are more righteous than everyone else, pose a grave threat.

Presently, Muslims are seen as terrorists or covert terrorists due to the actions of various extremist factions. I was astounded to learn that these groups employ preaching and brainwashing as the primary methods to recruit fighters willing to commit heinous crimes or even blow themselves up in the name of religion. Before I could understand this, I accompanied a friend to a secondary school in Ibadan, where we spied on the Islamic teacher in the school. After obtaining the principal's approval, we joined the teacher, whom the entire school called Alfa, in his class.

Alfa's passion for his religion was evident as he taught Islamic studies so easily that even non-Muslims would have easily related to his teachings. He emphasized the concept of haram, things forbidden for Muslims, such as pigs and animals with fangs. Additionally, he stated that as the world progressed, there were some things that, even though they aren't haram, Muslims should avoid eating, citing Pepsi as an example. Intrigued by this, I wanted to ask why he made that submission, but Alfa preemptively addressed my question. He said the Pepsi company provides funds to Israel, which is then used to buy weapons to attack Muslims in Palestine; therefore, Muslims should boycott Pepsi products.

After that class was over and the students were on recess, my friend bought a cold bottle of Pepsi, which he offered to one of Alfa's students. The boy blatantly refused, saying Alfa told them not to drink Pepsi. Shocked at the boy's strong will, my friend wondered aloud if that boy would hesitate to shoot someone if Alfa handed him a gun and provided him with a compelling reason to kill a particular set of people. I understood his point immediately.

Religion is a powerful tool, but religious leaders are in another league entirely. If the saying of Karl Marx, "Religion is an opium of the masses," is to be followed in this context, religious leaders are the dispensers of the opium. Unfortunately, if the opium dispenser is a nut head, he pumps his followers full of opium, the consequences of which can be disastrous.

This issue isn't exclusive to Muslims alone; even Christians are guilty of it. I've seen marriages end in divorce because one partner decides to mindlessly follow a religious leader. Take, for instance, a pastor who instructed a wife to deny her husband sex, and if at all they were to have sex, she must seek the pastor's consent! When the husband found out why he had been denied his rights, he sent his wife packing. Months later, the same pastor impregnated the woman and callously abandoned her.

In a world where many see religious leaders as demigods, believing everything that comes out of their mouths, even when unreasonable, we also have religious fanatics who have risen through the ranks to become religious leaders. When such zealots sit atop a religious organization, you have a terrorist sect not far below, and this is not restricted to Islam alone. The number of Muslim terrorists is just a few compared to the number of peace-loving and law-abiding Muslims. Even in countries and states where these terrorist sects operate, not all Muslims share the same ideology; many remain as humane as every other individual, shunning hatred and violence.

However, defending Islam and its adherents can be challenging because the atrocities of a few Muslim terrorists, mostly against non-Muslims or people they feel are not religious enough, cast aspersion on the global Muslim community. To worsen the issue, powerful Muslim states aren't doing enough to fight these terror groups, making it look like they are in support of the terrorist activities. If Muslims are sabotaging Islam, what can a non-Muslim do to help? We can only help sensitize the world against stereotyping Muslims. Not all Muslims are terrorists!

I recall an incident I witnessed at a Lagos secondary school. At the end of the school day, a little girl, still in her primary school uniform but also wearing a hijab, waited for her brother to finish his class so they could go home together. Trouble started when the vice principal came out of her office and ordered the girl to take her hijab off. A teacher intervened, questioning the vice principal's directive, but the vice principal insisted that the hijab wasn't part of the school uniform. The teacher reminded the vice principal about the state government's directive that Muslim students could wear hijabs with their school uniform. He added that the girl was from the primary school and had already closed for the day, so they had no right to control what the students wore. However, the vice principal insisted that the girl must take her hijab off regardless of all the reasons the teacher gave. The teacher and the vice principal got into a heated argument, which left the little girl scared, and she began to cry. I stepped in then and asked the girl to go with her brother, who had just come out of his class.

The hijab is an important piece of clothing for Muslim girls above toddler age as they must keep their hair covered from males who are not from their immediate family. Failure to do so is considered a sin, which is why Muslim organizations ensure that Muslim girls are allowed to use their hijab everywhere. I understood why the Muslim teacher came out to protect the little girl's interest.

After diffusing the situation between the vice principal and the teacher and ensuring that the girl and her brother had safely left the scene, I engaged the vice principal to understand why she insisted that the girl remove her hijab. She expressed her concerns about giving Muslims a free hand in the south, fearing they might want to replicate what the religious fanatics in the northern part of Nigeria are doing in a bid to Islamize the country. This was another conspiracy theory about Islamization! I had to ask her whether her actions toward the girl and the teacher had eliminated terrorism from their minds or if she had potentially planted the seed for terrorism in their minds instead.

Another example is the hijab crisis at the University of Ibadan International School, which led to the closure of the school for days to prevent a potentially violent altercation between some members of the school's protesting Muslim

FIG. 15. *Female Muslim Students* by Dr. Kazeem Ekeolu. Muslims adorn the hijab, as many see it as a sign of modesty. The right to wear it in Nigeria's Western secular schools has sparked various issues over the years and continues to be a topic of debate.

Parents Forum and some students. The Muslim community at the University of Ibadan had a significant presence on campus, with many female students choosing to wear the hijab as an expression of their faith. The University of Ibadan is known for its rich diversity and academic excellence and has always prided itself on being a beacon of tolerance, welcoming students from various cultural and religious backgrounds. However, the hijab crisis tested its claim of commitment to inclusivity and freedom. It became a big issue that divided the community and ultimately led to a court case that redefined the boundaries of religious expression and individual rights. This hijab issue sparked a national dialogue on religious freedom, diversity, and individual rights. It reminded the nation of the importance of upholding and protecting the fundamental principles upon which the country was built.

During my travels to regions where indigenous faiths emphasize a flexible cosmology with a focus on the supernatural, I've observed the thriving presence of Sufism. This is particularly notable in locations like Ibadan and various Yoruba cities. In contrast, Salafism, from my perspective, seems to have less resonance with many African societies. Salafism is characterized as a fundamentalist movement that insists on adhering strictly to the teachings of the Prophet and his companions to practice authentic Islam. Navigating the diverse religious landscapes of Africa reveals that while Sufism flourishes in environments that prioritize flexibility and spirituality, Salafism's strict adherence to historical practices may encounter difficulties in adapting to the region's cultural nuances. Ultimately, the coexistence and interaction of diverse religious traditions contribute to the rich cultural tapestry of Africa.

As an African, I have my shoulder in Islam, my head in Christianity, and my mind in indigenous Òrìṣà practices. I know about the Salafi community; I have moved closer to them and learned about them, much as I have done with other sects of Islam; nevertheless, I know I can never be accommodated in the Salafi community. Salafism has spread significantly across Africa over the past several decades, attributed to factors such as the shrinking nature of the world due to globalization, the influence of international educational-religious networks fueled by Arab petrodollars (particularly from the Gulf States), and local conditions in many African countries that have been favorable for those who would challenge traditional religious elites. This is especially true in places where Sufi traditions have weakened, although exceptions exist, such as in Senegal, where Sufism remains dominant. Many think this is what has saved Senegal so far.

As the world became more connected and social media platforms grew in influence, divisive ideologies began seeping into many hearts and minds. Radical interpretations of religious texts and extremist narratives are spreading like wildfire, fueled by fear, ignorance, and sometimes political agendas. Anti-Islam sentiments are beginning to take root in many corners of society. As an advocate of Pan-Africanism, my experience has made me realize that one of the main catalysts of this rise is a series of violent incidents perpetrated by extremist groups claiming to act in the name of Islam. These acts of terror strike fear into the hearts of people across the continent, causing a ripple effect of suspicion and mistrust. Many Africans, who had once embraced their Muslim neighbors as brothers and sisters, now find themselves questioning their allegiance, and a subtle shift is beginning to shake the Muslim community.

The once vibrant spirit of ecumenism is depreciating daily, and a seed of competition has germinated. Different sects and factions within Islam have started asserting their interpretations and beliefs as superior to others. The focus has shifted from unity to division, from collaboration to competition. With the decline in ecumenism, power struggles have emerged among the various sects, and each faction seeks to consolidate its influence, striving to outdo the others in terms of followers, resources, and influence.

I had the honor of attending a presentation by an imam where he covered several topics related to the strange spread of religious terms, which he deemed to be extremely blasphemous/unreasonable among the general Muslim population. He highlighted the emergence of terms like *Agbesinga Adini* or *Afewagbesinga Adini*, occasionally extended to non-Muslims by some Muslim interest organizations for financial reasons. This has contributed to the rise of discord among Muslims over what is right or wrong. As a result, religious and scholarly leaders and imams have engaged in backstabbing and spreading chaos, not only among themselves but also among their followers.

The imam discussed how some leaders have chosen titles such as "chief imam," "grand chief imam," and "superior imam" rather than the distinguished term "imam." This trend has led to unique practices, such as having many grand chief imams within a single community, a title that has no validity in Islam other than the prestige associated with it. He said this has also given rise to a more dangerous trend when students at neighborhood Arabic schools adopt titles like "mufti" (jurisconsult / head of scholars) or even grand mufti without being eligible Islamic scholars. The imam also remarked that in the not-too-distant future, mosques and Muslim communities may begin to adopt the title of "general overseer."

Islamic scholars and leaders debate and argue vehemently over doctrinal differences, causing rifts and animosity among the faithful. As the competition intensifies, the true essence of Islam becomes obscured. The values of compassion, tolerance, and justice that once defined religion seem to fade into the background; instead, ambition and the desire for dominance have taken center stage. This decline in ecumenism and the power struggles have profound consequences for the Muslim community. Internal divisions have fragmented and weakened the once-united front against injustice and inequality. As Muslims focused more on asserting their own beliefs, they lost sight of the shared values that bound them together, while other communities and faiths observed the diminishing power and unity within Islam.

The imam concluded by narrating how the enemies of Islam sensed an opportunity to exploit the situation, sow seeds of discord, and weaken the influence of Islam. They played upon the divisions, further fueling the competition and creating a vicious cycle of mistrust and hostility. The Muslim community has lost its ability to address social issues collectively, as sectarian divisions have prevented effective collaboration. The voice of Islam, once a beacon of hope and justice, is now disjointed and muffled.

Nonetheless, the story of declining ecumenism and power struggles within Islam should serve as a cautionary tale for future generations. It should remind them of the importance of unity, respect, and cooperation in upholding the true values of their faith. The Muslim community should learn from its past mistakes, ensuring that the bonds of ecumenism remain strong for generations to come. There used to be a flourishing community of Muslims united in their faith and sharing a deep sense of ecumenism. The power and influence of Islam were strong, radiating a sense of peace and justice throughout the land. People lived harmoniously, respected each other's differences, and worked together toward common goals.

Back to the story of the hijab crisis at the University of Ibadan: That time wasn't the only time religious altercations would storm through the sands of the peaceful environment. Another incident, narrated by a close associate, involved an intrusion from a Christian lady. The incident occurred on a Friday in August 2010 and could have probably escalated into a full-blown religious war, with possible repercussions across the entire nation. A Christian student, Seun Olubunmi Adegunsoye, disguised herself and gained entrance into the Central Mosque at the University of Ibadan during the Jummah service to speak against Islam and all those worshipping at that prayer, saying, "Except you accept Christ in your life, you are not safe. All of you here, no matter the number of the congregation members who accept Jesus Christ. Allah is not God. Jesus is God."

Adegunsoye's behavior was absurd and no different from what extremists do against other religions. It reflected the confusion among young people today about religion and how dogmatic they have become. Surely, the nation would have been calculating the number of lives lost if the incident had occurred in an unstable region. Although the lady was subdued, her action was an act of religious extremism, and it sparked a reaction from the Muslim Students' Society of Nigeria. They locked all the gates, paralyzing academic and social activities on campus for an entire day. As they marched around the campus, they demanded the expulsion of the intruder and the banning of preaching and other forms of worship in lecture halls, residential halls, and public places outside designated areas.

When I heard about Deborah Samuel, the student who was brutally murdered in 2022 in front of fellow students at the Shehu Shagari College of Education in Sokoto, I felt horrible. We have been told that Allah is the most powerful, wise, and majestic, but those who killed her thought they were helping God fight the insult thrown at Him by Deborah. Killing her on the claim that she insulted God showed that they seemed to doubt Allah's invincibility and capability to protect Himself. He couldn't defend himself against the female, so the killers reasoned that they had to do it for Him, believing that their actions would guarantee them a place in Paradise and that some affluent people in the community would reward them for fighting for God. The murderers exuded joy as they carried out the dastardly act of killing their classmate, and every step of the way, they filmed it and showed their faces.

At the newspaper stand, before we all dispersed from the fear that the bearded man was a suicide bomber, one of the bystanders had argued that the rise in extremist Islamic ideology isn't often emphasized enough despite its significance. According to him, a Fulani faction has adopted techniques comparable to Boko Haram's operations. They attack Christian leaders, villages, and churches while evicting Christian farmers from their farmland. This has resulted in killings and displacements, with Christians being disproportionately affected. While extremist Fulani attacks can sometimes target Muslims, Christians account for a huge percentage of victims. These religious disputes have far-reaching consequences, undermining conventional leadership, threatening national security, and causing huge economic losses. The steadily increasing violence has exacerbated religious tensions, leading to a rise in suspicion and mistrust between Muslim and Christian communities.

Resolving this religious dispute requires both top-down and bottom-up strategies. Nigeria is a country where Christians are murdered frequently, sometimes solely for their faith. Although Boko Haram has a homicidal hatred for Christians, most of its victims have always been Muslims, in part because the conflict happens in a region of the country where Muslims are the majority. Boko Haram attacks anyone whom it believes is promoting Western education, whether they are Muslims or Christians. Accordingly, these extremists routinely target schools, especially Muslim girls' schools. Political and Christian leaders have joined prominent Muslim voices in denouncing the violence.

There are more killings of Christians in the Middle Belt, where there are disputes over land, water, ethnicity, and religion. But why would a Muslim or Christian be slain in the Middle Belt? Is it because they belong to a small ethnic group and are mostly farmers or herders? Or is it because they follow Islam, like the majority of Fulani do, or Christianity, as many minor ethnic groups do? The answers to these queries are complex, as a particular religion and ethnicity can occasionally be associated with certain lifestyles or not. Fighting between armed factions in Kaduna State is commonplace, and it disproportionately impacts weaker populations, like the Christian minority.

It may come as a surprise that logical perspectives on a critical issue could come from a casual discussion at a newspaper stand. As my newspaper comrade continued to make his point, one of us lightheartedly joked, "Oga, you speak so much English, and you get points. Why do you not contest for the presidency?" We all laughed, and then my learned fellow continued to highlight that the criminal elements include cattle rustlers and bandits. While violence may occur along racial and religious lines, these disparities are not always the main motivators.

Africa is a vast continent experiencing a wave of change. With its rich cultural heritage, Africa has long been a beacon of tolerance and coexistence, embracing various religions and ideologies. Islam has been practiced on the continent for centuries, becoming an integral part of many African societies. Muslims and non-Muslims lived side by side, respecting and supporting one another. Mosques stood tall, their minarets reaching the heavens as symbols of unity and devotion. However, globalization has introduced new ideas that challenge our traditional values. Peaceful coexistence among different religious communities is beginning to decline.

In the face of this rising tide, however, many Africans have remained steadfast in their commitment to tolerance and understanding. Interfaith dialogues, community initiatives, and educational programs have emerged to dispel stereotypes and foster harmonious coexistence. Individuals and organizations have made concerted efforts to promote understanding and reconciliation between Muslims and non-Muslims, highlighting the common values and aspirations that unite them. Through grassroots movements, social media campaigns, and personal connections, the voices of unity and love have drowned out the cries of division. Ordinary Africans from different backgrounds and faiths come together to celebrate diversity, protect religious freedom, and promote a culture of acceptance.

Although the struggle against anti-Islamic sentiment is far from over, hope has sprouted in the hearts of those who have refused to let hatred define their continent. Africa stands at a crossroads, challenged to confront biases and

FIG. 16. Portrait of a young Muslim woman by Raji Babatunde Mohammed. Aside from wearing a hijab and other head cover, female Muslim students dress in attires that complement both their religion and Western culture. From the private collection of Omoba Yemisi Shyllon.

embrace the true essence of its cultural tapestry. The rise of anti-Islam sentiment in Africa has served as a wake-up call, urging Africans to reflect on their shared history of peaceful coexistence and to reject toxic ideologies that have sought to tear them apart. It serves as a reminder that true strength lies in unity and understanding and that the beautiful mosaic of Africa can only shine bright when all its pieces are embraced and celebrated.

With determination and resilience, Africans have embarked on a journey to reclaim their continent's legacy of harmony, inch by inch, step by step, building a future where anti-Islam sentiments would be nothing but a distant memory, a testament to the triumph of love over hate. Religion can be likened to the body of an elephant—the side of the elephant that we are on influences how we describe what we see. Faith and religion are as big as the body of an elephant, and every religion and its practices are built on different perspectives. Embracing this diversity is crucial for fostering mutual respect and peaceful coexistence among Africans.

Muslims are also harnessing every possible means of modernization. From an external perspective, Islam may seem rigid, with its guidelines outlined in the Quran and hadith. Every Muslim is expected to totally submit to the will of Allah, as this is what makes them "true" Muslims. However, this notion of total submission baffles my mind. For instance, would Kabiru in Ode Aje, who follows the masquerade procession during the day and gets home at night to observe Maghrib and Isha salat, be considered a true Muslim? Kabiru is not alone in this scenario; perhaps many of the new converts in Ode Aje while I was growing up belong in this category.

Who is a Muslim? Is it Eleha, who allegedly killed her co-wife's second child because she had visited a sorcerer who told her the boy would be the richest in the family? Out of jealousy, she invoked the boy's spirit at night after blowing powder given to her by the magician, and the next day, we learned that the boy had died. You know there are witches in Ode Aje. Some said Eleha was a witch before she converted to Islam, but I chose to ignore what I believed was a rumor.

In any case, despite the education and modernity brought by Christianity and Islam, indigenous beliefs in magic or voodoo persist among the people. Why would a self-proclaimed Muslim or Christian visit a magician or a sorcerer for help or visit a *babalawo* to know if they would be lucky or not with a business they want to embark on? I've read in the holy books that one should not worship or seek help from any other source besides God. Islamic law, for example, is there to see, read, and follow, although some say it's rigid and rarely flexible.

However, globalization has not only brought about changes in how Muslims do things around the world. With the establishment of modern universities, migration, and the secularization of the religion by the different sects of Islam, there have been significant changes in modes of dressing and music, to mention a few. The trend has not only stopped at establishing schools for Islamic learning and Western education at the elementary and secondary levels. It's surprising to see universities and other centers of learning with an Islamic outlook teaching both the *deen* (faith) and modern subjects. These institutions, unlike the traditional *ile kewu* model I attended as a child, are the results of modernism pursued by the faithful.

That hijab crisis between the teacher and the vice principal made me understand that many devout Muslims still want their hijab worn at all times, which has given rise to a number of lawsuits on whether the hijab should be incorporated into official attire. Sadly, this not only raises concern but also incites disputes. When I returned to Agege to visit Baba Agege, though I missed seeing him, as he was dead, I was taken aback by the high rate of indecent dressing and the exposure of sensitive body parts in many places in Lagos. I saw a lady wearing a hijab with a short skirt that barely covered her knees, drawing attention as she attempted to climb a motorcycle. All attention, including mine, was on her as onlookers rebuked her for her improper dressing until she walked away in shame. While this lady certainly defied the Islamic codes and prescribed dress, she also called forth the wrath of non-Muslims.

In a separate incident, I heard the story of a woman who wasn't called to the bar as a lawyer because she chose to wear a hijab, which was not part of the court's dress code. The matter was taken to court, and she won the case. Yes, it's a win for Muslim women who want to wear hijab for decency, but what can one say about the girl I saw in Agege wearing a short dress with a hijab? While the Islamic law regarding dressing is clear, some still choose otherwise. This may be a loss for their souls and maybe a loss for Islam; however, the number of times the Nigerian court has ruled in favor of people who want to wear hijab in schools and for official purposes is a huge win for Islam.

I know some sects and Islamic societies that have established secular schools and those mixed with Islamic teachings. These schools and higher educational institutions are established to navigate the challenges of the modern world without losing the knowledge of Islam and its practices. The recent developments and flexibility demonstrated by the Saudi Arabian government have sparked different opinions and debates. These changes span various aspects, including women's rights, law, education, and societal norms. However, it's important to note that some Islamic states continue to uphold Islamic principles across all sectors, even amid the push for modernization.

During the 2022 FIFA World Cup in Qatar, prohibiting alcoholic products in stadiums during matches triggered strong reactions in Europe, Africa, and other regions. Even in the beer parlors in Nigeria, passionate discussions ensued among football enthusiasts regarding the host country's strict stance on alcohol consumption. Sporting events like football heavily rely on sponsors who depend on advertising segments and viewers' engagements. However, being an Islamic state, Qatar found itself at a crossroads, torn between embracing modernity and adhering to Islamic principles.

Alcohol consumption is prohibited in Islam, just like fornication, but who doesn't know the level of sexual immorality that goes on when tourists travel to attend sporting events? However, the principle of "When in Rome, behave like the Romans" prevailed, as Qatar prioritized its Islamic principles by enforcing laws governing permissible and prohibited actions within its borders. But at what cost? If you want to see the wrath of *agbero* in Lagos, suggest a ban on sachet alcoholic drinks. Whether it's "Jekomo" or "Tesojue," they don't miss a chance to take their *paraga* (sachet alcohol drink), even though most of them are either Muslims, Christians, or traditionalists. Just as an *agbero* would react if a ban were imposed in car parks and garages in Iwo Road, Ojodu, and Oshodi, European football supporters wailed about the prohibition of alcohol around the stadium.

As I move from one place to another, I feel the connection between migration and religion. As a child, I practiced Christianity with Pasito and prayed all the daily salat during my visit to Baba Agege. Iya Lekuleja ensured that I gained knowledge of traditional practices. In places where religious customs and rituals hold significance, I admired all and couldn't help but wonder about some of the tenets of Islam, even when they seem to have innumerable interpretations. In recent years, the concept of secularization within Islam has expanded, with the increasing argument that it's feasible and desirable to reconcile religious values with the demands of a pluralistic society and changing times. The more I've observed beliefs and practices in various places, the more I've recognized the enormous diversity of viewpoints within Islam.

I will not be truthful if I don't share my childhood experiences with religions and their interactions with cultural activities like music and festivals. My experience with secular and religious songs, Islamic or Christian music, which I've dubbed the "Lips of Angels," reveals a connection between Muslims and music, alongside adherents of other faiths. However, some sects consider music to be improper in Islam, while others embrace it, with some even making it a profession. Artists in Nigeria's ever-changing music industry frequently spark controversy with their creative choices and music videos, a trend that has continued to this day.

One incident in 2022 involving Davido, a prominent Afrobeats artist in Nigeria, stirred up a storm of criticism. Davido faced backlash and anger for promoting a new song by his newly signed artist on social media. The song "Jaye Lo" by Logos Olori, whose real name is Olalekan Emeka Taiwo, mostly angered Muslims in northern Nigeria. Due to the controversy the song generated, I had to listen to it and watch the now-deleted video clip. It left me questioning the intention of the video director. Sometimes, music artists, particularly Afrobeat musicians, incorporate verses from the two holy books or the traditional religion into their songs, and some even use their platforms for praise and worship. This may be because many of these artists started their music career in the church as a choir member.

However, this wasn't the case with the song by Logos Olori. The music was totally disconnected from Islam or the mosque setting depicted in the video, so the question again is: Why was it shot in that manner? Another notable observation is that the video didn't seem to have bothered Yoruba or other Muslims in Nigeria, as most of the criticism came from the core north. In my earlier encounters with Muslims closer to the core north, I observed that they didn't see Islam only as a religion but as a way of life in its wholesomeness. This perspective from the post-jihad era in northern Nigeria is marked by a major shift in how Islam was practiced compared to its manifestation in the Southwest.

In this context, indigenous cultural practices seamlessly intertwined with Islam, particularly evident in places like Ilorin, which served as a melting point. The influence of figures like Sheikh Alimi was strong, leading to Islam becoming the most practiced religion in the current Kwara State. Conversely, my encounters with Muslims in Yorubaland reveal that they are more accommodating to external influences and see no offense from a religious standpoint.

Olori's video showed guys dressed in traditional Muslim garments suddenly breaking out in wild dancing after concluding Muslim prayers near a mosque. This move was widely interpreted as a blatant disregard for the sanctity of the mosque and a disrespectful portrayal of Islamic practices. The Muslim community in northern Nigeria was deeply offended by this video, perceiving it as a direct affront to their religion and a portrayal that crossed the boundaries of what is considered respectful. The criticism quickly gained momentum, and regardless of their religious background, many people joined the chorus of disapproval and called on Davido to act. They demanded that the video be removed from the internet and an apology be issued to Muslims for the disrespect to Islam.

The backlash placed Davido in a difficult position as he faced immense pressure to address the issue. Eventually, he bowed to the mounting pressure, removing the controversial video from his social media platforms and releasing a new video for the song. Yes, the contentious video clip has been deleted, but has this changed the narrative that those who profess to be "real" Muslims are often aggressive and confrontational in public and private settings? The underlying issue remains persistent, necessitating ongoing reflection and introspection among adherents. It's crucial for individuals to continuously assess their actions to ensure they align with the principles of the religion of peace.

In another 2023 event, the ban placed on the Isese Festival, honoring Yoruba traditional worship by the emir of Ilorin, is a testament to the "double conscience" story of Ilorin. Is Ilorin a Yoruba or Hausa-Fulani city? The ongoing religious dispute and the city's composition and history, from both a religious point of view and cultural affinity, highlight Ilorin's complex cultural and religious dynamics. The Isese Festival's central figure, a devotee of the Yoruba Òrìṣà religion, expressed concern over threats from enraged Muslims. Interestingly, the outrage on the Isese Festival wasn't limited to the Hausa-Fulani Muslims; Yoruba Muslims also posed threats to those who wanted the festival to be held in Ilorin. For them, it's an insult to their control of the city.

It's rather ridiculous that in a place where Islam was introduced through spiritual conquest, spearheading Fulani imperialism would disregard the freedom of expression in a constitutionally secular country like Nigeria. The Yoruba Muslims in Ilorin who see the Isese Festival as a threat to their religion denounce it as "idol worship," disparaging it as paganism. This polarization, which reflects a larger social split between traditional and modern, indigenous and imported religious practices, exposes the underlying tensions and identity battles inside Ilorin.

Declaring the Isese Festival illegal constitutes an insult to the cultural heritage of those who practiced the traditional religion in Ilorin even before the advent of Islam. The ancient city of Ilorin, once a confluence of diverse faiths and ethnicities, has sadly been reduced to a symbol of intolerance manifested as a presiding monarch. Respect for different worldviews, festivals, morals, and humanity is threatened, jeopardizing the possibility of harmonious coexistence. The crux of the issue lies in the refusal to accept the various dimensions of human awareness. By marginalizing minority religions in Ilorin, the city loses its claim as a melting point of culture and religion. Will the emir make it a requirement for non-Muslims to visit the market on Fridays in robes? Will the emir also compel them to cover their heads?

Growing up in Ode Aje, I experienced firsthand how living in a community where people coexisted in peace despite differences in worldviews made life better and enjoyable. We observed Ramadan and its festivity as an all-inclusive community, regardless of religious differences. Nobody ever from any other religion claimed the killing of rams during Eid Fitr or Adha festivals was illegal or idolatrous. Is the present-day Ilorin operating a different constitution in which freedom of religion, association, and movement is restricted to just a religion? Pronouncing the religion of a particular group of people illegal is one of the reasons terrorist groups like Boko Haram, ISIS, ISWAP, and other theological maladies that presently afflict our society are wreaking havoc and indignation throughout a hitherto tranquil society and undermining the existence of the religion of peace with their aggressive strain of Islam. Such behavior has turned different ecumenical cities and communities into a bloodied farce of cohabitation.

Secularization in Islam entails maintaining a strong adherence to Islamic principles while emphasizing individual liberty, human rights, and the pursuit of knowledge and understanding through studying the Quran and the hadith. I've been to places where people have shared varied opinions and interpretations of Islamic teachings, providing a way to reconcile faith with the desire for a more open and progressive society. Finding common ground and charting a course that would honor religion while meeting the changing demands of our communities is paramount. Secularization in Islam presents an opportunity to reinterpret and adjust to the changing environment rather than a betrayal of faith.

Recent discussions underscore the notion that secularization in Islam can uphold fundamental principles such as equality, justice, and compassion. Aggressively opposing patriarchal practices and fighting for the rights of women and other underprivileged groups have served as motivation for Islam's inclusive principles. People who have accepted new concepts participate in critical discussions, which can propel the secularization movement forward.

To promote a well-rounded education for all, Islamic communities should continue establishing schools and centers that offer religious and secular subjects. Additionally, encouraging interfaith communication through various platforms fosters mutual respect and cooperation among different religious communities. For those who have threatened individuals like Yeye Ajesikemi Olokun Omolara for their Yoruba religious beliefs, it's imperative to seek reconciliation and offer restitution for the grievous insults. Alas! Let the imam beg the masquerade, and the pastor pleads with the imam. From Ode Aje to Ojaba, Agege to Jebba, Ilorin to Kano, let peace reign! *No dey follow pastor dey beef imam* (credit to Kizz Daniel's "Barnabas"). No religion is of violence!

CHAPTER ELEVEN

The Last Sermon

"إِنَّ الدِّينَ عِندَ اللَّهِ الْإِسْلَامُ"
(Surat Al Imran 3:19)

Jannah Land,
A realm beyond worldly bounds,
A paradise of bliss where serenity resounds,
A celestial abode of beauty untold,
Where souls find solace as their stories unfold . . .

In Jannah Land,
No pain, no hardship, no tear shall fall,
In the land where blessings enthrall,
Where peace and tranquility forever reign,
A haven of bliss, free from all pain.

My journey into the realm of Islamic education began with a humble curiosity sparked by a desire to understand different perspectives. As an academic, I have traversed various institutions, delving into the depths of knowledge across disciplines. However, my encounters with Islamic tertiary institutions in Nigeria have broadened my horizons. Among these, Fountain University stands as a beacon of innovation, seamlessly blending Western educational models with Islamic principles. The ambiance of its campus makes it feel like a realm where spirituality and academic excellence coexist harmoniously, emphasizing that the pursuit of knowledge isn't just about acquiring skills but about nurturing the soul and embracing morality.

I was privileged to engage with students and faculty members who epitomized dedication and passion for learning. The vibrancy of academic discourse intertwined with the serenity of spiritual contemplation created an environment unlike any other. Receiving the honorary doctoral degree in public administration was a profound honor, one that I accepted with humility and gratitude.

As I stood before the audience, listening to the words of Vice-Chancellor Amidu Sanni, I was reminded of the significance of my journey. In my acceptance speech, I reflected on the moment and the underlying reasons behind my decision to embrace this particular award. For me, it was more than just a recognition of academic prowess; it was a testament to my support for an institution that embodied the values of inclusivity and tolerance. A rush of emotions flooded over me as the weight of the doctoral hood draped over my shoulders. For me, that hood symbolized not just academic achievement but also a journey of cultural exchange and enlightenment. That moment was a culmination of experiences that shaped my perception of education, spirituality, the power of diversity, and the fulfillment of dreams.

A dream can be anything where I was born. You can dream of being pursued by a masquerade, the invisible man from heaven, or your stepmother perceived as a witch trying to harm you. You can dream of buying a big, expensive car, only to find yourself settling for a Korope (a small commercial van). Sure, your enemies will laugh at you, but it beats wandering around with your legs. Many people attach spiritual, metaphysical, and emotional importance to their dreams. While a dream can be many things, some will remain as a fairy tale, while others can manifest into reality. For individuals with deep spiritual reverence, dreams can be taken seriously, especially for seers who communicate with the gods. However, it is important to understand that a dream is only a partial message that means nothing by itself without additional information, which can only be provided by the dreamer or the interpreter.

As a child, I frequently had nightmares, especially during my time in Ode Aje. The phrase *Ala go* (Dream is silly) is a metaphorical expression that captures part of their essence, dismissing dreams as foolish because they mostly consist of imaginative scenes. For instance, dreaming about great things and receiving huge amounts of money is widely believed to be stupid, as the money is gone when you wake up. Seeking clarity as to what a dream might suggest, people often consult a cleric or a *babalawo*, who they believe could help them decipher the meaning of the dreams.

One of the recurring features of my dreams was seeing myself standing before an audience of diverse races and backgrounds. I would see myself speaking to an enthralled audience, but I never heard my own words, which often left me unsettled when I woke up. Seeking interpretation, I narrated the dreams to a revered alfa then at Ode Aje, and he would look at me and say, “Ala go.”

FIG. 17. Sculptural representation of artist and trumpet by Fatai Abdulkareem. With the progression in human activities and tools, various forms of musical instruments are in today's music industry, from gospel music to *juju*, *fuji*, and *apala*, among others. Here, images of indigenous religions are set side by side with an Islamic representation without provoking conflicts. From the private collection of Omoba Yemisi Shyllon.

Looking back now, I think I'd be right to imagine that he laughed at me in his mind, thinking about the audacity of this local Ode Aje boy to dream he was addressing a global assembly. I must have reminded him of the story of Joseph from the biblical narrative, whose dreams were interpreted to mean his brothers and his parents would bow to him.

My dreams of what the future held for me continued, and I learned to hold my peace and watch as life's currents took me to where fate had prepared me. Throughout my life, I have seen my past dreams come to light. I've stood before presidents, kings, and mighty men, and this time, I hear every word I speak. True to the whims of destiny, the tapestry of my dreams has woven itself into the fabric of reality.

I recall being invited to speak at a special Islamic event. On the day of the event, I made my way to the mosque in my flowing pure white *jalabia* (long robe), where the imam and some other alfas eagerly awaited my arrival. They welcomed me in hushed tones, expressed their gratitude for my prompt response to their invitation, and handed the drafts of my sermon to me.

Stepping into the main hall, I couldn't help but notice the bewilderment etched on the faces of the congregation. It was as if my presence was a disruption. As the master of ceremony formally introduced me, I felt the stares from a disgruntled crowd. The disapproving stares bore into me as I mounted the podium, and I could feel their hostility. It was evident that I was perceived as an outsider, unwelcome in this sacred place. Mounting the podium, I could sense the palpable disappointment radiating from the audience. Their faces mirrored a silent hostility and a reluctance to accept me as the main speaker at the event.

Now, this hostility wasn't because they hated me. In fact, I don't even know who loves me! Their hatred toward me was because the imam had promised them that a scholar from Mecca would grace the event and deliver the sermon. So they were expecting a Mecca scholar, adorned with a Genesis beard, not an older man from Texas, even though I qualified as a scholar. Adopting a Yoruba proverb, *ipako o gbo suti* (the occiput does not see mockery as it has no eyes), I decided not to allow their attitude to bother me. I adjusted my white cap, boldly emblazoned with the letters "TF," embraced my identity, and began to speak to them from my heart to impart knowledge that transcends religion and personality.

The purpose of my sermon was to remind my audience of the profound teachings contained in Prophet Muhammad's (PBUH) final pilgrimage sermon, which he delivered to the Muslim Ummah on the ninth day of Dhul-Hijjah, the last month of the lunar year, on Uranah, Valley of Mount Arafat, in Mecca. This momentous occasion happened during the annual rites of hajj, now known as the "Farewell Pilgrimage." It was the Prophet's last message to the Muslim community on how to navigate life in his absence.

After praising and thanking Allah, the Prophet (PBUH) began his sermon on the day of Arafat with:

> *O People! Lend me an attentive ear, for I know not whether after this year I shall ever be amongst you again. Therefore, listen carefully to what I am saying and take these words to those who could not be present here today.*
>
> *O People, just as you regard this month, this day, and this city as sacred, so regard the life and property of every Muslim as a sacred trust.*
>
> *Return the goods entrusted to you to their rightful owners. Hurt no one so that no one may hurt you. Remember that you will indeed meet your Lord, and that He will indeed reckon your deeds.*
>
> *. . . O, men! The unbelievers indulge in tampering with the calendar to make permissible that which Allah forbade, and to prohibit what Allah has made permissible. With Allah, the months are twelve in number. Four of them are holy, three are successive and one occurs singly between the months of Jumada and Shaban.*
>
> *Beware of Satan, for the safety of your religion. He has lost all hope that he will be able to lead you astray in big things, so beware of following him in small things.*
>
> *. . . O People! No Prophet or apostle will come after me, and no new faith will be born. Reason well, therefore O People! and understand words that I convey to you. I leave behind me two things, the Quran and the sunna and if you follow these you will never go astray.*
>
> *All those who listen to me shall pass on my words to others and those to others again; and may the last ones understand my words better than those who listen to me directly.*
>
> *O Allah, be my witness, that I have conveyed your message to Your people.*

As part of this sermon, the Prophet also recited a revelation from Allah to the Ummah, which he had just received and which completed the Quran, as it was the last passage to be revealed:

> *This day the disbeliever's despair of prevailing against your religion, so fear them not, but fear Me (Allah)! This day have I perfected for you, your religion and fulfilled My favor unto you, and it hath been My good pleasure to choose Islam for you as your religion.* (Quran 5:3)

I continued with excerpts from the message:

> *All mankind is from Adam and Eve. An Arab has no superiority over a non-Arab, nor does a non-Arab have any superiority over an Arab; white has no superiority over black nor does black have any superiority over white, except by piety and good action.*
>
> *Every Muslim is a brother to every Muslim, Muslims constitute one brotherhood. Nothing shall be legitimate to a Muslim which belongs to a fellow Muslim unless it was given freely and willingly. Do not therefore do injustice to yourselves.*
>
> *Remember the day you will appear before God and answer for your deeds. So beware, do not stray from the path of righteousness after I am gone.*

As I read, I looked up to see that the disappointment on their faces had changed to guilt. It was obvious that the words had struck the right chord, just as I had intended. Even the imam and the alfas were not exempted, as they must have also realized the error in their decision to invite me. Turning toward them, I asked why they were willing to spend so much resources to bring a scholar from Mecca when they had capable individuals among their congregation and within the country who would have been more than happy to take on the task.

My question was rhetoric, so I didn't wait for a reply before I asked them again why they grumbled when they found out I was to deliver the sermon. Yes, I understood their disappointment; I wasn't the person they were expecting, but they took it too far with how they reacted. What was their chain of thought? That I wouldn't be as versed as my contemporary from Mecca? I reminded them of the timeless wisdom of Prophet Muhammad (PBUH), who emphasized that no race is greater than the other and no skin color is superior to the other, but that as humans, we can be superior to one another only in deeds and righteousness. This principle gave backing to my presence—the proposed lecturer wasn't better than me. It didn't matter that he was a direct descendant of the religion, and I was only an observer of Islam. It didn't make him a better Muslim. We could only be superior to each other if we were graded according to our good works.

I noticed a shift in the demeanor of the audience. Many of them sat up right now, their total attention fixed on me, and I could tell that they were taking in each of my words. I touched on how some of us perceive ourselves to be inferior compared to people of lighter skin, whether they are from Europe, Asia, the Middle East, or America. By considering ourselves as inferior or of lesser worth and unquestioningly deferring to their actions, we continue to perpetuate a cycle of self-deprecation, leading to internalized racism. This mindset is wrong and dangerous, especially as we don't grant these excesses to our people.

The average Black person believes that white individuals are more competent, so if there is an opportunity to choose between a Black and white person, the latter gets appointed—just like the imam and his alfas were going to bring in an imam from Mecca to deliver a sermon in a predominantly Black community. Despite having an array of local Black scholars, the foreign preacher was deemed more suitable and considered first. I reminded them that after Prophet Muhammad (PBUH) built the first mosque in Medina, he called upon Bilal, a Black freed slave, to make the first call to prayer. Rather than favoring his closest companions, Abu-Bakr, Umar, Uthman, and Ali, who had followed him from Mecca, the Prophet chose Bilal because he had the best vocal strength and, therefore, was more qualified. When inviting preachers, especially for a local event, the focus should shift from external attributes like their geographical location or the color of their skin to the substance of their message.

I continued with my sermon, also quoting from the last sermon of Prophet Muhammad (PBUH):

> *O People, it is true that you have certain rights with regard to your women, but they also have rights over you. Remember that you have taken them as your wives only under Allah's trust and with His permission. If they abide by your right then to them belongs the right to be fed and clothed in kindness. Do treat your women well and be kind to them for they are your partners and committed helpers. And it is your right that they do not make friends with any one of whom you do not approve, as well as never to be unchaste.*

To bolster these words from the Prophet, I asked the men if they offered support or assistance to their wives beyond financial provision. The women didn't let me finish my statement before they interrupted, their voices cascading like a sudden downpour. Before the men could answer, the women preemptively answered on their behalf in the negative. According to the teachings of Prophet Muhammad (PBUH), kindness toward women extends beyond mere provision for their upkeep and children. It encompasses actions such as helping them with household chores when they feel overwhelmed.

Women do a lot at home, juggling responsibilities such as cooking, looking after the children, and tidying the house, all while striving to maintain a balance in their personal lives and attend to their husbands. Husbands should help their wives in one way or the other to ease their burdens. If, for some reason, a man can't assist his wife with household chores, then it would be nice if he gets a domestic assistant for her. Men should be kind enough to listen to their wives and to do things that would make them happy. Above all, men should remain faithful and committed to their marriage. If a man's wife can no longer satisfy his needs and he has the financial and mental capacity to manage more than one wife, the Quran provides the option of marrying another wife. If a man lacks these qualities to satisfy his wife, then he has no reason to take another wife.

As the women in the audience continued to signal their agreement with what I was saying, I silently hoped they also absorbed the part where I mentioned the importance of honoring their husbands' rights, not associating with people disapproved by their husbands, and maintaining their innocence. I realized that when I started talking about the women's role in building a good home, it seemed I had shifted from being a feminist to a patriarch within one minute.

After the noise from both sides subsided, I continued my sermon, revisiting the teachings of the Prophet. This was centered around Islam itself and what makes a Muslim.

> *Believe in Allah only, pray to God in earnest by performing your five daily salats, fast during Ramadan, give out alms (zakat) to the poor, and perform Hajj if you have the means.*

Some people believe in Allah yet consult other sources—other gods or beings and religious leaders to solve their problems. This is an act of *shirk* in Islam. In your daily activities, put in the necessary work and look to Allah for its success. In matters of health and wellness, seek professional advice, go for regular checkups, and take your medications as needed, even as you look to God for healing.

As Allah's followers, don't identify as non-Muslims during Ramadan because you have a mixed-religion family, and suddenly remember that you have an imaginary ulcer that disappears after the fasting period. Also, some individuals will fast and break all the rules that make Ramadan sacred. They will curse, gossip, engage in adultery and fornication, and drink alcohol immediately after iftar but claim they are fasting. If you are in any of the categories, please do yourself a favor and just eat.

At times, we need to assess situations and take appropriate actions. For instance, you don't go about giving free hajj trips to people who need sustenance. Rather, you have to address their core challenges and help them achieve financial stability. They can't go to Mecca to acquire the title of "Alhaji" or "Alhaja" and only return to abject poverty, with their new title making it harder for them to get assistance.

One Muslim is not different from another Muslim. There is no difference between Muslims in Africa and the Muslims in Mecca and Medina. The only difference is the piety and good deeds individuals have achieved on their own. Don't feel inferior toward another race or skin color. Kindness toward women is important, and women should be free to make decisions. As I wrapped up the lecture that day, I stressed the importance of upholding the five pillars of Islam, asking all Muslims to hold them sacred and hoping to inspire a renewed commitment to these pillars. It was a call to action, a reminder of the fundamental principles that bind believers together and guide their spiritual journey.

Turning toward the organizers of the event to gauge their appraisal, I found them already on their feet, same with the audience, offering a standing ovation to appreciate me. What a twist of fate! The same audience that had initially grumbled at the start now showered me with applause. It felt surreal, like a dream unlike any other.

I am many things; my name depicts that—Oloruntoyin Ifalola. While some of my dreams are consistent with realities, my encounter with Islam transcends the confines of waking life; it comes in dreams, too. Since I have told different tales of my encounters in reality, let me also set sail and share other stories from the other world, the dreamland. Perhaps the Yoruba saying that "dreams are foolish" isn't entirely true, or maybe it's a means of discarding the essence of dreams, especially to those who cannot find meaning in them.

In one such dream, I found myself amid devout souls who had gathered for devotion and prayers, a scene that depicted the holy land. I am over seventy years of age, and I have, at different times, sponsored Muslim friends and families on pilgrimage, but I have never gone on one. In my dream, the words being uttered sounded strange in my ears, and at the same time, I thought I had heard them before. They sounded like words used during a pilgrimage, but I couldn't interpret the meanings.

Labbayka -llāhumma labbayka,
Labbayka lā šarīka laka labbayka,
ʾinna -l-ḥamda wa-n-niʿmata laka wa-l-mulka lā šarīka lak

Here I am [at your service] O God, here I am.
Here I am [at your service].
You have no partners (other gods).
To You alone is all praise and all excellence,
And to You is all sovereignty.
There is no partner to You.

Having a deep understanding of hajj, I can comprehend my dreams and narrate what they look like in detail when I am awake. It's a gift, as not everyone can narrate their dreams or find meaning to them. I might not have visited Saudi Arabia for hajj, but I know the intricate details: the actions, sayings, and deeds—all of which I'd read about in books. As pilgrims circumambulated in my dream, I joined the chanting, dressed in a white robe and with my white hair shaved. The chant continued:

> *Labbayka -llāhumma labbayka,*
> *Labbayka lā šarīka laka labbayka,*
> *ʾInna -l-ḥamda wa-n-niʿmata laka wa-l-mulka lā šarīka lak.*

As we stopped at the seventh round, I realized it was such an engaging exercise and not for the weak. It took strength and piety. At this moment, among individuals of diverse color, race, and title, the essence of what Prophet Muhammad's (PBUH) sermon was all about dawned on me. Islam doesn't segregate.

Moving to another setting, we were engaged in a vigil, a practice that some have claimed to be new to Muslims in Africa and other parts of the world. I partially agree and partially disagree with this claim, as every religion has its mode of worship detailed in the holy book of such religion. However, for most African traditional religions, there are no written holy books to guide worshippers.

I know some *dua* (prayers) are time-fixed, and this might have caused the perception that night prayers are exclusive to one religion. Vigil prayers seem to be peculiar to the Christian faithful, and some view such activities as an innovation to Islamic practices, but the stories and the prayers we attended at midnight for the last ten days of Ramadan as young children at Ode Aje seem to negate these claims. The modes of worship and activities may have evolved; however, I can't flatly conclude that Muslim vigil prayers are a recent adaptation from their Christian neighbor.

As I stood among the believers, the air heavy with the mingling fragrances of incense and the whispers of prayers, a profound sense of serenity washed over me. With each whispered invocation, I felt a connection to something greater than myself, a divine presence that transcended earthly bounds, listening to the melodious language of Arabic and reciting verses from the Quran with a reverence that resonated deep within the depth of my soul. With each prostration, I felt the weight of the world lifting from my shoulders as I poured out my hopes, fears, and aspirations before the Almighty. In the rhythm of the prayer, I found solace and strength.

The dream stretched on, and I lost track of time, consumed by the intensity of the moment. Each *rakka* of prayer felt like a journey in itself, a testament to the resilience of the human spirit and the power of collective devotion. In the quiet space of that dream vigil, I found myself praying fervently for Nigeria, my beloved homeland. With each whispered plea, I prayed to the Almighty to bestow his blessings upon the nation, to guide us through the darkness, and to lead us toward a future of peace, prosperity, and unity.

Just as the first light of dawn began to break, I woke up from the depths of my dream, my heart brimming with a sense of profound peace and purpose. Though the vigil existed only in my dreams, its impact lingered within me, serving as a reminder of the transformative power of faith and prayer.

As I awoke to the dawn of a new day, my thoughts shifted to other components that radiate the Islamic space. At various places and discussions, the search for better opportunities has moved many young individuals out of Nigeria through different avenues such as education, employment opportunities, better living conditions, as well as anything you can think of when the word *japa* (escape), sociolingo used to describe the massive migration of Nigerians to other countries, comes to your mind.

> *Japa,*
> *Japa,*
> *Japa,*
> *Japa this, japa that!*

If you don't see a friend, colleague, or family member for two weeks and you inquire about the person's whereabouts, the most likely response you get is *o ti japa*, meaning the person has absconded or migrated. This term is now commonplace in Nigeria, or at least among the Yoruba-speaking people. Once you are hit with that term when you go about asking for someone, it means the person has left the country in search of greener pastures. Can they be blamed, though? No, if you ask me. As much as we preach that things will get better for the country, we have to be honest and admit that the reverse has been the case so far. Some of these individuals do not see prospects in Nigeria, so for every little opportunity they get, they try to escape to countries they presume can offer them a better life. The alarming part is that they don't care about the financial, mental, or emotional cost associated with the *japa* to foreign lands.

At this point, I have come to terms with the fact that I can no longer dissuade people from seeking opportunities abroad. Time was when Nigerians only traveled abroad for education and tourism purposes. Citizens who were comfortable enough would send money to those in these foreign lands because the naira was strong in the international market. That was the reality then, unlike now. Citizens no longer feel at ease in their own country, grappling with low income and high cost of living. The naira is so weak that Nigerians who relocate abroad and earn "chicken change" in foreign currency are regarded as wealthy, depending on how much they make.

I remember hearing some young individuals discussing the new inroads into Arab cities. All they had to do was study and be efficient in the Arabic language, and then they could get jobs in places like Dubai as translators, earning sustainable income. While their sentiments and ideas might sound appealing, especially to me, listening to their conversations gave me further insight into how people go to other countries to work as cleaners and do all sorts of menial jobs that they wouldn't naturally do in their motherland. But I was shocked at some point when one of them pointed out that this method was open mainly to the alfas, who have spent most of their lives studying the Arabic language in the madrassas.

Nonetheless, he proposed a new method, which he described as tested and trusted because one of his friends was already in Dubai and working. All the friend had to do was pay to illegally enter Dubai through the desert and be smuggled into the country where a job was already waiting for her. This job would be facilitated by agents who would put her in the care of a family in need of domestic staff. She would get paid for her services, with the agent taking an agreed percentage of the earnings. In less than two years, she would have made the money spent on the trip three times over, even while paying the agent, too.

I was astounded. What kind of thought is that? A trip through the desert is not child's play, and this wasn't even factored into his thoughts. He only cared about getting money. This piqued my interest, and I joined the conversation, unable to resist the urge to intervene. I questioned the feasibility of surviving the rigorous journey through the desert, but he claimed that his friend who was there was a lady, and if a lady could survive the journey, a man should be able to do the same. He even ended it with a Yoruba proverb, *ibi lile la n'ba omo okunrin*, meaning men always court hard situations.

I further questioned him on how he planned to communicate, as the employers barely speak English. He beamed with laughter and pride and brought out his phone. He said his friend didn't speak Arabic, but she could communicate using an application on her phone. She would record in English on the phone, and the application would translate it into Arabic as voice output to her employers, who would also speak Arabic on their phones and play English feedback to the lady.

But how was he going to integrate himself into society without the necessary documents and not get caught and deported? He explained the family he intended to work with would confine him to the house. According to him, his friend in Dubai never went out except for a few nights when her employers needed her to clean up their mother's residence. She would sit behind the driver's seat and hide as they transported her under the cover of the night and ferried her back to the house before daybreak.

I was astounded! This was no longer human trafficking but also slavery—voluntary human trafficking and slavery. When I expressed my fears about the risks and the moral implications, my young friend replied by saying that the dirham is a strong and scarce currency, and he was ready to live as a captured prisoner for a whole year if that was how long it would take to earn the currency.

There are several reports of racist acts and inhumane treatment meted out to these domestic workers who can't come forward to make reports to the security, as they are illegal migrants and will be immediately arrested to be deported or maybe jailed. The saddest part of these stories is that some of these workers are sold to other places by their employers without their consent. When this happens, there is no more salary, and such an individual becomes a proper domestic slave exposed to all sorts of maltreatment. Imagine leaving your country where you are treated like a human for another where you are subjected to treatments they wouldn't mete out on animals, all in the name of chasing greener pastures. It is a stark reminder that the grass is not always greener on the other side.

The world has witnessed several innovations, and religion has not been left out. Islam has enjoyed the technological advances of the modern world, which have impacted our daily lives and transcended spirituality and morality. During the month of Ramadan in 2021, the Covid-19 lockdown changed the face of communication. It impacted the world so much that almost every human physical activity, including religion and education, was done virtually, which left a mark on the communication sphere of the world.

To paint the world with a sense of spiritual awakening during this Ramadan period, I found myself in a unique online congregation on Instagram. Typically, mosques would echo the rhythmic recitations of prayers during Ramadan; however, this year was different. The world has transformed, urging people to adapt and find solace and connection in unconventional spaces. And so, I embarked on a virtual journey that would redefine my understanding of communal worship. With a few clicks, I joined a live stream on Instagram hosted by a cleric. I could see the minaret picture background and hear the soothing melody of Quranic recitations that greeted me through my screen. This cleric, draped in the traditional garb, sat in the midst of his students.

In no time, the number of virtual attendees from across the globe increased to over one million. I marveled at the ingenuity that had brought us together.

Through the lens of a camera and the power of technology, we were listening to one voice and making the same supplications despite the miles that separated us. The cleric's voice, amplified by microphones, showed an authenticity that transcended the digital realm. But what truly captivated me was the seamless integration of spirituality and innovation. Alongside the prayers, the cleric pinned bank account details of the association to receive charitable donations, a modern solution to an age-old practice of giving *sadaqah* (charity). In that digital realm, the boundaries between the spiritual and the practical blurred, creating a space where acts of worship and kindness intertwined effortlessly.

Reflecting on the significance of that moment, I couldn't help but recognize how technology became the bridge that connected hearts and souls across continents amid a global pandemic. The virtual congregation wasn't merely a substitute for physical presence but a testament to the resilience of faith in the face of adversity.

In the silence that followed the closing supplications, I was filled with gratitude. Gratitude for the minds that dared to innovate, for the hearts that yearned for connection, and for the boundless blessings of a faith that knows no bounds.

Truly, dreams become reality!
I once wandered through realms unseen
With words of wisdom, I sought to preach
In tongues of truth, my lessons reach.

Taqwa, in every word I spoke
A mission grand, a divine yoke
But behold! From the seeds I've sown
Springs forth a truth once unknown
For dreams are not but fanciful things
They are the prophets of what life brings
And in their whispers, we find our call.

Rise from the sands where dreams belong
So let us dream, with eyes agleam
For in those visions lies the seam
That stitches faith into reality's shore
And dreams of yesterday are dreams no more.